D0927491

CHINESE SOCIALISM TO 1907

Chinese Socialism to 1907

by MARTIN BERNAL

CORNELL UNIVERSITY PRESS

Ithaca and London

First published 1976 by Cornell University Press.
Published in the United Kingdom by Cornell University Press Ltd., 2–4 Brook Street, London W1Y 1AA.

International Standard Book Number 0-8014-0915-2
Library of Congress Catalog Card Number 75-16809
Printed in the United States of America

To the memory of
DESMOND BERNAL and
ALAN GARDINER

Acknowledgments

I am deeply indebted to all at King's College, Cambridge, and to the China-Japan Program of Cornell University for their great kindness and tolerance and for allowing me more than enough time to complete this work. I should like to thank my teachers, Edwin Pulleyblank, Piet van der Loon, Robert Scalapino, Benjamin Schwartz, and the late Joseph Levenson. I am also extremely grateful to David Mozingo for his help and encouragement, and to Edward Friedman, Richard Howard, Donald Sutton, and Ernest Young for their thorough reading of earlier versions of this book, for their perceptive comments and criticisms, and for their encouragement. I should like to thank Paul Cheng for his patient copying of my appalling characters in Appendix III, Lynne Mulcock for typing the manuscript, and Jane Fior for her corrections, and my mother, Margaret Gardiner, for her proofreading. Finally, I must express my gratitude to Li Chin-hsiung of San Francisco for his extraordinary generosity in giving me several rare anarchist magazines.

MARTIN BERNAL

Cambridge, England,
and Ithaca, New York

Contents

CHINESE SOCIALISM TO 1907

Introduction

Is it possible for one culture to borrow from another? Clearly any concept or pattern of concepts becomes something new both in itself and functionally in a new cultural context. This is true both historically from age to age, and geographically from place to place. Thus at a certain level the "foreign origin" of an object or idea is unimportant or even misleading. To my mind, however, the persistence of certain elements of the original provides a useful background against which one can view the process of adaptation and transformation, and this process gives one of the best possible insights into the nature of the receiving culture. Furthermore, however radically the new object or idea may be altered in nature and function, it does affect the totality of the new culture.

How much impact has the West had on China? Here one encounters a problem of historiography. Nineteenth- and early twentieth-century Western historians of China generally emphasized the importance and progressive nature of foreign influences. Historians tended to attribute the foundation of Chinese civilization to invaders from the West and to give positive roles to invaders and outside cultural influences; they stressed the traditionalism and lack of initiative of the Chinese. This viewpoint, of course, provided a good progressive justification for Western intervention in China.

In the 1920s and 1930s a reaction set in. Western writers and scholars—particularly Americans—began to stress the originality and creativity of the Chinese, and outside influences were played down. In almost every way this was a healthy reaction to the implicit racialism of the early period. It seems to have represented a turning away from nineteenth-century imperialism and colonialism. The new trend, however, had what might be described as neocolonialist aspects, that is, a tendency to ally with local elites to preserve the existing hierarchies for the benefit of the elites and foreigners. Thus in scholarship there has been an inclination to rely almost entirely on the historiography of the Chinese ruling class. This could be considered as inevitable, since few other bodies of historical material exist. However, the positivist precision with which it is used—the huge apparatus of references and bibliographies—tends to give a spurious scientific objectivity to history that is in fact based on very partial material. For instance, reading the cultivated and charming letters of the Governor General of Hupeh and Hunan, Zhang Zhi-dong, one gains very little feeling of the mass destitution in the provinces he ruled or of the corruption throughout his administration, let alone of the torture practiced daily in courts under his jurisdiction. For information on these aspects of life it is often better to read foreign reports, even though these were often written to justify foreign intervention. For specialists, however, apart from their partiality, these reports have another disadvantage—any Western historian can read them. In order to maintain professional status, Western historians of China tend to stress the importance of documents made esoteric by being in Chinese, over anything more easily accessible.

The playing down of the importance of foreign influence is extremely convenient for Western writers who are uneasy about the morality of expediency of direct foreign intervention in China or the rest of the Third World and yet do not wish to condemn their own society outright. Where the Victorians had maintained that the merchants, soldiers, and missionaries had gone to China with the noblest motives and were beginning to transform it, the new school tended to argue that the Westerner's motives were varied and complicated, and that in any event their actions had had very little effect on the huge and creative mass of China. Thus it is a relief to "discover" that the foreign imports and investment had little impact on traditional crafts or that where the Victorians had attributed the defeat of the Taiping Rebellion to General Gordon it was "really" a triumph of the conservative Chinese official Zeng Guo-fan. According to what I believe to be an emerging third historiographical trend, both of these explanations are thought to be one-sided. The new tendency is to restate the importance of outside influences, notably imperialism, on Chinese history. However, this is not a return to the Victorian view, principally because the third school deplores most of what the old found admirable, and also because it tries to retain the second school's belief in China's own genius and vitality. Analyzing the defeat of the Taiping, the third school maintains that the victory was gained by a combination of the gentry of south and central China and the cash, weapons, advice, and direct military aid of foreign powers, notably Britain. The joint victory was reflected in the condominium of gentry leaders and foreigners who ruled China for the rest of the nineteenth century.

In a similar way, although the struggles between warlords after 1911 did have local roots, these conflicts can also usefully be seen as struggles between foreign powers. The anti-Japanese Yuan Shi-kai's position weakened with the growth of Japanese influence in China, while Britain was distracted from the Far East by the First World War. After the war, the pro-British and American Wu Pei-fu defeated the pro-Japanese Duan Qi-rui, as Western influence returned. At a more profound level there was foreign support for the warlord system itself, and all available resources were used to block any social or political force that threatened the system. The preservation of the corrupt and inefficient Manchu government had suited the foreign powers, not one of whom could have colonialized China directly. In a similar way, the encouragement of warlordism, the destruction of traditional handicrafts, and the draining of rural capital into treaty ports under foreign control were all beneficial to the foreigners and detrimental to China. In fact, they contributed powerfully to the creation of the hell that China became in the 1940s.

Chinese Socialism to 1907 is concerned with one of the very few areas where foreign influence on China has been beneficial. It is in no way controversial to assert that, despite the radical transformation it undoubtedly underwent in its transition, Western socialism has played a critical role in twentieth-century Chinese history. The English and American missionaries who wanted, among many other things, to promote social radicalism, and their associates, Kang You-wei, Liang Qi-chao, and Sun Yat-sen, began a process which, though it failed in the short run, became crucial after the May 4 Movement.

Mao Ze-dong once wrote that "before the October Revolution the Chinese were not only ignorant of Lenin and Stalin, they did not know of Marx and Engels." [1] Other modern scholars have tended to agree with him that before 1919, when the impact of the Soviet revolution first hit China, the socialist and anarchist movements there were futile, insignificant, and not worth studying. Observers at the time tended to hold the same opinion. Relatively few of them were interested in the schemes for drastic social reform of a small number of radical politicians. Students of the political scene were concerned with what they believed to be immediate and practical problems: the constitutional plans of the Manchu empire and the early republic, or the questions of financial and foreign loans. While it is true that men of political importance like Kang You-wei and Liang Qi-chao, the leading Reformists, were interested in socialism and anarchism, these interests were subordinate at that time.

Most historians of modern China are agreed that the date of May 4, 1919, is even more significant than the date of October 10, 1911, when revolution against the Manchu empire broke out. The May 4 Movement started in protest against articles in the Treaty of Versailles which were thought to be humiliating to China, articles which allowed Japan to keep the concessions in China she had seized from Germany at the beginning of the First World War. The Movement consisted of student demonstrations, merchant boycotts, and workers' strikes. Out of such activities and those of the simultaneous and related new culture movement came language reform, the beginnings of a demotic literature, and the foundation of both the Chinese Communist Party and the reorganized Kuomintang.

Many scholars have begun their studies of Chinese communism with 1919, or with the preceding three or four years as an introduction, but this approach excludes some interesting questions. If socialism did not become relevant to China until the twenties, what changes had taken place in Chinese society and intellectual life in the preceding decades to make that possible? Is it true that socialism could have had an impact on China only after Lenin had revolutionized Marxism and created a successful model for a revolutionary

---

1. Mao, "On the People's Democratic Dictatorship," *Selected Readings from the Works of Mao Tse-tung* (Peking, 1967), 304. For the Chinese text, see Takenouchi Minoru (ed.), *Mō Takutō Shū* (Tokyo, 1970), X, 294.

party? Is there any evidence of the effects of pre-Leninist Marxism in China? Within a decade of the foundation of the Chinese Communist Party, the larger part of the Chinese intelligentsia was Marxist. Had Marxist or other socialist ideas seeped into Chinese thinking before 1919? The later successes of Chinese communism make all of these questions very relevant to the present day.

It would also be interesting to know which parts of European socialist theory were accepted by the Chinese and which were neglected or rejected by them. For instance, theories of equal distribution of property or common ownership were welcomed and talked about, while class conflict was discussed much less often. Were the acceptable sections adopted because they were in accord with Chinese tradition, because they fitted the needs of various sections of Chinese society at the time or was it simply because the sources of information available to the Chinese emphasized these aspects? Through their selection of sources, and in the translating, Chinese students modified Western theories. Did these modifications form a coherent pattern? If they did, how did Chinese socialism differ from that of European countries, Russia, and Japan? Although Lenin exaggerated the similarities between Russian populism and the social policies of the Chinese revolutionaries, there were very real parallels between the two.[2] Furthermore, during the Russo-Japanese War and the Russian revolution of 1905 Chinese students became acutely aware of the similarities between the social and political structures of the two countries. The parallels between Chinese and Japanese social revolutionary ideas are particularly interesting, not only because both countries share the East Asian tradition, but also because between 1903 and 1919 the Chinese gained nearly all their knowledge of the West through Japan.

Another fascinating problem is the extent to which traditional Chinese ideas survived in early socialism and anarchism and in the later communism. Communism often was and still is equated with the traditional concept of *datong* "Great Harmony," representative of a legendary age in which there was no selfishness or private property. Socialism was also linked to a traditional form of com-

2. For Lenin's parallels, see "Democracy and Narodism in China," *Selected Works* (London, 1935), IV, 308–311.

munal agriculture called the *jingtian* system. In the earlier period the connection between socialism and these concepts was admitted or even boasted about. After 1919 the relationship tended to be disavowed, but it clearly continued to influence Chinese communism. The recent campaign against Confucius indicates that even today the symbols have potency, although some of them, like the *jingtian* system, now called a slave system, are reversed. Thus a knowledge of the ways in which before 1919 such concepts helped form the Chinese students' picture of Western socialism may enable one to understand later facets of the Chinese communist movement.

Chinese Socialism to 1907 is the first part of what I hope will some day become a three-volume history of Chinese socialism before the May 4 Movement. The projected second volume, on Chinese Anarchism and Terrorism before 1911, will be concerned with the anarchist movements in France and Japan—the last chapter of the present work is a brief summary of the beginnings of this. It is to include also a study of the assassination groups in Kwangtung in 1910 and 1911. The third volume is to be on the mass political parties that flourished in the short period of political freedom, which lasted from the autumn of 1911 to August 1913, when Yuan Shi-kai, with the support of the Western powers, suppressed it. The work will concentrate on Jiang Kang-hu and his Chinese Socialist Party of over 200 branches and possibly 400,000 members, which spread—in very dilute form—a mixture of the socialism and anarchism acquired by the progressive elite in the earlier period. The volume will also be concerned with the Chinese anarchist movement between 1911 and 1915, the year its leading teacher, Shi Fu, died and the May 4 Movement can be said to have begun.

The present work takes its place in the proposed trilogy as a study of the rise and fall of Western socialism in China. European socialism as seen by liberal and Christian sympathizers was introduced to the Far East by English and American missionaries. The United States was undoubtedly the Western nation most responsible for introducing socialism to China. Before 1900 its influence was direct, through personal contact and the Chinese publication of *The Review of the Times*. On the other hand, this Western influence was on a very small scale, although three of the key figures in early twentieth-century Chinese politics, Kang You-wei, Liang Qi-chao, and Sun Yat-sen, were deeply impressed by it. The second wave of influence came through Japan, where like-minded low-church missionaries and teachers from America led a small number of their most talented converts toward social democracy, and these converts formed the core of the early Japanese socialist movement. It was this movement, together with more conservative Japanese interest in German state socialism, that encouraged a significantly larger, but in absolute terms still small, group of Chinese to become interested in socialism. Though all of them were Westernizers, these writers and students came from a wide political spectrum, from Reformists to Revolutionaries.

The year 1907 is significant because it was then that the progressive consensus disintegrated. Many Reformists and Revolutionaries became cultural conservatives, and their political radicalism became muted. A few revolutionaries, like those in Paris, reacted violently against the cultural conservatism, becoming iconoclasts and radical Westernizers. But their faith in existing Western institutions was shattered, and many became anarchists. The social democracy and state socialism projected in the earlier period became irrelevant. After the fall of Western socialism in China, however, the movement was not obliterated without trace. Sun Yat-sen continued to proclaim his land policies. Even more important was the fact that although interest in social democracy was dead at the center, its ideas continued to spread among the middlebrow and the young long after that. Elements of it persisted in the later anarchism and in the vague ideas promoted by Jiang Kang-hu. Many names, words, phrases, concepts, and patterns of thought remained in the minds of men and women who lived on to play crucial roles in the Chinese revolution. Chen Du-xiu, one of the two founders of the Communist Party, Dong Bi-wu, the late acting president of China, Lu Xun, the great influential writer, and Yang Chang-ji and Xu Te-li, Mao's teachers who had a critical effect on his political development, were all fully conscious political-ly between 1903 and 1907. They knew personally many of the figures mentioned in this book, some of whose writings on socialism they certainly read. Mao's emphasis on the importance of the Oc-tober Revolution and the May 4 Movement is absolutely correct.

There is no doubt that a qualitative change did take place in 1919. Nevertheless, for men like Mao Ze-dong and Zhou En-lai the earliest semantic connotations of words like socialism, communism, capital, and class were established by the Reformists and Revolutionaries of this early period.

1 | Datong

Before coming to the introduction of Western socialism and associated ideas into China, it is necessary to describe a traditional Chinese concept which became inextricably bound up with socialism in China until well after the time of the May 4 Movement in 1919. The concept was that of *datong* ("Great Harmony" or "Grand Union"). The age of *datong* was described in the following passage attributed to Confucius from the *Liyun*, a chapter of the Book of Rites:

When the Grand Course was pursued, and common Spirit ruled all under the sky, they chose men of talents, virtue and ability, their words were sincere and what they cultivated was harmony. Thus men did not love their parents only, nor treat as children only their own sons. A competent provision was secured for the aged until their death, employment for the able bodied, and means of growing up to the young. They showed kindness and compassion to widows, orphans and childless men, and those who were disabled by disease, so that they were all sufficiently maintained. Males had their proper worth and females had their homes. (They accumulated) articles of value, disliking that they should be thrown away upon the ground, but not wishing to keep them for their own gratification. (They laboured) with their strength, disliking that it should not be exerted, but not exerting it (only) with a view to their own advantage. In this way (selfish) schemings were repressed and found no development. Robbers and filchers, and rebellious traitors did not show themselves, and hence the outer doors remained open and were not shut. This was (the period) of what we call the Grand Union *datong*.[1]

The chapter went on to describe another age called *xiaokang* ("Small Tranquillity"), which had come after *datong*, during which

1. Translated by James Legge, *Sacred Books of the East*, Vol. XXVII, *Li Ki*, Books I–IX (Oxford, 1885), 366.

there was order, and people loved their families, and there was social harmony of a kind. But it was a period in which men were selfish and did things for the profit and glory of themselves and their families. The age of *datong* presumably applied to the age of the legendary Five Emperors, while the age of *xiaokang* definitely applied to the three dynasties which followed them, namely the Xia, the Shang, and the Zhou. The description of *xiaokang* said: "Thus it is that selfish schemes and enterprises are constantly taking their rise and recourse is had to arms, and thus it was that Yu, Tang, Wen and Wu and the Duke of Zhou obtained their distinction."[2] The slighting reference to all of Confucius' favorite heroes and sages, and the general tone of the passage attacking the family and social grades, made some traditional commentators doubt that the passage could be ascribed to Confucius.[3] Despite these doubts, however, the *Liyun* was generally considered to be part of the Confucian canon and was given the respect due to a classic.

It is now believed that the *Liyun* was written long after Confucius in the third or fourth century B.C. and that it is full of Mohist and Taoist thought.[4] Aspects of these schools, particularly Mohist egalitarianism and "general love," and the Taoist longing to return to the simple life, seem to have been a part of the folk beliefs forming the substratum of Chinese philosophy. These, together with other aspects of the folk beliefs, notably the *yin-yang* cosmology, were introduced into the previously aristocratic and rationalist Confucianism during the late Zhou and the early Han periods.[5]

The great synthesizer of the high philosophy with the popular

2. Legge, 367. The distinction between *datong* and *xiaokang* is very similar to Dong Zhong-shu's concept of the alternation of periods of *zhi* and *wen*. See Fung Yu-lan, *A History of Chinese Philosophy*, 2 vols., translated by Derk Bodde (London, 1953), II, 63. This is further evidence suggesting that the concept of *datong* and *xiaokang* was part of the general religio-philosophic movement at the end of Zhou and the beginning of Han. For the interesting but not entirely convincing view that *datong*, Taoist simplicity, and Western golden ages originated from memories of primitive collectivist society, see Joseph Needham, *Science and Civilisation in China*, Vol. II (Cambridge, 1962), 127; and Hou Wai-lu, *Zhongguo Lidai Datong Lixiang* (Peking, 1959), 1–10.

3. Legge, 367.

4. Qian Mu, *Zhongguo Jin Sanbainian Xueshu shi*, 2 vols., (3rd ed.; Shanghai, 1948), II, 665; and Hou Wai-lu, 12–13.

5. Tjan Tjae Sam, *Po Hu T'ung, The Comprehensive Discussions in the White Tiger Hall*, 2 vols. (Leiden, 1949), I, 96–97. For a fascinating account of this synthesis see Needham, II, 232–253.

religion was Dong Zhong-shu (c. 179–c. 104 b.c.). Dong in effect changed the works attributed to Confucius from philosophical texts, useful for guidance, into gospels containing "a sacred message valid for all times." [6] The text that he considered the most important was the *Spring and Autumn Annals.* These were the annals of Lu (the home state of Confucius), written or compiled by Confucius himself. Dong Zhong-shu's chief work, in which he expounded most of his ideas, was based on the Annals and was called *The Copious Dew of Spring and Autumn Annals.* He believed that an understanding of the inner meaning of the Annals could explain all the phenomena of the world. Dong greatly amplified Confucius' principle of praise and blame, that is, praising the good men and actions in history and blaming the bad. Dong believed that Confucius, in the terminology he had used and in the events and persons he had included or omitted, had given a coded message that could save or help the whole world. [7]

For Dong and his students the most important key for the understanding of the Annals was the *Commentary of Gongyang.* This was supposed to have been transmitted orally from Confucius himself, but it can only have been written down in the second or third century b.c., and in very much the same philosophical atmosphere as that of the period in which Dong began teaching. [8] Because of the use it made of the *Commentary,* Dong's school of thought became known as the Gongyang school.

One of the special interpretations of the Annals by the *Gongyang* divided up the history of Lu into three distinct periods. These were the period which Confucius had seen with his own eyes, the period which he had learned about from hearsay, and the period he knew only from tradition. [9] According to the *Commentary,* Confucius used different terms and applied different judgments to each of the periods. Dong Zhong-shu emphasized this interpretation, and gave the exact dates which he considered divided the *sanshi* ("Three Epochs").

A further development of the theory came in a subcommentary

---

6. Tjan, I, 98.   7. See Fung Yu-lan, II, 7–87.
8. For the dating of the *Gongyang Zhuan* see Kang Woo, *Les Trois Theories Politiques du Tch'ouen Ts'ieou* (Paris, 1932).
9. Kang Woo, 90.

written by He Xiu (A.D. 129–182) on the *Commentary of Gongyang*. He based his interpretation on another theory of the Gongyang school, that of the "New Kingdom" of Lu. By very forced interpretations of the Annals they had decided that Confucius had received the mandate of heaven to found the new dynasty of Lu. According to the theory, Confucius was not a temporal emperor but a *su wang* (uncrowned king), the dynasty itself was thought to have several facets—it was supposed to be historical, but at the same time it had a mystic entity which was to be a model for the future.[10]

He Xiu's development of the theory of the three epochs went as follows. The first epoch, which Confucius had heard about from tradition, was a period of *juluan* ("Chaos"). It was a period in which the new kingdom of Lu was beginning to develop, but its civilizing influence was apparent only in Lu itself. For this reason there was a boundary or distinction between Lu and the other Chinese states. According to He, that was why Confucius had recorded events occurring only in Lu during that period.

The second period, which Confucius had learned about from hearsay, was one of *shengping* ("Rising Peace"). In this period the influence of Lu had spread to all the Chinese states. Therefore the boundary this time was between the Chinese and the barbarians. The proof of this was, according to He, that Confucius had recorded events in all the Chinese states in this period.

The third period, which Confucius had seen with his own eyes, was the epoch of *taiping* ("Great Peace"). In this period the influence of Lu had spread all over the world. There were no boundaries at all; Chinese and barbarians were all moved by Confucius' civilizing influence. That was why Confucius, writing about events in this period, dealt impartially with Chinese and barbarians.[11]

This theory was interpreted as having a symbolic as well as a

10. Kang Woo, 107–135. For excellent descriptions of *datong, taiping,* and their relationship, see Joseph Needham, *Time and Ancient Man* (London, 1965), 23–31; and Frederic Wakeman, Jr., *History and Will: Philosophical Perspectives of Mao Tse-tung's Thought* (Berkeley, 1973), 100–136.

11. Kang Woo, 94. The reason for Confucius' increasing range of interest as the historical narrative approached his own time was obviously the increasing amount of information available to him.

historic significance: the spreading influence of Lu was a moral guide and a future portent as well as a historical process. The theory of the three epochs had very little influence on Chinese philosophy or political thought in the following sixteen hundred years. Its significance lay in its belief in upward progress; in this it was unlike the two historical theories which dominated Chinese thought: the theory of descent from a golden past, and the theory of the cyclical rise and fall of dynasties.

During the later Han dynasty (25–220 A.D.), the *Commentary of Gongyang* became associated with a group of writings which were known collectively as the New Texts. After the burning of Confucian—and other—books and the burial of scholars by China's unifier, Qin Shihuangdi, in 213 B.C., Confucianism was banned for almost a century. After its revival under imperial patronage, and led by scholars such as Dong Zhong-shu, there were many doubts about the reconstruction of the original sources. Toward the end of the first century B.C. another tradition grew up claiming to be based on documents hidden during the destruction of the books. It emphasized different texts and commentaries and came to be known as the Old Text school.[12]

After the fourth and fifth centuries A.D., the New Text school and the *Commentary of Gongyang* were eclipsed by the Old Text school and the *Commentary of Zuo*, its preferred commentary on the *Spring and Autumn Annals*. During the period of division between North and South, 420–589 A.D., there was a general decline of Confucianism and a rise of Taoism and Buddhism, and in the restoration of Confucianism in the Tang and Song dynasties the Old Text school acquired a dominance that was made secure by the commentaries and annotations of neo-Confucian scholars.[13]

In the late eighteenth and early nineteenth centuries there was a revival of interest in the New Text school: Zhuang Cun-yu (1719–1788) began a study of the *Commentary of Gongyang*, and

12. For a discussion of this, see Fung Yu-lan, II, 133–167; Tjan, I, 137; Kang Woo, 186–190; and Wakeman, 102.

13. Wakeman suggests plausibly that the annotations of the great scholar Zheng Xuan (127–200 A.D.) helped blur the distinction between the Old and New Text schools, 108.

another scholar from Wujin in Kiangsu, Liu Feng-lu (1776–1820), wrote an explanation of He Xiu's subcommentary, in which among other things he described the theory of the three epochs.[14]

There are various possible explanations for this revival of interest after sixteen hundred years. On the level of pure scholarship, it came from a desire to strip away later commentaries and interpretations in order to reach the "true" nature of the ancients, who could be best understood through the writings of Han scholars—many of whom were New Text—who were closer to them in time. This research had a political aspect. In many societies radicals use and need the distant past—which because of its distance can be shaped according to their wishes—to justify their attacks on the present order.[15] It is almost certain that the revival of interest in the heterodox school was related to the social strains and disintegration of the late eighteenth and early nineteenth centuries. But this explanation is clearly not sufficient. A further possibility, for which there is no evidence, is that concern with the theory of the three epochs may have been stimulated by Western ideas of progress filtering into China through the Jesuits.[16]

In his *Intellectual Trends in the Ch'ing Period,* Liang Qi-chao quoted a poem written to him by a friend:

> Gong (Zi-zhen) and Liu (Feng-lu) evolved from Zhuang (Cun-yu)
> This line alone and dim
> Reached back to Dong Zhong-shu.[17]

The transmission of the texts of the Gongyang school over so many centuries shows that the "dim line" existed among the literate. Among the peasants the ideas associated with this tradition were

14. Liang Qi-chao, *Intellectual Trends of the Ch'ing Period,* translated by Immanuel C. Y. Hsü (Cambridge, Mass., 1959), 88. (This work is referred to hereafter as Hsü.) For more detail see Qian Mu, II, 523–568. For biographies of Zhuang and Liu, see *Eminent Chinese of the Ch'ing Period* (hereafter referred to as ECCP), ed. A. Hummel (Washington, 1943–1944).

15. See Marx, "The Eighteenth Brumaire of Louis Bonaparte," *Selected Works* (Moscow, 1958), I, 247.

16. Wakeman sees the revival of interest in more internalist terms, that some scholars wanted to break away from rigid neo-Confucianism as well as from a desire for practical as opposed to textual studies, 110. See also Hsü, 89.

17. For Gong see ECCP and *Gong Ding-an (Zi-zhen) Yanjiu,* ed. Zhu Jie-qin, (Hong Kong, 1971).

much stronger. But recurrent millenarian rebellions show that messianic beliefs and visions of an ideal communist future, connected with all the Chinese philosophies and Buddhism, obviously had credence among the ordinary people throughout the two millennia, separating the second century B.C. from the eighteenth century A.D.[18] Soon after scholars became interested in the *Commentary of Gongyang* and interpretations of it, the Taiping leaders began synthesizing Christianity with the same stream of apocalyptical Confucianism. The name *Taiping* itself—the last of the three epochs and a word associated with Han Confucianism—is significant.[19] The Taiping teachers definitely linked *Datong* to their vision of the Kingdom of God. A Taiping proclamation quoted the passage in the *Liyun* on *datong,* following it with these words: "But now it can be hoped for, the extreme disorder will be regulated, and the extreme darkness will be made light, such is the way of heaven." [20] Thus the Taiping teaching clearly shifted the age of *datong* from the past to the future. In their specific policies they constantly stressed the importance of working for the public good and not for private interest, and for all property to be divided equally among the people.

18. See Yuji Muramatsu, "Some Themes in Chinese Rebel Ideologies," in *The Confucian Persuasion,* ed. Arthur F. Wright (Stanford, 1960), 241–268. See Also Hou Wai-lu, 14–28.

19. See Vincent Y. C. Shih, *The Taiping Ideology: Its Sources, Interpretations, and Influences* (Seattle, 1967), 211–235; and Eugene Powers Boardman, *Christian Influence Upon the Ideology of the T'aip'ing Rebellion, 1851–1864* (Madison, 1952).

20. "Taiping Zhaoshu" in *Taiping Tianguo,* ed. Xiang Da et al. (Shanghai, 1954), I, 92. The proclamation is mentioned by Joseph Levenson in *Confucian China and its Modern Fate,* Vol. II, *The Problem of Monarchical Decay* (London, 1964) 106; and Shih, 119. The belief that the glorious new world will begin only after an age of extreme chaos and suffering is common to most millenarian sects. See Norman Cohn, *The Pursuit of the Millennium* (London, 1957), particularly 71–84.

It is true that the *Commentary of Gongyang* was studied in Canton, the Taiping leader Hong Xiu-quan's home region. In pointing this out, however, Levenson exaggerates Canton's importance as a center of New Text studies, II, 107. Changzhou or Yangzhou were more important, pace Wakeman, 113. Furthermore, only a few decades later Kang You-wei, studying in Canton, encountered the *gongyang* tradition only when he was over 30, and then it was from a Szechwanese. See below. As far as specifics are concerned I tend to agree with Shih when he states that apart from their name he sees "no trace of the gongyang teachings in the Taiping ideological system," 213–214. However, there is abundant proof that they were part of a broad millenarian movement of which both the *gongyang* tradition and the tradition of *datong* formed parts. There is also no doubt that after 1820 Kwangtung, bearing the brunt of British aggression, became an area of maximum social strain and hence of heterodox ideas.

The devastation in south and central China which accompanied the Taiping Rebellion and its suppression seriously hampered the development of Qing philosophy.[21] However, *gongyang* studies continued and the final flowering of the school came at the end of the nineteenth century.

The outstanding intellectual figure of the 1890s was Kang You-wei (1858–1927), the leader of the abortive reform movement of 1898. Kang, who came from a scholarly family, received a relatively orthodox education. His teacher, Zhu Ci-qi, one of the nineteenth-century scholars, emphasized the "practical studies" of the seventeenth-century writers like Gu Yan-wu and, opposing purely philological research and belles-lettres, insisted on social relevance. In 1878 at the age of 20, Kang, who had always had a mystical streak and tendency to see himself in messianic terms, went through an emotional crisis. He went for a time into retreat for meditation and study of Buddhism and Taoism. In the following years he became interested in the West and visited the foreign settlements in Hong Kong and Shanghai. He began radical speculation, not only on the problems of reforming China, but also on cosmology and society as a whole.[22] Although Kang claimed to have read the *Commentary of Gongyang* and He Xiu's subcommentary in 1880, it was not until 1889 that he was able to see its potential as a purely Chinese justification for his new synthesis. It was at this time that he first met Liao Ping, an ardent follower of the *gongyang* tradition. According to Liang Qi-chao, who had no liking for Liao, the latter made Kang change his ideas completely.[23] Perhaps plagiarism is too

21. Hsü, 84.

22. For Kang's intellectual development, see his "Kang Nan-hai Zibian Nianpu" (hereafter referred to as "Zibian Nianpu") which is reprinted in *Xuwu Bianfa*, 4 vols. (Shanghai, 1957), IV, 107–171. It is translated by Jung-pang Lo in *K'ang Yu-wei, A Biography and a Symposium* (Tucson, 1967), 17–144. For a bibliography on Kang's concept of *Datong*, see Lo, 472–475. See also Richard C. Howard, "K'ang Yu-wei (1858–1927): His Intellectual Background and Early Thought," in *Confucian Personalities*, ed. Arthur Wright and Denis Twitchett (Stanford, 1962), 294–316.

23. Hsü, 92. For Kang's reliance on Liao, see Kung-ch'uan Hsiao, "Kang Yu-wei and Confucianism," in *Monumenta Serica*, *XVII* (1959), 96–212, esp. 127–131. Hsiao has clearly demonstrated that Kang did not use *Gongyang* concepts or terminology before 1888, 106–116. In his autobiography Kang mentioned that in 1880 he wrote but destroyed an attack on He Xiu. See "Zibian Nianpu," 115; and Lo, 36.

For Liao, see Joseph Levenson, "Liao P'ing and the Confucian Departure from History," in Arthur Wright and Denis Twitchett (eds.), *Confucian Personalities* (Stan-

strong a word to describe the relationship, but ideas very close to those of Liao Ping were the basis of the two books which made Kang's reputation as a great though controversial scholar. The two, *On the False Classics of the Xin Dynasty* and *On Confucius as a Reformer*, appeared in 1891 and 1897 respectively. The first was concerned with the struggle between the Old and New Texts. In it. Kang tried to prove that the Old Texts were all forgeries made during the usurping Xin dynasty (9–25 A.D.), thus upholding the New Texts, including the *Commentary of Gongyang*.[24]

In *On Confucius as a Reformer* Kang came very close to the mysticism of He Xiu. He said that Confucius' references to the glorious past and the ancients had been made for purely didactic purposes and had no historical value. He took Confucius and the *Gongyang* school's emphasis on the differences of ritual and administration between the three classical dynasties, the Xia, Shang, and Zhou, to mean that Confucius believed in rigorous institutional reform. He also described the three epochs of "Chaos," "Rising Peace," and "Great Peace," saying that Confucius had outlined these stages for China and the world to go through.[25]

Thus Kang tried to reverse the mainstream of Chinese thought. He attempted to change Confucius from the guardian of antiquity who explained the golden past into a prophet and savior who forecast and set in motion a process leading to a glorious future.[26] By the 1890s, the period of his main political activities, Kang had assembled all the elements of his political and historical thought. It was at this time that he incorporated the concept of *datong*, which he equated with *taiping* ("Great Peace") as the final glorious age of a staged evolutionary process.

While he was activating the young literati and writing his books on Confucianism, Kang was drafting a far more original work, the final title of which was *Book of Datong*. Though it was probably completed by 1902, the book was so radical the Kang did not allow

---

ford, 1962), 317–325, and in Joseph Levenson, *Confucian China and its Modern Fate,* Vol. III, *The Problem of Historical Significance* (Berkeley and London, 1965), 3–15.

24. Hsü, 92–93.

25. Hsü, 94–95.

26. Joseph Levenson, *Confucian China and its Modern Fate,* Vol. I, *The Problem of Intellectual Continuity* (London, 1958), 80–82.

its complete publication during his lifetime. Sections were published after the 1911 Revolution in 1913, but the complete edition only appeared in 1935.[27]

According to Kang, in the new age all the barriers that had divided the world would be broken down so that men and even animals could live in harmony. The chapter headings of the work were: Abolishing National Boundaries and Uniting the World, Abolishing Class Boundaries and Equalizing All People, Abolishing Racial Boundaries, and Amalgamating All Races, Abolishing Sex Boundaries and Preserving the Independence of Individuals, Abolishing Family Boundaries and Becoming Heaven's People, Abolishing Livelihood Boundaries and Making Occupations Public, Abolishing Administrative Boundaries and Governing with Complete Peace and Equality, Abolishing Boundaries of Kind and Loving All Living Things, Abolishing Boundaries of Suffering and Obtaining the Utmost Happiness.[28]

The idea of a world-wide homogeneous society produced by this destruction of boundaries was very similar to the theories of the age of *datong* described in the *Liyun,* with everybody working for common not personal or sectional interests. Using evolutionary relativism he argued, for instance, that although the family had been a useful institution in the age of chaos, it was no longer appropriate for the age of *datong,* as its exclusiveness harmed the general good. Thus babies and children should be brought up in creches and nurseries, and the old and the sick should be looked after in public institutions. Kang's long and detailed description contained many specific proposals not mentioned in the *Liyun,* most of which would have been enormously shocking to orthodox Confucians. For example, not only did he foresee sexual equality and the economic and social destruction of the family, but he also advocated such reforms as the replacement of marriage by short-term contracts and the toleration of homosexuality.[29]

Kang's autobiography makes it difficult to discover the stages by

27. Kang You-wei, Introduction to *Datongshu,* edited by Zhang Xi-chen and Zhou Zhen-fu (Peking, 1956), 2 (referred to hereafter as *Datongshu*); and *Ta T'ung Shu, The One World Philosophy of K'ang Yu-wei,* translated by Lawrence G. Thompson (London, 1958), 26–31 (referred to hereafter as Thompson).

28. *Datongshu,* 3–6, and Thompson, 31–33.

29. *Datongshu,* 164–165 and 281–282; and Thompson, 164–165 and 252.

which, or the sources from which, he developed these radical ideas. Recent research, however, has made the picture much clearer. Between 1884 and 1887 Kang wrote a number of drafts describing utopian worlds; none were published, and only one has survived. His *Substantial Truths and Universal Laws* can be fairly described as a forerunner to the *Book of Datong*.[30] The world envisaged in *Substantial Truths* was regulated by universal principles that proceeded from geometric axioms rather than from human laws. But Kang also had an ethical criterion, maintaining that universal laws should be those most beneficial to human morality. In an attempt to transcend the ethical differences between East and West and between different ages, he argued that unlike the relative moral laws of specific societies those deduced in common by all mankind also had universal validity even if they could not yet be proved geometrically. These universal principles included sexual equality, the freedom to choose and change mates and, with the old and the young being looked after by public institutions, a society which would free men and women from the obligations of filial piety.[31] The radicalism of these proposals seems to have come from Kang's own original synthesis of Qing neo-Confucianism, Western, Taoist, and Buddhist thought.[32] The historian Hsiao Kung-ch'üan points out the similarity between Kang's ideal world and the "Universe of One Reality," the highest phase of the fourfold universe envisaged by the Hua-yen school of Buddhism—a world brought into perfect harmony through the operation of the "Ten Profound Theories" which taught, among other things, that

"all things have coexistence and are united to form one entity, that all beings commune with one another without obstacle, that each identifies itself with another thereby realizing synthetical identification."[33]

Kang's *Substantial Truths* contains no mention either of the three epochs or of *datong*.[34] Kang was converted to the New Text school

---

30. Thompson, 27; Howard, 311; Wakeman, 121–123; and Hsiao, 112–114.
31. Howard, 312; and Hsiao, 113.
32. In his utopias Kang appears to have been influenced by Dai Zhen, the major eighteenth-century philosopher. Dai argued against the Song neo-Confucians that "reasonable" desires should be satisfied rather than repressed. See also Hsü, 60.
33. Hsiao, 181.
34. Hsiao, 107–108; and Howard, 315.

only after reading Liao Ping's book *Studies in Old and New Learning* and after long discussions with Liao in 1889–1890. It is likely that Kang began linking the upward progress of the *Gongyang* tradition to that of his ideal worlds at about this time.[35]

The source of Kang's interest in *datong* and the timing of its incorporation into his intellectual scheme are much less certain. Kang stated that he began to study the *Liyun* in 1884 and to appreciate the significance of *datong* in 1885.[36] But his failure to use the term in any of his extensive writings during the 1880s makes the claim most unlikely.[37] The first independent evidence that Kang was using the term comes from his disciple, Liang Qi-chao, who wrote that, in 1891 when studying under Kang at his new school in Changxing lane in Canton, Kang talked about the works he was just writing which included *Gongli xu* ("Universal Principles") and a study of *datong*. However, the historian of philosophy, Qian Mu, points out that Kang's *Changxing xueji,* a course outline for the new schools, does not mention the *Liyun* or *datong*.[38] Thus it seems likely that Kang began using the concept of *datong* during or more probably shortly after 1891.

This dating suggests that the concept may well have come to Kang from a translated synopsis of Edward Bellamy's *Looking Backward* that appeared at this time in *The Review of the Times (Wanguo Gongbao)*.

The Review of the Times was essentially the creation of two missionaries, an American, Dr. Young J. Allen, and a Welshman, Dr. Timothy Richard. In 1875 Allen, a southern Baptist, established its earlier incarnation, *The Globe Magazine (Wanguo Gongbao),* in order to enlighten the Chinese, particularly the gentry, whose violent hostility to Christianity and the West was causing great concern to the missionaries.[39] In this journal, evangelism was mixed with

---

35. Hsiao, 126–130.

36. Kang, "Zibian Nianpu," 118; and Lo, 42.

37. Qian Mu, II, 638–639; and Hsiao, 107.

38. Liang Qi-chao, "Sanshi Zishu," in *Yinbingshi Wenji* (Taipei ed., 1960), IV, XI, 15–19, esp. 17. See also Qian Mu, II, 639.

39. For a biography of Allen, see Warren A. Candler, *Young J. Allen* (Nashville, 1931). See also Knight Biggerstaff, *The Earliest Modern Government Schools in China* (Ithaca, 1961), 160–161. For the *Review's* origin, see Chi-yun Chen, "Liang Ch'i-ch'ao's Missionary Education: A Case Study of Missionary Influence on the Reformers," Harvard *Papers on China,* XVI (Cambridge, Mass., 1962) 66–125, esp.

secular news and general information from both China and the West. Publication stopped in 1882, but in 1889 *Wanguo Gongbao* was revived as a monthly with a different English title, *The Review of the Times,* under the auspices of a new interdenominational organization, the Society for the Diffusion of Christian and General Knowledge among the Chinese (S.D.K.). As well as publishing *The Review of the Times,* the S.D.K. also brought out books and pamphlets on Western culture and technology, together with those on Christianity. Like the journal, these publications were aimed at the literati, and particular efforts were made to sell them at examination centers.[40]

Alexander Williamson, the first general secretary of the S.D.K., died in 1891. His place was taken by Timothy Richard,[41] a Welsh Baptist who had been in China since 1869. Richard and Allen, who had retained the editorship of *The Review of the Times,* became its leading contributors. During the height of the reform movement, from China's defeat by the Japanese in 1895 to the abortive Hundred Days of Reform in 1898, Allen and Richard became national figures. Their publications sold by the hundred thousand, and both their journal and society became models for those of the reformists. High officials and even the Emperor himself read their writings.[42]

In 1899 Kang told newspaper reporters that "he owed his conversion to reform chiefly to the writings of two missionaries, the Rev. Timothy Richard and Dr. Young J. Allen." [43] From 1895, Kang and Liang Qi-Chao were in close contact with Richard. It is even possible that Liang acted for a time as his Chinese secretary.[44] But even

---

69–75. The *Review* had a predecessor, *Jiaohui Xinbao, Church News,* which ran between 1868 and 1874. This was more exclusively concerned with evangelism and church affairs than its successor, although it too contained Chinese and world news like *Wanguo Gongbao*—though not so completely.

40. K. S. Latourette, *A History of Christian Missions in China* (London, 1929), 436–437; and Chen, 71.

41. For Richard, see his autobiography *Forty-five Years in China: Reminiscences by Timothy Richard DD* (London, 1916); and W. E. Soothill, *Timothy Richard of China* (London, 1924). See also Chen, 69–70.

42. Soothill, 183; and Chen, 67.

43. Richard, 254; and Chen, 86 and 95. One reason for imitating the missionaries was the reformers' belief that this could help avoid persecution. See also Chen, 77.

44. Chen, 86; and Richard, 255.

before then, however, the missionaries' influence on Kang had been profound. He wrote in his autobiography: "In 1883 . . . having bought *Wanguo Gongbao,* I began studying Western sciences."[45] There is also evidence to show that he read religious tracts. For example, *gongli* ("Universal Principles"), was the term used by both catholics and protestants to describe their doctrines.[46] Kang's study, which he expounded to Liang Qi-chao, and which also formed part of the title of one of his ideal-world schemes, was *Renlei Gongli* ("Principles for Mankind").

Bellamy's *Looking Backward* was first published in America in 1888. It rapidly became a best seller, and it was extremely important in the spread of socialism throughout the world. The story is of a young man who fell asleep in Boston in 1887 to wake up in the same city in the year 2,000. In the intervening century the world had become transformed. Private ownership of the means of production had been abolished. Private affluence and public squalor had been reversed, except there was now no absolute poverty. All men and women were educated by the state to the age of 21. Then they were employed by it, at first in manual labor, after which they were divided by aptitude and inclination into various professions. These had differences of status but received equal pay—or rather equal credit from a state system. Retirement was at 45—rationalization of labor made this possible. The country was ruled by a "board" elected according to trade. There was sexual equality, and women's economic dependence on men was abolished, but the nuclear family remained the basic social unit. Even though there were communal kitchens families ate in private dining rooms adjoining them. With brilliant anticipation of the way in which technology has been used to reinforce existing social structures, Bellamy described how families in *Looking Backward* listened to music or religious services at home, the sound being transmitted by special telephone. All in all, although the projection was radical for nineteenth-century America, it was still very much marked by it.

45. Kang, "Zibian Nianpu," 116, and Lo, whose translation of the title as *The Review of the Times* (hereafter referred to as ROT), is an anachronism, 38.
46. Thompson, 13–14; and Hsiao, 112. Wakeman translates *gongli* as axiom, and *gongfa* as universal principle, 121. For the Christian connotations of *gongli,* see Chen, 81.

The social and economic changes had not come about through revolution. All that had happened was that public opinion had decided that the monopolies were now so huge that instead of serving the interests of a few they should serve everybody by merging with the state. The transformation took place quite peacefully. The new corporate state was run with the efficiency of an army, an army designed, however, for purely civilian purposes, for the age of warfare had passed and other countries had undergone similar transformations. Thus, although Bellamy foresaw intense patriotism and although the ideology of the new regime was called "nationalism," in his transformed society there was complete freedom of trade and personal movement throughout the world.[47]

The Chinese translation, which first appeared in serial form in *The Review of the Times* between December 1891 and April 1892, contained all these points.[48] It is known that by 1896 Tan Si-tong and Liang Qi-chao had read the translation in book form. Liang gave it a mark of distinction as one of the most important books on the West available in China.[49] Thus it is almost certain that Kang read it. In view of his longstanding interest in *The Review of the Times* it is probable that he read the serialization when it first came out or soon after. Some time between 1896 and 1898 Kang's close follower, Tan Si-tong, wrote that "the Western [ideal world] of *Looking Backward* is almost the image of the *datong* of the *Liyun*."[50] It is clear that many people, possibly even Kang himself, saw an equivalence between the two schemes. But Bellamy's proposed society was very different from and in many ways less radical than Kang's, and apart from a few specific points, some of which will be discussed below, there appear to be few direct borrowings by Kang from Bellamy. Furthermore, Kang had been working on his utopian schemes five or six years before *Looking Backward* first appeared in China. However, Bellamy's anonymous translator used the term *datong* to describe the future world: at the beginning of the

47. *Looking Backward* (London and New York, 1888).

48. It was entitled *Huitou Kan* and appeared in issues XXV to XLIX.

49. "Xixue Shumubiao," in *Zhixuezhai Congshu* (1896), III, 3b, quoted in Chen, 112. Liang gave it the title *Bainian yi meng*. The S.D.K. and Tan Si-tong referred to it as *Bainian yi jiao;* see ROT, CXXXIII (4/99), 16; and Tan Si-tong *Renxue* (Shanghai, 1958), 76.

50. Tan Si-tong, 76.

first chapter he paraphrased the narrator who was supposed to be writing in the year 2000 A.D.

> At this time [the 1880s] Americans were divided into four categories, rich, poor, intelligent and stupid. By the law of the rich getting richer, either by buying shares or doing business, the descendents of the rich could enjoy their riches without working. What is more they saw themselves as honorable and respectable, treating the poor who toiled, like dumb beasts. They maintained that the division between rich and poor was one between intelligence and stupidity and that the distance separating them was like that between heaven and earth. Why, did they not know that the Lord created them with one body, and the rich and poor are brothers. How could the rich live so high and have no pity for the poor. Why, was this not the World of *datong (datong zhi shi)!* Truly they did not have noble methods and beautiful proposals for rich and poor to benefit equally.[51]

In a later instalment *datong* was used in a still clearer context. The narrator, delighted at the virtual disappearance of crime and even lying, exclaims: "This truly is the world of *datong*."[52] Here the translation is of the biblical, "new heavens and a new earth, wherein dwelleth righteousness," which the prophet foretold.[53]

This, together with the Taiping use of the term suggests that the transfer of *datong* from the past to the future was first made in Chinese translations of Christian texts. However, the term does not appear to have been used in any of the major nineteenth-century translations of the Bible.

As far as Kang Yu-wei is concerned it seems likely that it was the use of the term *datong* in association with Bellamy's world of 2000 A.D. that precipitated Kang's transfer of the concept from the past to the future, and its incorporation into his utopian schemes. The link between *datong* and Bellamy's world which—like Marx—combined the technological advances of capitalism with a collective morality may also have helped Kang break with the other ancient connotation of *datong,* that it was an age of simplicity. In the final version of the *Book of Datong* Kang, using the specific traditional vocabulary to describe these ages, reversed their order: "Now barbarous ages respect *zhi* simplicity. The age of *taiping* respects *wen* cultivation."[54]

51. ROT, XXXV (12/91), 15–15b.
52. ROT, XXXVIII (3/92), 16.
53. Bellamy, 152; and 2 Peter 3–13.
54. *Datongshu,* 247. For the alternation of the ages *zhi* and *wen* see note 2 above. It is interesting that Kang used the word *taiping* here, possibly the reversing of tradition if he had used the word *datong* would have been too blatant.

Kang was not alone in shifting the meaning of *datong*. During the following years, writers in *The Review of the Times* began to use it in the sense of "cosmopolitan" or for the spread of civilization.[55] The process was described, in terms strikingly similar to those used by Kang in the final version of the *Book of Datong,* by Timothy Richard in the introduction to his best-selling translation of Mackenzie's *History of the Nineteenth Century:* "God is breaking down the barriers between all nations by railways, steamers and telegraphs in order that all shall live in peace and happiness as brethren of one family."[56]

Five years later Richard and his Chinese secretary, Cai Er-kang, were using *datong* in the sense of social evolution or even sociology. In 1899 they published at least part of Benjamin Kidd's *Social Evolution* under the title *Study of Datong.*[57] Kidd's book was an attempt to find a scientific and humanist alternative to social Darwinism and Marxism. In the translation, *datong,* which was specifically linked to the *Liyun,* was used to mean the goal of social evolution, and its study was seen as one of the methods to achieve this.[58] By 1899, however, the influences went both ways and not merely from the missionaries to the Reformists. From 1897 Kang openly proclaimed himself a promoter of *datong*. In that year he and his colleagues established the Datong Translated Books Company.[59] In public, however, he appears to have used the term as a respectable traditional term for cosmopolitan and progressive. Early in 1898, overseas Chinese businessmen in Yokohama established a school for which Sun Yat-sen gave the name East West

55. See, for instance, Dr. Allen's article "Datong faren" on "the launching of cosmopolitanism" which describes the breakdown of tariffs and the convertibility of currency, in ROT, LVII (8/94), 25–25b.

56. Chen makes the connection between this and *datong,* 73.

57. The first four chapters appeared in ROT, CXXI (2/99) to CXXIV (5/99). The S.D.K. also published it as a book which sold 2,000 copies: see ROT, CXXXIII, (2/1900), 2. *Social Evolution* itself was first published in London and New York (1894).

58. ROT, CXXI (2/99), 12. The need to explain the term suggests both that the translation was not obvious and that the term was still relatively unknown. *Social Evolution* lays great stress on the peaceful but inevitable disappearance of "inferior races," that is, blacks and red Indians. It makes no mention of Chinese or Japanese. See Ch. II translated in ROT, CXXII (3/99), 15–15b. It is possible that this influenced Kang's similar but more humane views on the subject; see *Datongshu,* 117–126; and Thompson, 140–148. The influence of the translation of *Social Evolution* on *Datongshu* is also evident in the descriptions of the workers' sufferings and labor conflicts: ROT, CXXIII, 16.

59. Lo, 153.

School. Later, on Sun's recommendation, the merchants approached Kang You-wei, who thought the name inelegant and immediately changed it to *Datong* School.[60] This school became a center for Kang and Liang when they fled from China after the Empress Dowager's coup that autumn, and during their years of exile they gave many of their organizations the title *datong*.[61]

Thus for Kang the term appears to have covered a wide spectrum of ideas. Or as he would have put it, it held an inner and an outer meaning. Externally, it meant progress and internationalism. Internally, it retained much of its traditional radical social content. However, by its totality, and immediate impracticability, it allowed Kang to act in the short run in a cautious or even conservative way and it was this political caution that made him refuse to publish the *Book of Datong*.

Kang seems to have known something about socialism and communism from *The Review of the Times*—and presumably from other sources—and from the 1880s, he clearly saw a relationship between these theories and his vision.[62] The *Book of Datong* contains several references to communism as a forerunner and a natural extension of democracy.

The Rise of Democracy as a Forerunner of datong: The upward progress of democracy is natural. When America was established, the French Revolution succeeded it, and other countries followed. Constitutions became widespread, republics flourished, theories of communism *(junchan zhi shuo)* emerged and unions/labor parties *(gong dang)* arose daily.

In an autocracy people are selfish and it is difficult to cooperate. But, once there is democracy, cooperation is easy. If when the people are seeking their profit, benevolent men proclaim the happiness of *datong* then they can work with the minds of others. Once the scheme is proclaimed people will

60. Lo, 254; and Feng Zi-you, *Geming Yishi*, 5 vols., 1939–1946 (Taipei ed., 1953), 148; and Harold Z. Schiffrin, *Sun Yat-sen and the Origins of the Chinese Revolution* (Berkeley, 1968), 155. See also Liang Qi-chao, "Datong Xuexiao Kaixiao ji," *Qingyi Bao*, X (11/9/99), 5–6b.

61. There was another *Datong Xuexiao* in Tokyo (Lo, 195) and a *Datong Ribao* established in San Francisco in 1902 which quickly became revolutionary. See Zhang Jing-lu, *Zhongguo Jindai Chuban Shiliao*, 2 vols. (Peking, 1957), I, 86; and Feng, *Geming Yishi*, II, 33.

62. For references to socialism in ROT, see Ch. 3 below. It is interesting to note that Thompson, who previously saw no relation between socialism and the *Datongshu*, now believes that it may have existed. See "Ta-tung Shu and the Communist Manifesto: Some Comparisons," in Lo, 341–354, esp. 341.

turn toward it, like water flows downhill. Therefore the rise of democracy, the flourishing of constitutions and theories of collective communism *(he-qun junchan zhi shuo)* are all the first sounds of *datong*.[63]

The belief that transformation will come, simply because enlightened men will demonstrate that existing society is irrational, is very reminiscent of Bellamy. But, where Bellamy was consistent in giving his ideas maximum publicity, Kang, believing that the time was not ripe, did all he could to hide his.

Although, at one level, Kang saw socialism as the logical extension of political democracy and hence of Western progress, he also completely accepted the radical and liberal analysis that the situation in Europe was getting worse and that there was a widening gap between rich and poor.[64] Bellamy, too, stressed this, and his book vibrates with his sympathy for the poor. However, he hated anarchistic and labor extremists. Indeed, one of the characters in *Looking Backward* argues that the agitators were subsidized by the monopolists to put people off reform. For his part Kang, believed that, although justifiable, labor conflicts could cause harm to progress.

In human struggles, if there is injustice, outcry is natural. Therefore, the struggle in recent years, from workers forming parties to press the owners, which is surging through Europe and America is only just beginning. The unification of labor parties must become greater. I am afraid that there will be a disaster of blood and steel. The struggle will not be between weak and strong countries but between groups of rich and poor. Hence within a century all eyes will be on this. Therefore socialist *(renqun)* and communist theories *(junchan zhi shuo)* increase and this will be the greatest problem. But, as long as the selfishness of the family is not eliminated and the ideas of private production are still current, there is almost no way of solving this extraordinarily great problem.[65]

This sentiment appears elsewhere.

63. *Datongshu,* 70; and Thompson, 86. The end of this passage is quoted by Rong Meng-yuan in his "Xinhai Geming qian Zhongguo Shukanshang dui Makesizhuyi di Jieshao," in *Xin Jianshe* (1953), III, 5–12, esp. 6.

64. *Datongshu,* 32–33, where he describes the slums of the East End of London, Paris, New York, and Chicago as hells, not in Thompson! See also 235–236; and Thompson, 212, esp. 213.

65. *Datongshu,* 236; and Thompson, 213.

If one proclaims the method of communism *(gongchan zhi fa)* and there are families and states there will be selfishness. If there is a family one looks after one's wife and family. If there is a state then to have soldiers' taxes increase. If you wish to practice communist theories *(gongchan zhi fa)* with these systems it is like pointing a chariot north when you want to go south.[66]

Kang's reasons or rationalizations for arguing that socialist or communist movements were limited and futile were very different from those of Bellamy, and his attack on the family has an almost "Cultural Revolutionary" ring. His reasoning is much more radical than Bellamy's argument that activism hampered the proposals of enlightened men, which alone could bring about real change. The totality and perfection of Kang's scheme discouraged any attempt to realize it. But he would not admit the impracticability of his schemes. Indeed, his one reference to a Western socialist by name was to the utopian anarchist Fourier, whose intentions he admired but whose schemes he condemned for being impracticable.[67]

If Kang saw Western socialist theories as partial and incomplete intimations of *datong,* others equated them. Liang Qi-chao was one of the two pupils Kang allowed to look at his manuscript of the *Book of Datong.* In 1901 Liang published a biography of his teacher in a special centenary issue of his magazine *Pure Criticism* which he had founded in Yokohama after his flight from China in 1898. The biography contained a detailed summary of *datong* which provided the first public information on it.[68] A section headed "His

66. *Datongshu,* 235; and Thompson, 212. It is interesting that Kang should have two such similar passages so close together. However, the difference in vocabulary suggests that the second passage is a later interpolation. *Junchan zhi shuo* is a term used in Chinese sources, while *gongchang,* the word later adopted as standard, came from Japan only at the turn of the century. For the Japanese origin see Saneto Keishō, *Chūkokujin Nihon Ryūgakushi* (Tokyo, 1960), 399.

67. *Datongshu* 235; and Thompson, 211. Kang describes Fourier as an Englishman. Kang's disagreement was with Fourier's advocacy of the establishment of ideal communities within the existing society. His own scheme was for the whole world. He realized it would be impossible on a smaller scale. For a discussion on the differences between these two kinds of utopian thought, see Arthur E. Beston "Patent Office Models of the Good Society: Some Relationships Between Social Reform and Westward Expansion," in Stanley Katz and Stanley Kutler, eds., *New Perspectives on the American Past* (Boston, 1969), 444–465, esp. 445–446.

68. *Qingyi Bao,* C (12/21/01). The journal has been reprinted (Taipei, 1967); pagination, according to the reprint is 6395–6440. The biography has been reprinted

Philosophy is the Philosophy of a Socialist" *(shehuizhuyipai)* begins:

Kang's philosophy is one of socialism. The socialism of the west begins with Plato in Greece which is also the beginning of the theory of communism *(Gongchan zhi lun)*. During the eighteenth century Saint Simon and Kant and their followers spread it. Its organization developed and it became a great hidden political force. Kang has never read their books but his ideal has many similarities with theirs.[69]

Liang was almost certainly right when he stated that Kang had not read any socialist books. There is no doubt, however, that quite apart from any socialist influences through Bellamy, Kang must have read about socialism in news items at least in *The Review of the Times* if not in other journals. Liang's own knowledge was not much more sophisicated. His references to Plato and Kant show that his own knowledge of socialism was not systematic. Nevertheless, it would be excessive to accept Sun Yat-sen's statement, made in 1906, that "six years ago Mr. Liang did not know anything about socialism." [70]

Liang's parallel between *datong* and socialism was an example of a mode of thought that appeared throughout his writings at the time. Like most of the reformers, Liang believed that all kinds of modern Western concepts were essentially similar to ones that had existed in ancient China. This "analogy of cultural values," to use Joseph Levenson's term, was extremely important to them in their desire to bolster up China and her culture against the West. As Levenson put it, "Western experience has shown that it is a good thing but Chinese must not believe that they were incapable of thinking it up for themselves." [71] But the analogy of cultural values must not be taken too far. In a letter to the translator, Yan Fu, in

---

and translated into English by Daiming Lee under the title *The Great Chinese Philosopher K'ang Yu-wei* (San Francisco, 1955). See also *Qingyi Bao*, 6417.

69. For Liang's use of the Japanese forms *shehuizhuyi* and *gongchan zhi lun,* see ch. 4 below.

70. Quoted by Hu Han-min, using the pen name of Min-yi, in "Gao Feinan Minshengzhuyizhe," *Min Bao,* XII (3/6/07), 108.

71. Joseph Levenson, *Liang Ch'i-ch'ao and the Mind of Modern China* (London, 1959), 43.

1897 Liang admitted that analogies could not be exact, but he justified drawing them by saying that they were useful for teaching purposes.[72] It is also possible that the Reformists gained the habit from their missionary mentors who constantly sought Chinese analogies in order to explain and justify the introduction of Western concepts. Nevertheless, Liang and the others were undoubtedly influenced in their perception of Western ideas and institutions by the Chinese analogies chosen for them.

In making the analogy of cultural values between *datong* and socialism Liang was only the first to state what later became a commonplace. The Kuomintang historian, Feng Zi-you, reported that before Sun Yat-sen invented the "principle of people's livelihood" in 1905, he advocated the "principle of *datong*" *(datongzhuyi)*.[73]

In 1908 Liu Shi-pei, one of the founders of the Society for the Study of Socialism, referred to the *Liyun* passage as an example of early Chinese communism.[74] In June 1911 Jiang Kang-hu, the future leader of the Chinese Socialist Party, said at the opening of the Society for Research into Socialism that "Socialism is the principle of *datong*. It is not a principle with divisions. It does not have racial, national, or religious boundaries. Everything is public and there is no self. Everyone is looked upon with the same benevolence."[75]

72. *Liang Ren-gong Xiansheng Nianpu Changbian Chugao,* compiled by Ding Wen-jiang, 2 vols. (Taipei, 1962), I, 41–42 (referred to hereafter as *Liang Nianpu*).
73. *Geming Yishi,* III, 216.
74. *Heng Bao* He Zhen and Liu Shi-pei, eds. (Tokyo, 1908), II (8/5/08).
75. *Hongshuiji* (San Francisco, 1913?), 25b–27, esp. 25b.

Wen-jiang, 2 vols. (Taipei, 1962), I, 41–42 (referred to hereafter as *Liang Lianpu*).

2 | The Review of the Times

Kang You-wei's known association with the *Review,* and his vocabulary when describing socialism, strongly suggest that he gained his knowledge of the latter from *Wanguo Gongbao* in both its incarnations as *The Globe Magazine* and *The Review of the Times.* This journal, like other Chinese-language newspapers growing up in the treaty ports at this time, printed news items about socialism, anarchism, and nihilism among their reports from the West almost as soon as these subjects became newsworthy in Europe and America in the 1870s.[1] The references were sparse and scattered, and it was not until the 1890s that *The Review of the Times* developed anything approaching a unified vocabulary to translate the Western terms. Furthermore, most of the reports were of events for which no background information was provided. Thus, while a casual reader could have acquired no real knowledge of the Western movements, enough information was available for systematic readers like Kang You-wei, Liang Qi-chao, and Yan Fu to get some general sense of them.

The circulation and readership of the treaty-port Chinese press in the late nineteenth century is not clearly known, though it must have been under ten thousand. At its peak *The Review of the Times* had a circulation of over 39,000 and a readership that was many times greater.[2] Before 1895, however, figures were clearly much lower, and it is likely that despite attempts to reach the gentry most copies were

1. For descriptions of this press, see Ge Gong-zhen, *Zhongguo Baoxueshi* (Hong Kong ed., 1964), 64–112. For the Western-language press see F. H. H. King and Prescott Clarke, *A Research Guide to China-coast Newspapers, 1822–1911* (Cambridge, Mass., 1965), esp. 28.
2. See the "Annual Report of the S.D.K.," ROT, CXXXIII (2/1900), 1–2b; and Richard, 231–232.

sent to churches and missions where the converts, most of whom were poor, would have found its literary style very difficult.

In 1871 the *Review's* predecessor, the *Church News*, reprinted reports of the Paris commune. Reflecting the opinions of the Western press these reports were extremely hostile to the communards who were generally described as rebel bandits, and no attempt was made to explain their goals or ideas.[3] Socialists, anarchists, and nihilists continued to be described in these terms in the *Review's* earlier incarnation, *The Globe Magazine*. However, the 1878 news items began to give more details. Interest was stirred by the attempt made by a German named Nobiling to assassinate the Kaiser, an incident which Bismarck used as a pretext to ban the rapidly growing German Social Democratic Party. In May, *The Globe* published a telegram from London stating that "in France there is a party which has as its principle no division between rich and poor *(wufen pinfu)*. The assassin *(cike)* was one of this party."[4] Later it was stated that he was "a rebel among the sect *(jiao)* who are against the division of rich and poor,"[5] implying that there were also peaceful men of this kind.

In the following weeks the terms *saihui* and *saidang* began to be used to describe Western socialist, anarchist, or anticzarist groups. *Sai,* which originally meant to "to repay" or "to give thanks," became, when compounded with *hui* (meeting), associated with religious ceremonies. In the late nineteenth century the compound was used to translate the Western terms for exhibition, meeting, or society. From this, in very much the same way as the Japanese *shakai,* the compound word developed the extended meaning of socialist. The phonetic similarity between these two terms shows that one of the reasons for their selection was their phonetic resemblance to the European word socialism. *Saihui,* however, retained its general significance of "society" when used in contexts that had nothing to do with socialism. Nevertheless, Nobiling and others were called *saihuizhe* socialists.[6]

3. *Jiaohui Zinbao,* III, 166 and IV, 9b. This last item describes the ferocity of the women of the commune.
4. *The Globe Magazine* (hereafter referred to as GM), X (1877–1878), 556b.
5. GM, X, 598.
6. CM, X, 681. In the same way, it is no coincidence that the first syllable in the Japanese word *kyōsanshugi* is similar to that of communism, though in general there

In the summer of 1878 there was a report from America which stated that a *saihui* was forming parties to cause strife. Furthermore this development was linked to "the disturbances in France eight years ago." [7]

Another report spoke of *saihui* (socialist) rebels.

In America socialist rebels are causing great alarm. People do not know where it will end. . . . Alas in America and many European countries there are many of this society. They all want to overthrow the State and level high and low, rich and poor.[8]

A similar report of the spread of socialism in Europe came from Russia. In this report the origin of the movement was seen as the French revolution of 1848.[9] This was also the conclusion of the most detailed description of socialism published at the time:

As for parties in France and Germany how can we assess their strength. Over the last 30 to 40 years in France there have been disturbances and struggles for power. Some people say that if the power of the princes and nobles has changed, among the people [differences] between the rich and honorable and the poor and humble have not, thus there is no advantage. They say that in the past centuries the poor have become poorer and the rich richer. Therefore in the great cities there are beggers and sickness, crime and suffering without number for which there is no cure. They also say that the great action of the future will be to liberate the workers who are at present slaves. In 1848 these things caused the French Government to totter. After this scholars were dissatisfied with this method and tried to oppose it. So that people would abandon these ideas and gradually turn toward the right and be as before. But it is not easy to destroy their theory and the party's hopes are like dreams. The party declined in France but grew in Germany. There were bold spirits who talked grandly about politics and formed a workers assembly *(gong zuo zhi yihui)* to destroy wealth . . . [line obliterated]. . . . They only talk about overthrowing governments and property. They only discuss the benefits of this life and do not think of those after death.

Now Germany has the broadest learning in Europe. It has thousands of studies. The reason for this becomes evident if you look at Germany's situa-

---

is no doubt that meaning was much more important than sound in the selection of new terms.

7. GM, X, 650. It is possible that this is a reference to the First International which was transferred to the United States of America after the Hague Congress in 1872.

8. GM, X, 681.

9. GM, X, 673b.

tion. In recent years everything has become more expensive and the people have become increasingly poor. How can society *(saihui)* be cured. Nowadays the Germans are a free people according to the English model. But previously the Germans relied on officials, as children do on their parents, not trusting their own talents and intelligence. Thus the strength of freedom is lacking. It is only that their philosophies and speculations are greater than those of other countries. There is a great gap between their thought and their action. This is why these parties greatly flourish. Moreover the power of the German military is strong and it oppresses the people who have to go through conscription to learn military skills. This is the basis of these parties.

In sum, most people do not accept the delusions of these parties and realize the danger in following their methods to overthrow the government fearing that they will damage the country. However, it is necessary for officials to investigate the background and see to it that the multitude can gain peace and happiness. Then the state and livelihood will flourish.[10]

This passage, which probably comes from one of the American digests of socialism, reflects many of the radical Christian attitudes toward socialism as well as Anglo-Saxon prejudices about or perceptions of Germany. The reference to "workers assembly" probably meant the First International. Another report printed in the same year was more specific. It referred to the banning of the German *Suxier Demokelate* (Social Democratic Party).[11]

During the early 1880s there was no sensational socialist activity in Germany, and *The Globe Magazine* like the Western press concentrated its interest in radicals upon the Russian nihilists.[12] With the resumption of publication in 1889 the situation had changed, and *The Review of the Times,* while continuing to publish articles on anarchism and nihilism, also published frequent reports on the Western labor movement, especially on the agitation for an international holiday on May Day and the associated struggle for an eight-hour day.[13] The news items were generally short and con-

10. GM, XI (1878–1879), 15b–16.

11. GM, XI, 178.

12. They were sometimes called by the traditional terms of *luandang, nidang,* or *pandang,* but more often they were referred to by the transliterations *niheilisite, nixili,* or *nitang.* See GM, XI, 615b; XII (1879–1880), 133b, 278, and 432–433; XIII (1880–1881), 396, 450; XIV (1881–1882), 152, 196b, 225, 297, 351, 387, 396b, 423; XV (1882–1883), 44b, 197, 206b, 275b, 304, 312b, 386, and 421.

13. Anarchists were given the insulting title of *yanajiside;* see ROT, LXVII (8/94), 29, and LXX (11/94), 26b. For reports on England and Germany, see ROT, XII

cerned with isolated events rather than with political trends or theories.

It was not until 1899 that there appear to have been any references to Marx or other socialists by name. This new information came in the abbreviated translation of Kidd's *Social Evolution*. In a rather garbled summary of a section of the first chapter, the translator wrote:

They [the poor] combine to have many strikes to coerce the rich . . . these "demos" *(judong)* are more savage than the clamor of war. The leader of all these workers is the famous Englishman Makesi (Marx). Marx' theories state that the power of the rich will extend across state boundaries to all of the five continents. If we do not control it their power will continue spreading and there is a real fear that the wealth of the world will be in their hands. But if we should reach this time the power of the rich would be exhausted. The poor masses *(qiongli)* reaching this desperate stage will have no alternative to remove their power and satisfy the people *(anmin)* and save the world.[14]

In the translation of *Social Evolution*, the term *anmin xue* was used to translate socialism in both its senses of reform and radical action. In Chapter III there is the passage:

I am afraid that the conflicts in the present world will become more intense than before. This statement is not empty. If one looks at modern trends of scholarship there is the new school of socialism *(anmin xin xue)*, like that set out by Germany's Marx in *Capital (ziben)*, like that set out in *Progress and Poverty (jiupin)* and America's George and the equality *(junfu)* of Bellamy and by the English Fabians. All these able writings state that although there is legal and political equality there is still extreme distance between rich and poor.[15]

The passage went on to describe the appalling conditions of London slums.[16]

Kidd's views that socialist theories were serious—though wrong—and required answering and that the social problem was critical and required alleviation were common to a wide range of enlightened

---

(1/90), 24b; XVIII (7/90), 24b; XXIII (12/90), 26b; XVII (4/91), 22b–23; XXXI (8/91), 22; XL (5/92), 23; XLIV (9/92), 24b, and many others.

14. ROT, CXXI (2/99), 13–13b; the summary is of Kidd, 11–13.

15. ROT, CXXIII (4/99), 16; the summary is of Kidd, 68.

16. This passage clearly influenced Kang You-wei. See *Datongshu;* see also Ch. 1, note 64, above.

men in the West, including the editor and most of the contributors to *The Review of the Times*. Like true Victorians, the later hammered home the message that national strength and progress depended on individual freedom, initiative, and responsibility. Nevertheless, like many others they found it impossible to accept the ruthlessness of social Darwinism.[17] The missionaries, in their articles on strengthening and enriching the nation (which became so influential among the Chinese reformers), insisted on the need to nourish the people and to avoid the Western dangers of "the rich becoming richer and the poor having no benefit." Thus one sees the "horror of assassinations of high officials." [18] As Timothy Richard wrote:

Now states have people as the basis and the people consider food as heaven. Therefore if crowds are starving and roaming around there will sometimes be waves of banditry. Truly if there are no means to make a living, men will be forced to stand up and take the dangerous road [become bandits].

He went on to describe Bismarck's social reforms and how these had quieted the people.[19]

The ease with which these ideas were translated into classical Chinese shows how congenial they were to Mencian Confucianists. For them it was both morally right and politically expedient for the ruler to satisfy the material needs of the people. For most Confucians, state socialism was far easier to comprehend and support than the ruthless selfishness of laissez faire and social Darwinism.

From time to time the editors of *The Review of the Times* went beyond their own beliefs to rather more radical ideas. In the summer of 1898 they published the first systematic exposition of any form of socialism in China. In 1897, while on leave in Europe and America, Timothy Richard hit on the idea of writing to a number of Western thinkers asking them to make proposals for China's reform. These he obtained with some difficulty, translated into Chinese, and

17. For a fascinating discussion of these issues in late nineteenth-century China, see Benjamin Schwartz, *In Search of Wealth and Power: Yen Fu and the West* (Cambridge, Mass., 1964). It is worth stressing, however, that among the reformers the belief in the importance of individual freedom for national strength was widely current at a theoretical level.

18. ROT, XLIII (8/92), 10; the quotation is from a series by the Rev. J. Edkins, DD, for which the English title was "How to Enrich the Nation." In Chinese it was *"Fuguo Yangmin Ze"* ("Policies to Enrich the Nation and Nourish the People").

19. "Bao min Xinfa lun," ROT, XXXIV (11/91), 4b–5.

published in a pamphlet entitled *The Renaissance of China;* this was serialized in *The Review of the Times* in the winter of the following year.[20] Most of the letters he received were from educational officials and university presidents who urged their Chinese readers to concentrate on more education and the eradication of backward customs. The longest and most detailed proposal came from the Reverend J. Bruce Wallace, a Congregational minister who had formed his own Brotherhood Church in London, a body which stood for socialism and untheological religion. According to one authority, Wallace advocated the formation of cooperatives which would extend to take over the state. The views set out in his letter, however, were from the mainstream of English socialism of the 1890s and very close to those of the Fabians.[21]

The letter began by setting forth two methods of national industrial development: private enterprise and state development. But it was maintained that the two methods could be combined: "Those things that are not suitable for private enterprise should go *(gui)* under state management and vice versa. In short this is the only way for the people to have sufficient food and clothing and equally enjoy the fruits of their labour."

The letter went on to state that although it was cheaper to develop through private enterprise it was a mistake to do so, because the developers were interested only in their profits and not in satisfying the people. By using big machinery, which only the rich could acquire, the poor came under their power and were savagely exploited. Thus the social problem became critical. With government enterprises the people would be protected and "just as scientists knew good methods of production they also know good methods of distribution." Government enterprises, Wallace maintained, could be employed for the common good. At the time, in all industrial coun-

20. "Xinghua Boyi," ROT, XVIII (11/98), CXIX (12/98) and CXX (1/99). For its compilation, see CXVIII, 10b–11.
21. Henry Pelling, *The Origins of the Labour Party, 1880–1900* (Oxford, 1965), 178. For more on J. B. Wallace, see K. S. Inglis, *Churches and the Working Classes in Victorian England* (London, 1963), 291 and 298. The author of the letter is described as the editor of the *Anmin Bao* in London, the Reverend Hualashi. J. B. Wallace should not be confused with A. R. Wallace, the founder of evolutionary theory who was a socialist, or with the Fabian leader, Graham Wallas, though the views expressed bear a striking resemblance to those of the Fabians. I am indebted to Sarah Smalley for information on this.

tries, there were a few idle rich and many who were desperately poor; the Christian message of selflessness was being neglected and men were entirely selfish. If China wanted to organize, she should study the advantages and disadvantages of the West. She should take the former and leave the latter, unlike Japan which had copied all the faults. Wallace then listed a seven-point program for China.

1. Land should be nationalized, with compensation. All land rent should go directly to the state which would use it for public developments, railways, offices, libraries, schools, etc. The author specifically rejected the idea of leasing land to businessmen for development.

2. Since what appeared to be free competition was often in reality a monopoly, enterprises like railways, shipping, gas, water, electricity, and trains should go to the state. But the most important utilities were the post office and long-distance railway lines. He gave as an example the successful municipalization of the Glasgow trams.

3. Banks should be nationalized.

4. China should establish a regular currency based on silver or gold and not use inconvenient copper cash.

5. Since the rich, by mechanization, force people out of work, the state should own industries which would stop the sufferings of the poor (in an unspecified way) and increase public wealth.

6. The state should set up large industries. There should be no direction of labor. The work force should be adjusted by increasing or decreasing wages.

7. There should be general education.

The letter continued with an attempt to explain the concept of surplus value. Wallace described the inevitable resentment of European workers toward the Chinese workers who undercut their wages and went on to attack cheap exports, arguing that a country should only export goods after its own people had been properly supplied. The conclusion was that private enterprise led to selfishness and war, and with public enterprise these could be avoided.[22]

As has been stated above, Wallace's program is very close to that of the Fabians. Like them, Wallace began with land and insisted, in opposition to the Land Nationalizers, that land was only one of the

22. ROT, CXX (1/99), 1–3b.

natural monopolies that should belong to the state. The letter was un-Marxist in its acceptance of a mixed economy. There was of course no mention of revolution, and unlike both Marxists and anarchists, Wallace saw the existing state as a neutral force capable of working for good rather than as a "gaoler for the ruling class." [23]

There is a striking similarity between Wallace's program and that developed by the Revolutionary Alliance between 1905 and 1907. There is no reason to suppose, however, that Sun or the other leaders of the Alliance were directly influenced by it, though this is possible. It is much more likely that the similarity comes from the fact that both were in the mainstream of Western European socialist thought.

The Review of the Times also transmitted a side branch of Western socialism which had a more direct impact on the Chinese revolutionaries, that of land nationalization or single tax. In its issue of December 1894, the *Review* published the first of a long series of articles advocating these ideas for the world in general and for China in particular. The author was W. E. Macklin, a medical missionary who appears to have been Canadian, though he was sent to China in 1886 by an American denomination, the Disciples of Christ.[24] The Disciples began in the early nineteenth century in the region between the Appalachians and the Ozarks as a fundamentalist sect believing in a return to the primitive Christianity of the New Testament. However, by the time of the Civil War it had become virtually indistinguishable from any other low-church denomination in the south and mid-west, both theologically and socially. For precisely this reason it is likely that many church members were sympathetic to Henry George's proposals for a single tax on land;[25] in any event, Macklin himself was an ardent advocate of the scheme and of all attacks on property in land.

23. For Fabian views at the time, see Margaret Cole, *The Story of Fabian Socialism* (London, 1961).

24. ROT consistently referred to Macklin as British. Presumably this included Canada as part of the Empire. There is no reason to doubt Schiffrin on this. See his "Sun Yat-sen's Early Land Policy," *The Journal of Asian Studies,* XVI, No. 4 (8/1957), 549–564, esp. 555 (referred to hereafter as "Early Land Policy"). See also Latourette, 398.

25. For a description of the Disciples of Christ, see William Tucker, *J. H. Garrison and the Disciples of Christ* (St. Louis, 1964).

The writings of John Lilburne and the other Levellers in the 1640s show that the belief that unearned income from land rent is immoral, while wealth gained from labor or trade is perfectly decent, is almost as old as bourgeois morality itself.[26] Even John Locke, the philosopher of private property, wrote:

> 'tis very clear that God, as king David says, Psalm 115:16, *has given the earth to the children of men,* given it to mankind in common. . . . Though the earth and all inferior creatures be common to all men, yet everybody has property in his own person. This nobody has any right to but himself. The *labour* of his body and the *work* of his hands, we may say are properly his.[27]

In the eighteenth century, at least partially inspired by Chinese ideas transmitted by the Jesuits, the French Physiocrats argued that since agriculture was the source of all wealth, there should be an *impôt unique* on land.[28] In England, Thomas Spence, a clergyman from Newcastle, proposed that all the land of the country should be given without compensation to the parishes which would rent it out.[29]

In the nineteenth century, the belief in the distinction between income resulting from nature and income resulting from labor became very widespread. This appears to have come about for two reasons, one theoretical and one practical. David Ricardo's theory of rent did not condemn it but drew attention to the fact that it was unearned and hence apparently different from other forms of income. Even more influential was the agitation against the landowners in the campaign for the repeal of the Corn Law, the railway boom, the massive increase in urban land values and the huge profits made by speculators who simply bought and sold land without improving it. These practices caused even fierce champions of private property like Herbert Spencer to write that the state, in reclaiming land, "would be acting in the interest of the highest type of civilisation." [30]

26. C. B. Macpherson, *The Political Theory of Possessive Individualism* (Oxford, 1962), 154–155.

27. "The True End of Civil Government," V, "Of Property," in *Social Contract: Essays by Locke, Hume, and Rousseau,* ed. Sir Ernest Barker (New York, 1962), 17.

28. See H. Higgs, *The Physiocrats* (London, 1897).

29. H. M. Hyndman, *The Nationlisation of the Land, 1775–1882* (London, 1882).

30. Charles Gide and Charles Rist, *A History of Economic Doctrines,* 2nd ed. (London, 1958), 560.

A less well-known, but in many ways more interesting, thinker along these lines was Patrick Dove. Although an Englishman, he inherited estates in Scotland. His interests ranged from German philosophy to small-bore rifles; he was the best kind of Victorian eccentric. Dove appears to have been a natural radical—he was expelled from school for leading a revolt—and was appalled by the Highland Clearances, which virtually depopulated over half of Scotland. He was also enraged by the use of Malthusian doctrine to justify the official reluctance to help the millions of crofters who starved during the Irish potato famine—which also affected western Scotland where he lived. He came to the conclusion that the famine, far from being the classic example of the theory that population expands beyond the increase of natural resources, was in fact caused by official neglect and exploitation of the peasants.[31]

In the late 1840s Dove went to Germany to study philosophy, where he imbibed not only German evolutionary relativism but also an appreciation of continental socialism and communism—which he believed to have many good points.[32]

He returned to Scotland and completed two major works, *Theory of Human Progression* and *Elements of Political Science,* which appeared in 1850 and 1854 respectively. The subtitle of the first was *Natural Probability of a Reign of Justice.* In it, he maintained that, on the basis of the Bible, science was advancing and that "political science," which was measured by "equity," just as mathematics was by numbers, would reach its acme. This progress would inevitably destroy property differences just as surely as the reform of English law had removed legal privileges. His main target was the landowning class, which he saw as completely parasitical. Following the bourgeois antifeudal tradition, he maintained that property—the right to possess, give, lend, or exchange an object—belonged to its creator. Thus, the fruits of labor clearly belonged to the laborer. Capital, which he, like most classical economists, saw as labor that

31. P.E. Dove, *Theory of Human Progression: Natural Probability of a Reign of Justice* (Edinburgh, 1850), 313–325.

32. Dove, *Theory,* 254–255. There was also a good deal of interest in social evolution in Edinburgh at the time. One of Dove's ideas that seems to have socialist origins is that wage workers were still serfs, because although they were not tied to one master they were tied to the landowners—not the capitalists—as a class. See also Dove, 356–359.

had previously been expended, also belonged to its creator or those to whom he had given or left it. Land, however, was created by God and given by Him to mankind as a whole. Thus private land-ownership was usurpation. In his eyes, land rent, which increased with population and the wealth of society as a whole, was a form of "surplus value" or robbery by the landowner of the value of the labor or its derivative, capital, which rightfully belonged to those who produced it.[33] Dove's solution was for the state to obtain the the land, which would then be rented out at periodic intervals to the highest bidder, though it was assumed that somehow these would be small-scale operators. Thus free-market forces in the periodic change of rents would appropriately encourage or discourage people going into agricultural production. The rent going to the government would be used for public works which would advance civilization and increase rents, thus creating a virtuous circle that would lead to the millennium on this earth as foretold in the Bible.[34]

Dove's works were little known, and the theories of "land nationalism" of the latter half of the nineteenth century appear to have grown up independently. There were three major strands, all of which held that land prices would certainly continue to rise, either because industrial progress was inevitable, or because land was limited, or both. According to Ricardo's theory, rent was the difference between the product of good land and that of the worst land, given equal labor. Thus, the poorer the land forced into cultivation, the larger the rent for the owner of good land. All three theories also endorsed the notion that unearned income was un-justifiable or positively harmful.

In 1870 John Stuart Mill launched the Land Tenure Reform Association to deal with the problems of what he called the "unearned increment." Its program can be roughly summarized as follows:

1. The State should take by taxation all increases in land rent after an official valuation had been made. (Mill accepted that there were other types of rent, but none were so "long lasting, profitable or unjustifiable as land rent.")

2. After the first valuation, periodic re-evaluations would be

---

33. Dove, *Elements of Political Science* (Edinburgh, 1854), 261–330.

34. Dove, *Elements,* 322–330. Dove does not specify that the landowners would be bought out, though this is implied. Cole accepts that this is the case, II, 370.

made, and all increases in values which were not created by the landlords' own development should go to the state through taxation.

3. If the landlords were dissatisfied with the amount of taxation, they should have the right to sell the land to the state at a price fixed at the original valuation.[35]

The second theory, or group of theories, was that of the land nationalizers: Gossen, Walras, and Alfred Russel Wallace. Walras and Gossen, who came to their conclusions independently, believed that the state itself should become a speculator and should buy all the land at its present price, a sum which represented its present value plus the amount the owner believed it would gain in the future. Their belief was that land values would increase more than the owners could envisage and therefore the state would benefit.

Wallace's theory was more social than economic. He believed that if the state bought and owned the land, it could give every citizen the right to cultivate a certain amount of it. This would mean that the worker could always subsist on the land and would, therefore, not be entirely at the mercy of the capitalist.[36]

The third theory, by far the best known, was that of Henry George. George, who spent much of his early life in the rapidly developing state of California, was appalled at the paradox that the more development there was, the greater poverty there seemed to be. He came to the conclusion that land rent was the root of the problem. Landlords and speculators swallowed all of the profits made by industry and progress. His solution was for the government to confiscate all money coming from land rent, excluding that made by the landlords' own improvements. In some ways George's scheme was more radical than the others in that it proposed that all land rents, not only future increments, be taxed away. The money raised by these means would be enough to supply all the government's financial needs, so that with this "single tax" all others could be abolished. In that case, without taxation, industry and commerce would boom. Free enterprise, far from being stifled by the plan, would flourish. As he modestly put it, the scheme was a "simple yet

35. Gide and Rist, 562.

36. Gide and Rist, 562, quoted in Schiffrin, *Sun Yat-sen,* 55, and "Early Land Policy," 558.

sovereign remedy which will extirpate pauperism, abolish poverty, give remunerative employment to whoever wishes it, afford free scope to human powers, lessen crime, elevate morals and taste and intelligence, purify Government and early civilization to yet nobler heights." [37]

W. E. Macklin's first two articles, which he related in Chinese to his secretary Li Yu who then wrote them down, were general surveys of the advantages of a single tax on rent, and came out in December 1894 and July 1897. In July 1898 and February and March 1899 he published articles on different policies of "political economy" from a Georgian point of view. In 1899 he published a pamphlet summarizing George's major work, *Progress and Poverty,* two sections of which appeared in *The Review of the Times.*[38] Macklin also claimed to have published, at about this time, abridged Chinese translations of Spencer's *Social Statics* and Dove's *Elements of Political Science.*[39] It is certain that he translated an extensive summary of Dove's *Theory of Human Progression,* which appeared in the *Review* in monthly issues between March 1902 and November 1903.

Macklin clearly saw himself as an orthodox follower of George and Dove, and not in any way a socialist. He was a firm upholder of private property and of the rights of capitalists. Where there were divergences between Dove and George, he tended to side with the former, as for instance on the issue of the ownership of underground minerals. Macklin agreed with Dove's agrument that these, being created by God, were in the public domain, while George fudged the issue and left them to the private mine owners.[40] This, together with the failure to attack socialism directly, left it open for Chinese readers to blur the two.

37. Quoted in Schiffrin, "Early Land Policy," 560. For a sympathetic recent view of Henry George, see Steven B. Cord, *Henry George, Dreamer or Realist* (Philadelphia, 1965).

38. ROT, CXXV (6/99), 12b. The section "Di, Gong, Ben, Sanshuo" and "Lun Dizu Guigong zhi Yi" appeared in ROT, CXXIV (5/99), 5–9 and CXXV (6/99), 10b–12b, respectively.

39. See the *Single Tax Year Book,* 1st ed. (New York, 1917), 188–192, quoted in "Early Land Policy," 555.

40. See ROT, CXXV (6/99), 11b. His Chinese form for George was generally Zhoerji or the short form Zho. Dove was named Duofei. For Macklin on minerals, see ROT, LXXI (12/94), 5b. For Dove on this, see *Elements,* 322; for George, *Progress and Poverty,* 5th ed. (London, 1883), 55–57.

The translations were filled with interpolations designed for Chinese readers. References to and analogies with the Chinese classics were frequently made. Confucius was often cited for his famous statement, "Do not fear poverty, but fear inequality."[41] This was linked to the proposition common to many radical Western economists—though bitterly opposed by Marx—that the economic problems were ones of distribution not of production.[42]

Macklin's second article contained an analogy which quickly became the standard equivalent for any radical land policy and even for socialism:

God created the world for mankind to enjoy in common. . . . When there was the Well-field *(jingtian)* system there was no tax on passes or towns . . . the people profited . . . there was enough for armies and education. Only in later generations did Shang Yang and his ilk (the legalists administering the State of Qin) destroy it for private benefit.[43]

The Well-field system was much closer to the center of Confucian orthodoxy than was *datong*. Its classical description was by Mencius:

A square *Li* is divided in the shape of the character 井*(jing*—in English, well). The *jing* is 900 *mou*. In its center there is *gongtian* (common field). Eight families each have a hundred *mou*. They all cultivate the common field. Only when the common business is completed will they presume to manage their private affairs. That is how you distinguish a country man.[44]

Mencius said that this was an ancient system he believed should be revived. There has been much impassioned argument as to whether or not the Well-field system actually existed. It is now generally agreed that the system or something like it did exist in China, although it had disappeared before Mencius' time.[45] But, its

41. See, for instance, ROT, CXXII (3/99), 4. At this time the radicals preferred not to look into the reasons for Confucius' concern about inequality which was made clear by the succeeding phrase "Do not fear poverty, only fear disorder." See *Lun Yu,* Bk. XVI, 1. In the political movement of 1973-1975, attacking Confucius and Lin Biao, the *jingtian* system has been condemned as belonging to slave society and Shang Yang has been praised for destroying it in the interests of the "progressive" land owning class. See *Peking Review* (2/22/74), 6.

42. For this connection, see ROT, CXIV (7/98), 9.

43. ROT, CII (7/97), 6.

44. Mencius, Bk. III, pt. I, Ch. III, 19. The word *gong* is ambiguous. It could mean the Dukes, or the public, a point of great social significance.

45. See Henri Maspero, *La Chine Antique* (Paris, 1927), 108-110.

symbolic significance far transcended the historical one. The Well-field system became idealized and closely identified with the golden age of the past. It was, as Levenson wrote, "a standing reproach to less deserving ages."[46] Mencius was only the first of a long line of philosophers and statesmen from Dong Zhong-shu in the Han period to Gu Yan-wu in the Qing dynasty who wanted to restore the Well-field system directly or gradually.

Even in the early twentieth century the ideal retained its potency. Its significance was such that Huang Xing, one of the major leaders of the Revolutionary Alliance, almost succeeded in having the Chinese character *jing,* the symbol of socialism, as the ensign of the Chinese national flag.[47]

46. "Illwind in the Well-field: The Erosion of the Confucian Ground for Controversy," in Arthur F. Wright (ed.), *The Confucian Persuasion* (Stanford, 1960), 268–287.

47. Chun-tu Hsueh, *Huang Hsing and the Chinese Revolution* (Stanford, 1961), 50–51.

3 | Sun Yat-sen

After the failure of the reform movement of 1898 the influence of *The Review of the Times* was greatly diminished. Its channel of information from the West was overwhelmed by the flood through Japan, though its influence persisted into the early twentieth century through Sun Yat-sen.

Sun, who had been close to English and American missionaries since boyhood, probably began to read *The Review of the Times* soon after its revival in 1889 when he was a student at the College of Medicine for Chinese in Hong Kong.[1] Sometime before 1892, toward the end of his time at the college, Sun established contact with the influential comprador, writer, and official, Zheng Guanying, who was an important promoter of the *Review*.[2] In 1894 when he abandoned medicine for politics Sun wrote a long letter in which he attempted to present his proposals for reform along Western lines to the allegedly progressive Governor General Li Hong-zhang asking to be appointed to his staff. It appears that it was only when Sun failed to obtain an interview, let alone employment, with Li that he turned toward revolution. Sun's connections with the *Review* are confirmed by publication of his proposals in two instalments in October and November 1894.[3] The main theme of Sun's proposals was that the imperial government should employ talented men, in particular those like Sun himself, who had the Western skills necessary to modernize China. There was a state

1. For Sun's early life, H. Z. Schiffrin's *Sun Yat-sen* is invaluable. For his study in Hong Kong, see 20. See also Luo Jia-lun, *Guofu Nianpu* (Taipei, 1965), I, 40.
2. Ssu-yu Teng and John K. Fairbank, *China's Response to the West: A Documentary Survey, 1839–1923* (Atheneum ed.; New York, 1963), 113–116.
3. Schiffrin's dating (*Sun Yat-sen*, p. 55) here is wrong. There was no joint issue for September–October.

socialist, or at least an antilaissez faire, aspect to his program. In the section on agriculture Sun maintained that the government had an economic responsibility for the people and should be active in promoting reforms. Giving himself the sanction of the distant past—in true radical fashion—he wrote:

> Our China's agricultural administration: In ancient times there were special officials; later generations have herders of the people. That is to say, before the Three Dynasties when the people's livelihood *(minjian yangsheng)* was incomplete they considered that good government was to nourish the people. After the Three Dynasties when the people's livelihood was complete, they considered that good government was letting the people nourish themselves and not interfering with them. This is why our China's agricultural administration is going to pieces.[4]

The idea for the "people's livelihood" (in the shorter form of *minsheng),* which was to become the third of Sun's Three Principles of the People, appeared throughout his letter to Li Hong-zhang. Although it is a traditional term, it is likely that the idea for its use came to Sun through the Reformists or possibly from its use in Dr. Edkins' long series of articles on "How to Enrich the Nation" which had appeared in *The Review of the Times* during the preceding three years.[5]

In his analysis of Chinese agriculture Sun described the terrible living conditions of the Chinese peasants and agreed that the government should introduce Western techniques to increase the area and fertility of arable land, but he made no suggestion for any alteration in property relations.

In November 1894, the month that the *Review* printed his letter, Sun founded the first branch of his Society to Restore China's Prosperity, the first of his revolutionary organizations, in Hawaii.[6] In January of the following year he returned to Hong Kong and, together with another Westernized Chinese, Yang Qu-yan, began organizing a rising in Canton to take advantage of the dislocation of the Sino-Japanese War. The rising, which was nipped in the bud in October 1895, was to have relied on secret society members and unemployed laborers, and had at its core a group of protestants, or associates of missionaries, like Sun himself.[7]

4. ROT, LXIX (10/94), 4.   5. See for instance ROT, XLIII (8/92), 7.
6. Schiffrin, *Sun Yat-sen,* 42.   7. Schiffrin, *Sun Yat-sen,* 89.

When this failed, Sun fled to Japan, Hawaii, America, and then England, which he reached late in 1896. Within days of his arrival there he found himself a prisoner in the Chinese legation in London.[8] The furore that surrounded his release, brought about by British public opinion and government pressure, and the skill with which Sun handled public relations after his "kidnapping" gave him an international reputation as *the* representative of "Young" (or progressive) China which was to be of inestimable political value. Describing the period, Sun later wrote:

After I escaped from danger [his kidnapping] I lived for a time in Europe to investigate its politics and customs, and I met the great men both in and out of power. During these two years I heard many different ideas. Only then did I realize that if one only makes a country rich and strong and develops the people's rights (political liberty) as with the European powers, one can not raise people to happiness. That is why the bold spirits in Europe still have a movement for social revolution. If we wanted to win perpetual ease in one great effort, we should have to solve the problem of the people's livelihood at the same time as the problems of nationalism and people's rights.[9]

Sun's teacher and friend, Sir James Cantlie, confirmed the fact that Sun studied hard in England.[10] There is also no doubt that while there he was interested in the socialist and land-nationalist movements. He met some influential British radicals, notably the veteran Irish patriot and organizer of the National Land League, Michael Davitt, M.P., as well as the Russian revolutionary Felix Volkhovsky.[11] Nevertheless, Sun's description of his political evolution is oversimplified. This seems to have come from the desire, which he shared with many others, to make it appear that his ideas came directly from the West and could only have come from personal contact, thus giving him and the handful of Chinese who had been to Europe and America a monopoly over Western knowledge.

8. For the conflicting stories on how he got there, see Schiffrin, *Sun Yat-sen,* 105–116.

9. *Guofu Quanji,* 2 vols. (Taipei, 1955), II, 84. Sun did not spend two years in Europe but only about ten months. See Hatano Yoshihiro, "Shoki ni Okeru Son Bun no 'Keikei Chigen ni tsuite,'" in *Shakai Keizai Shigaku,* XXI, 5.6, 479–502. 482. See also *Guofu Nianpu,* I, 75–76.

10. Sir James Cantlie and C. Sheridan Jones, *Sun Yat-sen and the Awakening of China* (London, 1912), 248.

11. Schiffrin, *Sun Yat-sen,* 128–135.

In fact, it is almost certain that Sun was aware of the social problems of industrial nations well before 1897. This knowledge came either from *The Review of the Times* and other Chinese and English publications or from discussions with his missionary friends. His interest in the *Review* is shown by his particular concern to meet Timothy Richard while in London.[12] An indication that he had been thinking along these lines comes in a report from the porter at the Chinese legation, who said that in trying to persuade the porter to help him in his escape Sun had compared himself with "the leader of our socialist party here in London and claimed that he headed a socialist party in China."[13] Thus it appears that by the beginning of his stay in London Sun had already identified himself and his revolutionary movement with international socialism. It is also very likely that Sun read Macklin's first article, which appeared in the *Review* in December 1894 one month after the publication of his own letter. Thus, it is probable that he knew about single-tax theory before his travels in the West and that from the beginning he saw it as part of socialism and in no way incompatible with it.

Sun's ideas on socialism and land nationalization continued to develop after he left Europe, particularly during his stay in Japan from August 1897 to July 1900. From interviews he gave in 1912 it seems that he read Macklin's translation of *Progress and Poverty*, and it is very likely that he read many of his other publications on the single-tax idea during this period.[14]

During the last decades of the nineteenth century there was also some single-tax activity in Japan. Various speeches by Henry George were translated into Japanese as early as 1887, and excerpts from *Progress and Poverty* appeared in 1891.[15] As with many Fabians in England, several Japanese socialists were first led toward socialism by Georgism.[16] Interestingly, one of the most active

12. Richard, *Forty-Five Years in China,* 350.

13. Schiffrin, *Sun Yat-sen,* 116. Sun denied having said this, but this denial must be seen in the light of his sensitivity to English middle-class opinion.

14. *Minli Bao* (1/1–2/12), 5; and *The Public,* an American single-tax journal (4/12/12). See Schiffrin, "Early Land Policy," 555.

15. For the development of Georgism in Japan, see H. Z. Schiffrin and Pow-key Sohn, "Henry George on Two Continents," in *Comparative Studies in Society and History,* II (1959–1960), 85–109, esp. 95–101.

promoters of the movement in Japan was W. E. Macklin's brother-in-law, the Reverend Charles E. Garst.

Sun's most probable source of ideas on this topic, however, was his close companion Miyazaki Torazō. The Miyazaki brothers—there were eight, although only four survived into adulthood—were all radicals. The eldest was killed fighting government troops in Saigo Takamori's great revolt in 1877. The two youngest brothers became interested in the movement for pan-Asianism—under Japanese guidance—to resist the West. In 1896 one of the two died, leaving the youngest, Torazō, to take over his contacts and carry on the work. It was about this time that Torazō met the important politican Inukai Ki. Through Cantonese contacts Torazō heard about Sun Yat-sen, whose international reputation made him appear to be a suitable leader for a revived pro-Japanese China. Torazō went to see Sun soon after his arrival in Yokohama in September 1897. The two took to each other immediately and remained friends for life. Torazō introduced Sun to Inukai who was also impressed by him and who used his influence to obtain official funds for Sun which were channeled through Torazō.[17]

The Miyazakis were brought up in the countryside near Kumamoto in Southern Kyūshu. In the 1870s and 1880s they were appalled by the sufferings of the peasants during the rural depression. The oldest surviving brother, Tamizō, was especially moved and indignant, and vowed to work to relieve their sufferings. In the early 1890s he read some of George's writings and became converted by them. In the spring of 1895 he and a friend established the first group promoting Georgism in Japan, the Society for Research into the Land Problem. In February 1897 he went to the United States, then to England and France, not returning to Japan until February 1900.[18] By this time Sun was in the midst of planning for his next

16. Kōtoku Shūsui, "Yo wa Ika ni Shite Shakaishugisha to Nari Shi," *Heimin Shimbun* (1/17/04), 10. Reprint (Tokyo, 1962), 85.

17. The main source for Miyazaki Torazō's early life is his *Sanjusannen no Yume* (Tokyo, 1941). See also Marius B. Jansen, *The Japanese and Sun Yat-sen* (Cambridge, Mass., 1954), 54–68. Jansen is mistaken on the date of Sun's arrival. See Schiffrin, *Sun Yat-sen*, 140–148.

18. For the life of Miyazaki Tamizō, see Miyazaki Ryūsuke, "Oji Tamizō no koto domo" in *Jimbutsu Kenkyū Shiryō*, 2 vols. (Tokyo, 1966), I, 110–113.

rising, so that is unlikely that he and Tamizō had much contact at this stage. It is almost certain, however, that Tamizō discussed his ideas with his one surviving brother, and it is possible that Sun read some of the writings on the subject which Tamizō completed before his trip to America.[19]

Since these writings are not available, it is impossible to know the details of his plans at this stage, though an estimate of their general nature may be gathered from the program of the Society for Restoring Land Rights which Miyazaki founded in April 1902. Its aim was "to return to mankind the rights of equal enjoyment of land so that each invididual would have an independent base"; its principle: "Our League considers that things made by man's labor should be enjoyed by the maker, but that things created by nature should belong to mankind to be enjoyed equally."

The League's program emphasized the following three points: (1) The individual should have a fixed amount of land to enjoy; population and land area should be assessed and compared, and land should be divided equally. (2) Everyone has the right to land; when men and women become adults they should receive some. (3) Anyone who holds more than an equal portion of land should be compensated according to the value put in by human labor; the surplus should be transferred.[20]

This program is clearly land nationalist as opposed to single tax but is very unlike any programs of the Western land nationalizers, with the possible exception of that proposed by Wallace. However, Miyazaki's scheme does have points of resemblance with the ancient Chinese Equal-field (juntian) system, and it is possible that the program is a compound of this and the Western proposals.

The Equal-field system, which was at least loosely inspired by the Well-field (jingtian) system, was established by the Wei dynasty at the end of the fifth century A.D. The dynasty ruled a territory with extremely serious economic problems. Some regions were suffering from overpopulation while others had been devastated and depopulated by decades of fighting. There were also serious social problems arising from the existance of semifeudal lords who had es-

19. Miyazaki Ryūsuke, 110. For reasons to justify the possibility, see below.
20. Miyazaki Ryūsuke, 111. The program was translated into Chinese in 1906. See *Min Bao*, II (5/8/06).

tablished themselves with huge land holdings during the years of insecurity. To meet these problems a drastic agricultural reform was proposed: "to have no land out of cultivation, no hands left idle, to ensure that the best agricultural land should not be monopolized by the rich and to ensure that the poor should reach a minimum subsistence level."[21] This was to be achieved by each householder holding land for himself, his wife and children, and for his slaves and his oxen. The inclusion of these last show that the main motive of the reform was agricultural efficiency rather than social justice. Further, there were to be two kinds of landholding: small "permanent fields," which could be inherited and were to contain houses and trees—especially mulberry trees for silk production—and larger portions of land which were allocated to each individual on coming of age and were withdrawn on death or retirement at the age of seventy.

The regulations of the Equal-field system varied from period to period and region to region, and it is impossible to know to what extent they were implemented. Nevertheless, it is certain that they were applied at least in North China from the end of the fifth century to the crisis in the middle of the Tang dynasty in the eighth century.[22]

Although there is no proof of derivation, the tone of Miyazaki's program and its calling for an equal allocation of land to individuals on reaching adulthood, a proposal which does not appear in any Western theory, do bear a striking resemblance to the Equal-field system.

It appears that Sun's economic program was relatively close to that of Miyazaki during this period—1897–1900. Although he wrote nothing on it at this time, accounts exist of discussions he had about it. Feng Zi-you, the historian of the revolution, who was very close to Sun during his stay in Yokohama wrote:

In 1899 and 1900 Sun talked with Zhang Tai-yan [Bing-lin], and Liang Qi-chao, and as students in Japan we often talked about our country's old and new social and land problems. The Well-field system of the three dynasties,

21. Quoted in Etienne Balazs, "Land ownership in Fourth and Fifth Century China," in *Chinese Civilization and Bureaucracy* (New Haven, 1964), 101–125, esp. 108.

22. See Mark Elvin, *The Pattern of the Chinese Past* (London, 1973), 54–68.

Wang Mang's Royal-fields and prohibition of slavery or Wang An-shi's "Green sprout Tax" and Hong Xiu-quan's "Public Granaries" were all discussed.[23]

Liang Qi-chao gives a more specific description of a discussion in 1899:

Sun Wen told me "The peasants today generally give half of what they get to the landlords. That is why their farming is in difficulties. After land nationalization *(tudi guoyou)* all who can till can receive land [or: to receive land one must be able to till it] and then pay some rent to the state directly. After that with no landlords to exploit them as middle men, the peasants can be prosperous." [24]

The revolutionary scholar, Zhang Bing-lin, gave a similar but more detailed picture of Sun's ideas at the time.[25] In answer to a question from Zhang about reducing taxes:

Sun Wen said, if (land) concentration is not checked, to talk about fixing taxes is only curing the symptom. Now the landlord takes part of the tenant's profit but reducing the profit he does not accept the whole tax. Therefore two thirds are taken from the tenant. . . . The great gap between rich and poor is an incitement to revolution. Nevertheless the properties of rich and poor workers and merchants should not be levelled. . . . The hauler and the master of an ocean ship both transport for others but one is like a draught animal and the other like a lord. How can they be equal? Work and trade have skill and to want to equalize the rich and the poor is the greatest

23. *Geming Yishi,* III, 213. Wang Mang, 33 B.C.–23A.D., a nephew of a Han empress, and high minister and regent for several years, usurped the throne and tried to create a new dynasty. In 9 A.D. he attempted to nationalize the land, breaking up large estates and giving the land to peasants who would pay taxes direct to the government. He also tried to restrict slavery. These policies were beyond the strength of the central government. Wang Mang fell from power and was killed in 23 A.D. Wang An-shi, 1021-1086, a reforming chief councilor, tried to improve the conditions of the peasants and increase government revenue by reassessing taxes and providing cheap credit for the poor, cutting out the money lenders. For Hong Xiu-quan, see above.

24. Liang Qi-chao, "Shehui Geming guo wei Jinri Zhongguo suo biyao hu," in *Xinmin Congbao,* LXXXVI (12/06), 5-52, esp. 32. Liang understood the ambiguous clause in the first sense.

25. For Zhang, see Charlotte Furth, "Kuang-fu: The Thought of Zhang Bing-lin and the Revolution of 1911," in *The Limits of Change: Essays on Conservative Alternatives in Republican China* (Cambridge, Mass., 1975); and Howard Boorman, *Biographical Dictionary of Republican China,* 4 vols. (New York, 1967-1971), hereafter referred to as BDRC.

stupidity in the world. Now land is natural. For the rich, without capital or labor, to enjoy the fertility of everything and to have a huge gap between them and the impoverished requires a method for equalization. The method of later kings was that those who did not personally till the lands should not have open fields *(lutian),* gardens, or ponds but should work like menials. Men should only have ten *mou* (of permanent land?) and only twenty *mou* of open field. If one man takes land and cultivates it, it is not his fertility. . . . He should have what his labor creates but not what is created naturally. Therefore a merchant should be rewarded only according to his labor. He cannot buy its fertility. Those who do not crop should not own a foot of arable land. Therefore taxes are not established and without the effort of confiscation land is equalized.[26]

To this, Zhang claims to have replied: "Excellent! If land is not equal, even though taxes are reduced the people will not be happy."

He went on to denounce the Suzhou scholar, Feng Gui-fen (1809–1874), who had obtained tax reductions for his region, the benefit of which went almost entirely to his gentry cronies.[27] After this, Zhang set out a specific land policy, the Equal-field method:

All land owned by people should not be left wild. All land that is not worked should pay each year 2/10ths of its value assessed at three years rent according to its quality.

All open fields; those who do not personally cultivate them should be made to sell them to the civil authorities. All gardens and woods that have been inherited should be retained and not sold. Ponds should be treated like open fields. In households headed by women those who can cultivate should cultivate. If they cannot they should sell. There should be no tenants for open land.

The profit of all heaths that are cleared for open fields, gardens, or ponds, with many dikes and embankments even though they are not personally cultivated their profit should be exclusive for fifty years. At the end of this time they should sell it at a value of ten years' rent. All mines and factories, even though they are not personally established regardless of size, should be

26. Zhang, *Kaoshu* (Shanghai, 1904; reprinted Taipei, 1968), 144–145. The *mou* varied from period to period and region to region. It was usually approximately one-sixth of an acre.

27. For the traditional view of Feng as a philanthropist, see ECCP; and Mary Wright, *The Last Stand of Chinese Conservatism: The T'ung-chih Restoration, 1862–1874* (Stanford, 1957), 165–167. For convincing backing for Zhang's attack on Feng, see James Polachek, "Gentry Hegemony: Soochow in the T'ung-chih Restoration," in F. Wakeman, *Conflict and Control* (Berkeley, 1975), 211–255.

freely owned. They should not be comparable with open fields, gardens, or ponds.[28]

Zhang's descriptions were clearly greatly influenced by the Equal-field *(juntian)* system. The references to the "later kings" pointed to the Wei and its successor dynasties whose rulers did not live in the classical age. "Open-field" *(lutian)* was a term used by the Wei for the temporary allocations of land. It seems improbable that Sun himself was influenced to this extent. As far as can be ascertained he did not refer to the *juntian* system, although he made frequent allusions to the *jingtian*. Furthermore, Zhang was quite capable of inserting these esoteric references to give Sun—and his own writings—extra style. Nevertheless, Miyazaki Tamizō's use of the system, and Sun's later use of the world *jun,* in reference to land policies make it quite possible that Sun was aware of and saw the uses of this precedent.[29]

Zhang did not directly attribute the Equal-field method to Sun, but the program's tone, content, and context make it seem that to some extent at least it did represent Sun's views. Taken together with Zhang's and Liang Qi-chao's description of Sun's economic policy, it does fill out a plausible and fairly coherent picture of Sun's views on the subject at the turn of the century. These can be summarized as follows: he saw a clear distinction between land rent on the one hand and profit and wages on the other; thus he was against any attempt by the state to interfere with business. He advocated land nationalization, with compensation, for cultivated lands. And he wanted speculators with undeveloped lands to be taxed, either into giving up their holdings or into developing them.

In late 1902 or 1903 Sun introduced his social policy into the program of his Society to Restore China's Prosperity.[30] Previously it had been made up of the three points: Drive out the Manchus,

28. *Kaoshu,* 145–146.
29. See Yang Zhi-jun in "Zhang Tai-yan di Lishiguan he tadi Fajia Sixiang," *Wen-wu,* III, 1975, 14–18, 17. There is a remote possibility that Miyazaki learned about the *juntian* system from Zhang, although this is extremely unlikely.
30. Rong Meng-yuan states that Sun was already using the term when he established the society's branch in Hanoi in December 1902 but gives no reference. Feng Zi-you disagreed with this hypothesis, maintaining that it was introduced at the foundation of the *Geming Junshi Xuexiao,* which was founded in Tokyo by some revolutionary students, Sun, and a handful of Japanese officers in the early autumn of 1903. See Feng, *Geming Yishi,* IV, 205.

Restore China, and Establish a Republic. To these he now added Equal Land Rights *(pingjun diquan)*. This almost appears to be a compound of Restoration of Land Rights *(tochi fukken—tudi fuquan* in Chinese), the title of Miyazaki's society founded in Tokyo in April 1902, and that of the organization's aim: the restoration of equal *(byōdō—pingdeng* in Chinese) enjoyment of land.

The only description we have of the meaning of this policy before the foundation of the Revolutionary Alliance in 1905 comes in a letter Sun wrote to a student revolutionary in December 1903.

I have carefully read your letter asking about socialism *(shehuizhuyi)*. It is an issue I think extremely important and cannot forget for a moment. What I advocate is Equal Land Rights. This is something that we can practice in our country today. Recently in Europe and America there have already been some attempts to practice it. But in those countries there has been concentration [of land] and it is difficult to oppose the power of the landlords. . . . As our country has not applied machinery to the land and productive forces still depend on human labor and are not all in the hands of the owners, the gap between rich and poor is not like that in Europe and America where the rich can rival a country and the poor cannot stand an awl.[31] Thus it would be easier for us to practice than for them.

Now Europe and America's development to this tragic state of division means that in the future there will certainly be a great conflict to level it. Now everything in the world tends to establish equality. Education is the way to equal knowledge. Houses and clothes equalize the body's temperature. By extension everything is like this, hence it can be stated categorically that today's inequalities in Europe and America will bring on a conflict leading to equality. Thus today we talk of reform in our country to avoid the development of a still worse catastrophe. This is something men of benevolence cannot bear. Therefore I wish at the time of the revolution that this shall be included as one of the points on our program.[32]

The letter avoids giving specific details of the program, a significant point in itself. But it tells us a great deal about Sun's thinking and ambiance at the time. The fact that Sun needed to write the letter at all, shows that from the time of their introduction Sun's

31. A classical reference referring to the situation under the Qin dynasty. See Sima Qian, *Shiji,* "Liuhou shijia."

32. *Jingzhong Ribao* (4/26/04), 2. An almost complete file of *Jingzhong Ribao* has been reprinted in 5 vols. (Taipei, 1968). Note the flavor of Dove in the references to equity.

social policies were questioned by fellow political revolutionaries. Equally, it shows Sun's belief in their importance. As in 1899, Sun insisted on the significance of land and rent as opposed to capital and profit. However, his emphasis appears to have shifted.

In the 1890s he was concerned with the plight of the Chinese peasants. By 1903 he seems to have been less worried by their situation. Indeed, he argued that China's backwardness was an advantage—an early example of the "poor but blank" theory. This lessening anxiety came about at the same time as his increasing—it was already there before—concern with development along Western lines. Thus at least in his public statements he saw his land policy as a prophylactic, a method of avoiding social division and not in any way a revolutionary doctrine.

For the next twenty years Sun's major social, as opposed to political, concern was still the danger of concentration of landholding causing social divisions during and after China's industrialization.[33] Why should this have preoccupied him to the exclusion of other more immediate problems? Sun was born in the relatively urban county of Xiangshan. He left home when he was thirteen and never returned to the countryside for any long period. The rest of his life was spent in Canton, Macao, Hong Kong, and Shanghai or in Western or Japanese cities where he usually lived in the overseas Chinese communities. The only time spent outside towns was at his brother's farm in Hawaii, but this farm was a commercial enterprise unlike anything in rural China.

This background may help explain Sun's concern with the difficulties of urban workers and the Western type of social problem and would account for Sun's desire to tax the profits made in the boom in urban land prices. Living in coastal cities into which money was pouring from the interior, and in Japan and the west coast of America, Sun had as good a view as did Henry George of the development of progress and poverty. Sun's urban point of view also led him to exaggerate the importance in terms of the national

33. In 1924 under Soviet and Communist influence he returned to concern for actual problems in the Chinese countryside. For his famous speech on "land to the tiller" see *Guofu Quanshu* (Taipei, 1960), 1004–1006. For a description of this policy and its relation to Equal Land Rights, see Yamamoto Hideo, "Son Bun Shugi Tochi Kakumei Riron no Hatten Kozō," in *Kindai Chūkoku no Shakaito Keizai*, ed. Niida Noboru (Tokyo, 1951), 160–163.

economy of the speculators' unearned gains. Sun appears to have believed that a good part, if not the whole of China, would become as highly developed as Shanghai, as he said at a public meeting in 1906:

If in the future the whole country changes, land values will definitely rise with civilization. At this time, land that is worth $10,000 will become worth hundreds of thousands or millions. Fifty years ago in Shanghai, land on the Huangpu Bund was not worth very much, now every *mou* is worth hundreds of thousands of dollars. This is very clear proof.[34]

Another factor in Sun's choice of the theories of Henry George and the land nationalists was his milieu and the nature of his political support. Many of his friends never joined the Society to Restore China's Prosperity, and many members of the society were men who met Sun only once and had a very vague idea of the purpose of the organization.[35] The society's composition, however, is interesting as a general guide to the type of man with whom Sun had contact and from whom he could hope for support.

Before 1903 nearly all his connections and political support came from overseas Chinese or from men in Hong Kong, Macao, or Canton who had little dealing with land either as landlords or tenants. Two hundred and ninety-three members of the Society to Restore China's Prosperity have been identified.[36] Of these, 123 or roughly 42 per cent were listed as *shang*, the traditional Chinese term for merchant. Most of these seem to have been small-scale retailers, presumably without enough capital for land speculation. For them at least Sun's plans to cut taxes would have been directly beneficial. The second largest occupational group in the society was that of *gong* artisans: there were 55 of them, just under 18 percent of the total. These too had an interest in Sun's schemes if only an indirect one. Sun promised that with the limitation of all taxes except land tax, trade and industry would boom. His proposal, like those of the Western reformers, appeared to benefit both employers and labor at the expense of the landowners. Sun implied that in the new state the

---

34. Sun, *"Min Bao* Zhounian Jinian Yanshuo ci," *Min Bao,* X (12/20/06), 86–96, esp. 91 (referred to hereafter as "Zhounian ci").

35. Shelley Hsien Ch'eng, "The T'ung-meng Hui, Its Organization, Leadership, and Finances, 1905–1912," Ph.D. Thesis, University of Washington, 1962, 18.

36. Feng, *Geming Yishi,* IV, 24–67.

merchants would share their new prosperity with all the people. Thus for the merchants and artisans, who together made up over 60 per cent of the society's membership, Sun's land policy—if they were able to understand it—was probably an additional attraction.

Dissatisfaction with Sun's land policy might have come from two quarters. On the one hand, opposition could have come from the secret societies. Thirty-six names, that is, over 12 per cent of the members of the Society to Restore China's Prosperity, were listed as *huidang* (secret society) members. The actual proportion is likely to have been much higher because their names would not be known. Before 1905 Sun certainly thought that this group should be considered as the basis for any revolution. Sun is reported to have said "the *literati* cannot rebel, soliders cannot revolt. . . . he considered that a rising of the secret societies was reliable." [37]

The economic position of secret society members varied enormously, but most of them were lumpen proletarians, people on the fringes of urban life or landless peasants. As such they would have been interested in immediate distribution of property rather than in Sun's vague and complicated long-term plans. However, given their political level, it is unlikely that they spent much time discussing Sun's policies or that they understood the economic part of his program. Some may have believed that Sun's Equal Land Rights meant distribution of land and not have understood his later qualifications, and it is possible that Sun did not try to resolve their confusion on this.

It is likely that secret society members did not demand immediate land reform. An indication of this comes from the program of the Dragon Flower Society. This was a Chekiang secret society reorganized in 1904 by the revolutionary leader Tao Cheng-zhang and other intellectuals.[38] The thinking behind the social policy in

37. Zhu He-zhong, "Ouzhou Tongmeng Hui Jishi," in *Geming Wenxian,* joint vols. I–III (Taipei, 1958), 251–270, esp. 256. See also Feng, *Geming Yishi,* IV, 246; and Song Jiao-ren *Cheng Jia-sheng Geming Shilue* (Shanghai, 1912), 2–26 and 66. Quoted by Wang De-zhao, "Tongmeng Hui Shiqi Sun Zhong-shan Xiansheng Geming Sixiang di Fenxi Yanjiu," in *Zhongguo Xiandaishi Congkan* (Taipei, 1960), I, 65–188, esp. 73.

38. See Tao Cheng-zhang, *Zhean Jilue,* reprinted in *Xinhai Geming,* ed. Chai De-geng and others, 8 vols. (Shanghai, 1957), III, 1–22, esp. 20. See also Mary Backus Rankin, *Early Chinese Revolutionaries: Radical Intellectuals in Shanghai and Chekiang, 1902–1911* (Cambridge, Mass., 1971), 150–155.

this society's program shows some similarity to that behind Sun's Equal Land Rights, by which it may or may not have been influenced. Unlike the programs of Sun's organizations, that of the Dragon Flower Society was written in the spoken language, so that it could be understood by a reasonable proportion of its members, and presumably it was to some extent designed to attract maximum support. The third point in the society's program read: "We want to make land become the common property of all. We will not allow the rich to seize it. We will do this so that our 400,000,000 brothers and their sons will not produce classes of rich and poor and everyone will have food and security." [39]

If this in any way represents the feelings of the society's members, it would indicate that they were interested in some type of land reform. It also indicates that they did not object to the intellectuals' picture of China as being without a gap between rich and poor, or of a China in which social action should be taken to prevent future calamities rather than to cure present ills. If the Dragon Flower Society, ostensibly basing itself entirely on the secret societies, tolerated this program, it is very unlikely that any articulate group of Sun's supporters demanded a more immediate or drastic land reform than that provided by the Equal Land Rights scheme.

While the majority of merchants supporting Sun were poor and stood to gain from his economic plans, there was a minority of rich men with investments in land. This minority was disproportionately important because of the revolutionaries' need for funds.[40] Sun's position with regard to this group was particularly precarious because of the very effective rivalry of Liang Qi-chao and the Reformists who captured many of Sun's sources of financial support.

Most of the students abroad or in Shanghai came from rural families with land holdings. As we have seen from Sun's need to reply to a student on his policy of Equal Land Rights, there were doubts about it from its inception from men who completely supported Sun's revolutionary nationalist and political ideas.

In the spring of 1905 before Sun's return to Japan and the foun-

39. Tao Cheng-zhang, "Longhua Hui Zhang Cheng," reprinted in *Xinhai Geming,* I, 534–544, esp. 540.

40. See for instance "Geming Furen li Ji-tang," in Feng, *Geming Yishi,* III, 160–165. See also Shelley Ch'eng's description of Sun's fund raising and finances, 14–18.

dation of the Revolutionary Alliance, Sun persuaded some Chinese students in Europe to join a revolutionary group that included in its oath the four principles of the Society to Restore China's Prosperity. However, almost immediately after Sun left, these students formed another group called the Public People's Party. This party's oath of admission included the first three policies but not that of Equal Land Rights.[41] The founders implied that their policies were formed to attract new members and prepare them for the Revolutionary Party itself. Another indication that political revolutionaries had doubts about Sun's social policies occurs in the memoirs of Hu Han-min, one of the poorest students and later an active supporter of Sun's socialism. Hu wrote: "I and Liao Zhong-kai said to him (Sun), 'we have not the slightest doubts about the basic aims of revolution, nationalism, and political freedom, but we still do not quite understand the points of Equal Land Rights and socialism.'"[42]

Feng Zi-you wrote that in 1905 "several people were doubtful about the one item of Equal Land Rights. Sun had to speak for over an hour to convince them on this subject."[43]

Thus it seems clear that most of the pressure on Sun came from one direction: from people who thought that his policies of Equal Land Rights and socialism were too radical, if not completely unnecessary. This may have had important effects on Sun's policies as he put them forward. There is no reason to doubt Schiffrin when he writes that Sun's tendency to spare contemporary landowners came from a fear that his rich merchant backers with landholdings might be antagonized.[44] It is also likely that Sun may have modified his social policies as a result of arguments with cautious students.

Despite these modifications Sun stuck to his social policy throughout his life. Why should he have done this? The first reason was clearly his poor peasant origin. As he told Miyazaki Torazō: "If

41. Zhu He-zong, 256; and Feng, *Geming Yishi,* IV, 240.

42. "Hu Han-min Zizhuan," in *Geming Wenxian,* III, 386. Liao Zhong-kai's widow, He Xiang-ning, when she recalled the conversation, said that only Hu Han-min doubted Sun's social policies; see He Xiang-ning, "Wodi Huiyi," in *Xinhai Geming Huiyilu,* 6 vols. (Peking, 1961), I, 12–60, esp. 17. For Hu, who became a violent right winger in the 1920s, and Liao, a left-wing martyr in whose assassination Hu probably connived, see BDRC.

43. Feng, *Geming Yishi,* II, 149.   44. Schiffrin, "Early Land Policies," 553.

I had not been born the son of a poor peasant family perhaps I would have neglected this important question. We shall never know."[45] Linked to this was his fundamental belief in justice, and the conviction probably articulated in the early 1890s through contact with his missionary friends and *The Review of the Times* that social justice was an absolutely necessary complement to political freedom. The second and related reason was that Sun was not content for the Chinese revolution to be a purely national movement. He wanted it to be part of world progress as a whole. His contacts with the West led him to believe that the greatest world force for progress was socialism. His statement in 1896 to the porter at the Chinese legation indicated that he saw himself as one of the many leaders of world socialism. From his letter of 1903 to the student revolutionary it is clear that he saw Equal Land Rights as the form of socialism applicable to China. Unlike most socialist politicians, but like many ordinary people, Sun believed that land nationalism and even single tax were parts of world socialism, not perversions of it.

This identification with the world socialist movement was manifested on his second trip to Europe in the spring of 1905 when Sun visited the Secretariat of the Second International in Brussels. A short article describing their discussion appeared in the Flemish socialist newspaper *Vooruit* on May 18, 1905, and in its French language equivalent *Le Peuple* a few days later. The discussion seems to have been in English, and language difficulties and the writer's utopian views of China must have affected the report. Nevertheless, much of the report appears to be authentic:

This week I had the chance to be the mediator between our comrade Sun Yat Sen, chief of the Chinese Revolutionary Socialist Party and our friends Vandervelde and Huysmans.[46]

Comrade Sen has come to Belgium to ask for the affiliation of his party

45. Quoted in Xia Dong-yuan "Lun Qingmo Geming Dang ren Guanyu Tudi Wenti Sixiang," in *Xinhai Geming Wushi Zhounian Lunwenji,* 2 vols. (Peking, 1962), I, 299–322, esp. 299; see also Li Shi-yue, "Sun Zhong-shan, 'Pingjun Diquan' Zhenggang di Chansheng he Fazhan,'" *Guangming Ribao* (10/27/55).

46. The writer's name was Sander. For Vandervelde and Huysmans, see G.D.H. Cole, 5 vols., *A History of Socialist Thought* (London, 1954–1956), III, 45–50, and 646–651 and 663. I am grateful to Marianne Rachline for giving me a copy of the article.

to the Bureau of the Socialist International which Comrade Huysmans is the Secretary. . . .

Comrade Sen first of all explained in outline the objectives of the Chinese socialists. . . . The first point of their program is then, China for the Chinese. Drive out the usurping strangers! (Manchus). In second place the land is entirely or almost entirely common property in China. That is to say there are few or no great landowners, but the land is rented by the commune to the inhabitants according to certain rules. What is more the Chinese have a very simple fiscal system: Everyone pays only according to his means and the burden does not weigh uniquely—as in Europe—on the great mass of the propertyless.

Our yellow comrades wish to improve this system still further in conformity with the principles of our party to prevent forever one class expropriating another as has happened in all the European countries. . . .

The Chinese workers find themselves in a state that is exactly identical to that of our guilds in past centuries. They are all organized and better off than in any country in the world and, like those of medieval artisans, the lives of Chinese workers today are far from being pitiable. There are few poor people but there are even fewer who are really rich.

The guilds are against the use of machines. . . . The Chinese are not at all stupid. They are among the most happy people in the world. They know what European workers have to suffer under capitalism and they do not wish to become victims of the machines. This is the cause for their backward situation.

Chinese socialists on the other hand want to introduce European modes of production and to use machines, but without the disadvantages. They want to build a new society in the future *without any transition*. They accept the advantages of our civilization but they refuse to become its victims. In other words, with them the medieval mode of production will pass directly to the stage of socialist production without passing through the misery of the exploitation of workers by the capitalists. "In several years" said comrade Sen "we will have realized our wildest dreams because all our guilds are socialist. Then when you are still straining to realize your plans we shall be living in the purest collectivism. This will profit you equally because beyond the fact that the example will be attractive the world will be convinced that integral collectivism is not a vain dream or a utopia. In this way more conversions will be obtained than through many years of writings or hundreds of meetings."

Furthermore, there are 54 socialist journals in Chinese.[47]

47. *Le Peuple* (5/20/05). For the attitude of the Second International toward China, see *La Deuxième Internationale et L'Orient,* ed. George Haupt and Madeline

If this report of Sun's ideas is to be trusted, they have a startlingly prophetic quality despite his extraordinary romanticism about the contemporary situation in China. Although the Marxist terminology could well have been that of the journalist, Sanders, Sun's statement is one of the earliest examples of the concept of "skipping historical stages" and of advancing directly from feudalism to socialism in China. This possibility—for other countries—had occurred to socialists much earlier. In 1877 Marx, writing about the growth of capitalism in Russia, said that she would lose "the finest occasion that history had ever offered a people" and would now be obliged "to undergo all the meanders of the capitalist system." [48] Sun's statement also showed his belief that the socialism resulting from the Chinese revolution would help its development in the West. This concept too was new for China. But the idea that revolutions in countries like Russia could be signals for those in the West had also been considered by Marx and other socialists. However, unlike Sun, they maintained that unless the Western proletariat came to their aid, these other revolutions were bound to fail. [49]

The extraordinary claim that there were fifty-four socialist newspapers in China was also included in a summary of the report published in the Japanese socialist newspaper *Straight Talk* in August 1905. [50] Later, at a meeting in Tokyo arranged by Miyazaki Torazō and other Japanese pan-Asianists Sun, who had returned to Japan a few weeks earlier, established full contact with the student revolutionary movement that had grown up in Shanghai and Japan. [51] On August 20, at a formal meeting with about a hundred

Reberioux (Paris, 1967); and *Marxism and Asia,* by Stuart Schram and Helene Carrère d'Encausse (London, 1969), 125–133.

48. Marx's letter to the Russian periodical *Otechestvennye Zapiski* in Marx and Engels, *Werke* (Berlin, 1962), XIX, 108, quoted by Stuart Schram and Helene Carrère d'Encausse.

49. See Schram and d'Encausse, 11.

50. *Chokugen* (8/06/05), 3. It was this statement that inspired Kita Ikki, the future Japanese fascist leader, to become involved in China. See Tanaka Sogorō, *Nihon Fasshizumu no Genryu, Kita Ikki no Shisō to Shōgai* (Tokyo, 1949), 27. For more on Kita, see George M. Wilson, *Radical Nationalist in Japan: Kita Ikki, 1883-1937* (Cambridge, Mass., 1969).

51. For Sun's earlier contacts with the student revolutionaries see Schiffrin, "The Enigma of Sun Yat-sen," in Mary Wright (ed.), *China in Revolution: The First Phase, 1900-1913* (New Haven, 1968), 443-474.

people present, the three leading revolutionary groups, the Restoration Society based on East China, the Society for China's Revival from Hunan and Hupeh, and Sun's Society to Restore China's Prosperity federated to form the Revolutionary Alliance.[52] Students of gentry origin, as opposed to petty bourgeois overseas Chinese, dominated the new organization from the start.[53] However, Sun's long revolutionary experience, his international reputation, and his Japanese backing ensured his election as leader and the adoption of his four-point political program by the Alliance.

In October, Sun wrote the introduction to the first issue of the Alliance's new periodical, *The People's Journal.* In this he set out his program as nationalism *(minzuzhuyi)*, democracy *(min-quanzhuyi)*, and socialism *(minshengzhuyi)*. *Minzuzhuyi* and *min-quanzhuyi* had been seen as the two principles of the revolutionaries for at least a year,[54] but this appears to have been the first use of the term *minshengzhuyi*. As we have seen above, Sun used the term *minsheng* freely in his letter to Li Hong-zhang in 1894 at a time when he saw the people's livelihood as a necessary component of national self-strengthening. The reason for the replacement by *minshengzhuyi* of the accepted Japanese term for socialism, *shehuizhuyi*, which Sun had been using for at least two years was clearly its euphony with the other two. Furthermore, the trio made up *sanminzhuyi*, the "Three Principles of the People," with its obvious parallels to Abraham Lincoln's "of the people, by the people, for the people."[55]

Presumably because he felt there would be no difficulty in convincing his readers of the necessity for nationalism and democracy, most of Sun's introduction was devoted to socialism. After stating that in the modern world political problems had been replaced by economic ones, he wrote:

52. See Hsueh, *Huang Hsing,* 38–55; and Wu Yu-chang, *The Revolution of 1911* (Peking, 1962), 71–77, as well as Schiffrin, *Sun Yat-sen,* 344–366.
53. See Li Da-nian, "Xinhai Geming yu Fan Man Wenti," in *Lishi Yanjiu* (5/1961), and in *Xinhai Geming Wushi Zhounian Jinian Lunwen ji,* 2 vols. (Peking, 1962), I, 188–203, esp. 199.
54. See the letter published in *Jingzhong Ribao* (12/20/04), 1.
55. The term *sanminzhuyi* was not introduced until at least a month later. See Feng, *Geming Yishi,* III, 215.

As for the social problem *(minshengzhuyi)* which has become increasingly serious and difficult to turn back, only China has not yet suffered from it deeply and can remove it easily. Hence, either in view of the past experiences of others or of our own future dangers we must simultaneously apply all things that benefit our people. . . . Europe and America may be strong but their people are suffering. Look at the way in which unions, strikes, anarchists and socialists *(shehui dang)* flourish everyday. The social revolution can not be far. . . .

From the start Sun distinguished between *minshengzhuyi* (the social problem and its cure) and the radical or revolutionary *shehui dang* socialists who justifiably but regrettably disrupted society. The existence of the two terms, *minshengzhuyi* and *shehuizhuyi,* allowed Sun and the Chinese revolutionaries to resolve the Western ambiguity between state socialism and the beliefs and actions of the socialist parties. However, this resolution did not take place immediately, and the terms continued for the next two years to be used interchangeably as in the phrase "the reason why the socialist, *shehui dang,* proclaim *minshengzhuyi.*" [56]

Sun's introduction continued: "Our country's cure for the social problem could be the first to develop, and if we look at this evil before it springs up we could carry out a political and social revolution at one blow." [57] The introduction gave no details about Sun's social program. The Alliance's "proclamation of military government" which was drawn up at about the same time was more specific. Its section on Equal Land Rights reads:

The good fortune of civilization is to be shared equally by all the people in the nation. We should improve our social and economic organization and assess the value of all the land in the country. The present value of land will still belong to the owner. But all increases in value resulting from reform and social improvements shall belong to the state to be shared by all the people in order to create a socialist state *(shehui di guojia)* where each family within the country will have enough. No-one will be without his place *(suo).*

56. Sun, "Zhounian ci," 89. Schiffrin and Scalapino claim that at the beginning the two terms were identical; see "Early Socialist Currents in the Chinese Revolutionary Movement," *Journal of Asian Studies,* XVIII (3 May 1959), 321–342, esp. 334. I believe this to be a slight over-simplification.

57. Sun, "Fakan ci," *Min Bao,* I (11/26/05), 1–3.

Those who dare to monopolize the livelihood of the people will be cast out.[58]

Schiffrin has argued on the basis of this passage that Sun was not advocating land nationalization, and there is no doubt that it is ambiguous.[59] However, a piece by Sun's close follower, Hu Han-min, published in April, indicates that Sun was in fact advocating it. The article, which was entitled "The Six Great Principles of the People's Journal," contained six sections. According to Hu the first three of these corresponded to Sun's three principles.[60] The third section, instead of being entitled *minshengzhuyi,* was called *tudi guoyou* (land nationalization).

The article began with a description of the new social and economic problems and continued: "There are many socialist theories but they all aim at leveling economic classes. They are generally divided into 'communism' *(gongchanzhuyi),* collectivism *(jichanzhuyi),* and land nationalism." By communism Hu meant anarchocommunism and by collectivism, social democracy.[61]

Only constitutional democracies can adopt collectivism for in these the ruling authority resides in the state and the state machinery is controlled by a representative legislature. Thus there is no inequality involved if a democratic state, in reflecting social psychology, should adopt collectivism in order to promote the welfare of the people. Such of course cannot be said of a regime which allows any political classes. Not all collectivist theories

58. Quoted in Zou Lu, *Zhongguo Guomin Dang Shikao* (Taipei ed., 1965), 45. In *Xinhai Geming* the proclamation is referred to as a revised edition of the 4th month, 1906.

59. The passage is translated in Teng and Fairbank, 228. In it they render the phrase *reng shu yuanzhu* as "shall be received by the present owner." Schiffrin states "the word 'received' implies government purchase of the land which I do not believe is the intent of the manifesto." See "Early Land Policies," 551. Although I accept that "still belong" is a better translation of *"reng shu,"* I think that other statements by Sun and Hu Han-min show that purchase of the land was involved. Schiffrin's punctuation on this point is peculiar in that he includes *suoyou,* which clearly belongs to the next sentence, in this phrase.

The word *suo* in the phrase "no one should be without his *suo,"* which Teng translates as "employment," I believe means position with hints of the more literal sense of "place," and "piece of land" with their land-nationalist connotations.

60. Hu, "Hu Han-min Zizhuan," in *Geming Wenxian,* III, 373–442, esp. 388.

61. Hu, *"Min Bao* zhi Liu da Zhuyi," *Min Bao,* III (4/15/06) 1–22, esp. 11. This threefold division which Schiffrin and Scalapino call curious (326) was in fact quite common; see for instance Miyazaki Tamizō's article in the following issue of *Min Bao,* "Yicong" section, 1–12.

can be applied to China at her present stage of development. But in the case of land nationalization we already have a model in the "Well-field" system of the Three Dynasties and it should not be difficult to practice something indigenous to our racial consciousness in this period of political change.[62]

Hu gave the moral justification for land nationalization: "It is not man made, any more than sunshine or air and it should not be privately owned." He described the rise of land ownership, and the increase of land prices with the advance of civilization, and the need to check this process in its early stages. Hu's preventative measures were closer to those of the land nationalizers than to those of Henry George. He believed in the nationalization of the land itself, not only of rent:

There are various measures for carrying out land nationalization but the main purpose is to deprive the people *(renmin)* of the right to land ownership, while permitting them to retain other rights (such as superfices, emphyteusis, and easement). These rights must be obtained by permission of the state.[63]

His description of the benefits brought about by the scheme was very similar to that of Sun, with strong overtones of the Equal-field system:

Only self-cultivating farmers can obtain land from the state. In this way the people will increasingly devote themselves to farming and no land will be wasted. Landlords who in the past have been nonproductive profiteers will now be just like the common people. They will turn to productive enterprises and this will produce striking results for the good of the whole national economy.[64]

Hu's views on socialism were very similar to, if not identical with, Sun's. It has been noted above that in September 1905, only six months before the article was written, Hu had doubts about Sun's policy in this respect. As he later explained it: "At that time the economics taught by the professors at the [Tokyo] School of Law and Politics were really capitalist theories and the books we studied

62. *Min Bao,* III, 12. The words *wuzhong zhi suo guyouzhe* have been changed in many texts to *wu zexi suo guyouzhe.* See *Xinhai Geming,* II, 264, and the translation in *Sources of Chinese Tradition* compiled by Theodore de Bary et al., text ed. (New York, 1964), II, 104. This interesting piece of editing indicates the decline in respectability of "racial" theories during the twentieth century.
63. *Min Bao,* III, 13.   64. *Min Bao,* III, 13.

only went as far as social reformism, that is why I was doubtful about it." [65]

During the next year or so, Hu was Sun's private secretary and was "close to him every day." Thus it is very likely that starting with this *tabula rasa* Hu's ideas on socialism were very largely derived from Sun. [66]

Hu's frankness roused some hostile reaction. For instance, Liang Qi-chao's opposition to socialism is supposed to have dated from the third issue of *The People's Journal* in which the "Six Great Principles" appeared. [67] Perhaps it was concern about this reaction that made Sun obscure and modify his position in his next major statement on his social policy. This came in a speech he made in December 1906 at a meeting called to commemorate the first anniversary of *The People's Journal*. [68] After describing the origins of socialism and the way in which the growth of the division between rich and poor was caused by industrialization, he pinpointed the problem: "Why can the West not solve the social problem? Because it has not solved the land problem. With all progress of civilization, land values increase . . . the poor have no fields to till and they have to depend on (industrial) work to make a living." He then showed how much land prices increased with industrial progress. He went on to state the way in which he thought socialism should be applied to China:

We must plan a method to solve it (the social problem) today and this is something we comrades must pay attention to. I have heard people say "socialism will kill half of our 400,000,000 people and seize the rich men's fields for the other." [69] This is loose talk and fails to understand its central meaning. One should not pay attention to them. Sociologists *(shehuixuezhe)* are not united as to the way to solve it. I believe that one should use the method of fixing land prices. For instance if a landlord has land worth a thousand dollars, its value should be fixed at that or up to two thousand. One can reckon that in the future the value will go up to ten thousand

65. "Hu Han-min Zizhuan," 386.
66. "Hu Han-min Zizhuan," 386, and Yamamoto, 153.
67. Hu Han-min, "Gao Feinan Minshengzhuyizhe" (hereafter referred to as "Gao Fei"), *Min Bao,* XII (3/07), 45–156, esp. 76, quoted by Rong Meng-yuan, 8.
68. Schiffrin and Scalapino mistook the Chinese calendar for the Western calendar when they wrote that the speech was given on 10/17/06; see Schiffrin and Scalapino, "Early Socialist Currents," 334. It was in fact 12/2/06.
69. This was a quote from Liang Qi-chao. See ch. 7 below.

dollars. In that case the landlord ought to receive one or two thousand dollars so that he has a profit from what belonged to him and no loss. But the eight thousand dollar profit would go to the state. This will be a great benefit to the national economy and the prosperity of the people and the evils of a rich minority gaining a monopoly would be stopped for ever. This would be the simplest and most convenient method to practice.[70]

This was only true for China: "Land prices in every Western country have already been expanded to the utmost so unfortunately there is no standard and it would be difficult to apply." In China, Sun thought, this method brought another advantage:

After this method has been applied, the more civilization advances the richer the state becomes. All financial problems will be easy to solve. All existing taxes will be remitted and prices will gradually go down. . . . After China has practiced the social revolution private individuals will never pay taxes, there will only be this one item of land tax and China will become the richest country in the world and no other country will be able to equal this social state.[71]

Sun's position, though slightly modified from that put forward, still retained the principle of land nationalization. Despite his reference to a single tax on land, Sun did not merely call for the expropriation of rent, and the policy was not like that of Georgism. It was much closer to the land nationalist policies of Walras and Gossen. However, at this stage Sun and his followers did not spell out the way in which their policy should be implemented.

70. "Zhounian ci," 90. Sun used the word *Shehuixuezhe* to include nonsocialists like Spencer and Dove. See Hu Han-min, "Gao fei," 101.
71. "Zhounian ci," 90.

4 | Socialism in Japan before 1906

In one day in May 1901 the first national socialist party in Japan, the Social Democratic Party, was founded and then closed by government order.[1] But Japanese interest in socialism started long before that and on a far greater scale than in China. Probably the first use of the word *shakaishugi* (socialism) came in a book called *Principles of True Government,* by Katō Hiroyuki in 1870, only two years after the Meiji restoration. Katō was an important early translator from German. He began by being a liberal, but his admiration of Prussia seems to have led him to change his opinions and become a supporter of the government, and the most important intellectual opponent of the liberal popular rights movement.[2] There is no sign that Katō sympathized with socialism even during his early period.

Shugi was a Japanese neologism—later transplanted to China as *zhuyi*—meaning "principle idea," and was used to translate the European suffix "ism." *Sha (or she* in Chinese) is an ancient word. Its written form is made up of two elements, the spirit pole signifying religion and the sign for earth—which itself comes from a phallic-shaped pole associated with the altar to the soil. Thus the word has deep associations with the land and the community attached to the land. In combination with *kai* (or *hui,* in Chinese), the word for meeting, the term *shakai* or *shehui* meant village fair or communal

1. Cyril H. Powles, "Abe Isoo and the Role of Christians in the Founding of the Japanese Socialist Movement, 1895–1905." Harvard *Papers on Japan,* I (Cambridge, Mass., 1961), 89–130.

2. Robert A. Scalapino, *Democracy and the Party Movement in Prewar Japan* (Berkeley, 1962), 54. See also "Nihon Shakaishugishi," by Kōtoku Shūsui and Ishikawa Kyōkusan, serialized in *Heimin Shimbun,* II–LVII; reprinted in *Meiji Bunka Zenshū,* XXI, *Shakai Hen* (Tokyo, 1929), 331–370, esp. 334.

meeting. Thus *shakaishugi* was a reasonably apposite translation of socialism for Katō and his colleagues to choose. The only major semantic difference was that *shakaishugi*, which became the standard word for socialism in all East Asian languages, retained traces of its rural communal origin.

The first advocacy of socialism came in the foundation of a party called Eastern Socialist Party in 1882. The party leader, Tarui Tōkichi, was a radical supporter of the Liberal party that emerged with the popular rights movement. It is not certain where he obtained his political ideas. These seem to have been rather contradictory and included anarchism and nationalization of the banks.[3] A year later another party was formed with a similar title that was a deliberate pun on the word *Shakaitō*, which meant Socialist Party. This was the *Shakaitō*, or Riksha Party, organized to agitate for better conditions among riksha men.[4] Neither of these parties seems to have had much influence in a period of great political turbulence, the time from 1880 to 1884 during which parties and political groups were springing up everywhere.[5] However, Tarui and other radicals from the popular rights movement went on to be an important element in the Japanese socialist organization.

At the same time an increasing number of translations and articles began to appear on European socialism. In 1881 an article was published in the Christian magazine, *The Universe;* entitled "On the Origins of the Modern Socialist Parties," [6] this article gave a general account of the life and theories of Karl Marx (who was still alive at the time). In 1882 T. D. Woolsey's *Communism and Socialism* was published, and many books were also published on other European reformist and revolutionary movements.[7] Books came out on Bismarck; and most of Henry George's books were translated before the Sino-Japanese War of 1894–1895.[8] Societies for the study of

3. Sakai Toshihiko, *Nihon Shakaishugi Undō Shi*, reprinted in *Nihon Kindaishi Sōsho*, No. 7 (Tokyo, 1954), 56.

4. Sakai, 56.   5. Scalapino, *Democracy*, 68.

6. Kosaka Masaaki (ed), *Japanese Thought in the Meiji Era*, translated and adapted by David Abosch (Tokyo, 1958), 179. The magazine was originally called *Kirisuto Kyō Zasshi*.

7. For a very full list of translations of European books on socialism, see Shioda Shobei (ed.), *Nihon Shakaishugi Bunken Kaisetsu* (Tokyo, 1958). See also Shimoide Hayakichi, "Shakai Bunken Nempyō," in *Meiji Bunka Zenshū*, XXI. 603–621.

8. Kosaka, 201.

social problems sprang up almost every year between 1895 and 1901. In 1896 a group of professors at Tokyo University founded the Japanese Association for the Study of Social Policies. This association followed the German "Socialists of the Chair," or state Socialists, in believing in state interference to protect the workers from the full effects of laissez faire, in order to avoid class conflict and protect the state and the essentials of capitalism.[9] The society was purely a study circle, but because of the respectable positions of its leaders and members its recommendations were extremely influential in the government and civil service, and as Bismarckian state socialists the group later became one of the most powerful enemies of the socialists.[10]

One year later the Society for Research in Social Problems was founded. This society, which had much broader and more humanitarian aims than the Japanese Association for the Study of Social Policies, was established by Tarui Tōkichi and one of the most important of the later leaders of Japanese socialism, Kōtoku Shūsui. Kōtoku was also connected with the earlier liberal movement and was a pupil of Nakae Chōmin, a famous liberal intellectual and the translator of Rousseau's *Contrat social*.[11]

In October 1898, Kōtoku and several of the Christian members of the society founded a group called the Socialist Research Society. The society's leader was Murai Chishi, a professor of English at Tokyo University. Another leading figure in the group was Abe Isō, a clergyman who had spent several years studying in America, and the whole society was dominated by American-trained Christians.[12]

It is hardly surprising that Japanese Christians should be concerned with the "social problem," but is interesting that a significant number of them should have turned toward socialism. The basic reason for this seems to have been the practical failure of Christianity to deal with social problems, either in the industrialized West or in industrializing Japan. The need for a solution to these worldly problems led some of the Japanese Christians to think of socialism

9. Hyman Kublin, *Asian Revolutionary: The Life of Katayama Sen,* (Princeton, 1964), 108.

10. Kublin, 136.

11. For Kōtoku and his background, see F. G. Notehelfer, *Kōtoku Shūsui: Portrait of a Japanese Radical* (Cambridge, 1971).

12. Powles, 104; and Kosaka, 324.

as a way to practice *Hakuai* (brotherly love). As Abe wrote: "Christian humanism provided me with the basis which would one day bring me to socialism. Now I realize that social welfare was insufficient as a means for the destruction of poverty." [13]

And another Christian socialist, Kinoshita Naoe, wrote that "while I had become a fervent believer in brotherhood, the earthly tragedy of the struggle for existence was inexplicable by theology. . . . It was the economic theory of socialism which afforded me solace." [14]

It was already a socially unorthodox step to become a Christian in Meiji Japan. The socialism of the Christian socialists came from this radical predisposition and from their American mentors, many of whom were interested in socialism. For instance, the Reverend Dwight W. Learned gave the first lectures on socialism in Japan at the Christian Community University in the early 1880s. Many of the other missionaries seem to have been in the liberal and practical wings of their Protestant or Unitarian churches, and they naturally introduced their students to the books that appealed to them.

Bellamy's *Looking Backward* had an influence on Japanese Christians even before it was translated into Japanese in 1903. Abe Isō, who saw it in the early 1890s, said after he read it that "it was as if a blind man's eyes had been opened and he had been able to look up at the sun in the heavens." [15] Even more influential in Japan were the books by American Christians on socialism in general, like Richard Ely's *French and German Socialism* and W. D. P. Bliss's *Handbook of Socialism*. These books were surveys of the socialist movement as a whole, giving short descriptions of each major school of socialism and the socialist parties in each country. The authors tried to be sympathetic toward socialism and impartial toward the different schools. Naturally, they had their prejudices. They believed that evolutionary social democracy was the true form of socialism and supported it against false socialisms. Bliss, for ex-

13. Abe Isō, *Shakaishugisha to Naru Made* (Tokyo, 1932). This passage is translated in Powles, 102. For background on radical Japanese Christians see Irwin Scheiner, *Christians, Converts and Social Protest in Meiji Japan* (Berkeley, 1970).

14. From an article in *Heimin Shimbun* called "Yo wa Ika ni Shite Shakaishugisha to Nari Shi." This passage is translated in Kosaka, 331.

15. Abe Isō, *Shakaishugisha to Naru Made*. This passage is translated in Powles, 103.

ample, wrote that "Marx in the greatest deed of his life drove out the anarchists from the Congress of the Hague . . . and saved socialism from the scourge that anarchism has since proved to modern Europe."[16] Bliss and Ely also had their own ideas concerning the "true," as opposed to the apparent, nature of social democracy, maintaining that it was really evolutionary rather than revolutionary, and spiritual rather than material. Ely said, "As Socialism is expected to come as a result of evolution to a greater or less extent brought about and guided by the wishes of men, it is not to be anticipated by the modern socialists that it will come all at once."[17]

By modern socialists, Ely meant here the Fabians, with whose views he and the other Christian socialists often coincided. Ely and Bliss thought that the essence of socialism was unselfishness and love and not, as other people thought, class conflict.

Socialism is essentially and has been from the start a humanitarian movement. It is not, whatever some would make it, a class movement of the have nots against the haves. The major part of its foremost leaders, Owen, Saint Simon, Gall, Marx, Lassalle, Morris, Hyndman, Vollmar, Bakunin, Kropotkine, belonged originally to the haves. Weitling "the father of German Communism" declared that he was converted to Communism by the New Testament. If German Socialism has become completely materialistic, not enough emphasis has been laid on the fact that with Marx, Lassalle and Bakunin their Socialist philosophy was derived primarily from Hegel, the most spiritual of modern philosophers. . . . In France Fourier, Lamennais and Cabet were profoundly religious.[18]

It would be fair to say that American, and these American digests of European socialism in particular, were the most important sources for the Japanese socialists at this period. Sakai Toshihiko (Kōsen) wrote: "The first book I read was Ely's 'French and German Socialism.' . . . For the first time the way was illuminated for me, and it was this thought that made clear all the other thought in my mind."[19]

16. W. D. P. Bliss, *A Handbook of Socialism* (New York, 1895), 45. It is interesting to note that postcultural-revolutionary Chinese studies should also stress this episode. See *Bakuning,* ed. Nankai Daxue Lishixi (Peking, 1972), 45–48.
17. R. T. Ely, *Socialism and Social Reform* (New York, 1894), 82.
18. Bliss, 41.
19. "Yo wa Ika ni Shite Shakaishugisha to Nari Shi," translated in Kosaka, 331. The book which the non-Christian Kōtoku said converted him was A. E. Schäffle's

There are reasons for this American predominance. The Christian socialists were educated in American institutions and some, like Abe Isō, had spent much time in America, and English was their first foreign language.[20] The American books were comprehensive and simple, as opposed, for instance, to the works of the Fabians, and the Japanese government's ban on the translation of the works of the socialists themselves may also have been a factor. The main point seems to have been that the American authors' predilections fitted those of the Japanese Christians.[21]

The terms of the Socialist Research Society, "were only to study the possibility or otherwise of applying the principles of socialism to Japan." [22] It was not necessary to be a committed socialist to join. The society, which never seems to have had more than twenty members, discussed many aspects of socialism, from the socialism of Saint Simon to land tenure in New Zealand.[23] Information about all these subjects was available in Bliss and Ely.

By January 1900 most of the society had become convinced Social Democrats, and it was decided to form a new society, the Socialist Association, to which only socialists could belong. Murai Chishi resigned, and Abe Isō was elected president. The society decided to hold public meetings and lectures, and two of its members, Kōtoku Shūsui and Kawakami Kiyoshi, started writing articles to popularize socialism in the newspaper, *The Daily News,* where they worked as journalists.

During the year 1900, various members joined in the society's first agitation, a campaign against legalized prostitution; among others. Abe Isō and Shimada Saburō made speeches to arouse the workers. The society also made increasing contact with trade unions and their supporting groups, the earliest one of which was the Association for the Promotion of Labor Unions formed by Katayama Sen, Shimada, and various others, mostly Christians, in 1897. The

Die Quintessenz des Sozialismus. This book is also a digest by a sympathetic non-socialist. It is almost certain that Kōtoku read the book in its English translation which came out in New York in 1890.

20. Powles, 102.

21. Kublin, note on 179. One Japanese socialist did have a relatively sophisticated understanding of the Fabians: see Kawakami Kiyoshi, "The Political Ideas of Modern Japan," in *Bulletin of the State University of Iowa, Studies in Sociology, Politics, History* (1903), Vol. II, No. 2, 181–193.

22. Powles, 107.   23. Powles, 108.

association had coordinated the various organizations of skilled workers, and their activities increased the number of unions and strikes in the period from 1895 to 1901 during which the tensions of industrialization were mounting.

In April 1901 it was decided to form a Social Democratic Party to link the unions with the socialists in the approved German manner. The manifesto of the party was published in Katayama Sen's newspaper, *Labor World,* and in six other leading dailies.[24] It was supposed to have been based on the *Communist Manifesto,* but as one writer put it, "it is far more the product of British and American socialism than of the European tradition."[25] The new party was overwhelmingly Christian. All of the party's six founder members except for Kōtoku were or had been active in their churches, and Abe Isō, a Christian minister, was its leader.

The ephemeral Social Democratic Party in 1901 lasted for one day. From then, until the foundation of the Japanese Socialist Party in February 1906, there was no socialist party in Japan. This does not mean that socialism was dead during this time. In fact, despite the small number of people involved, this period can be described as the heroic age of Japanese socialism.[26]

After the prohibition of the Social Democratic Party, Abe Isō and other socialists revived their old association, the Socialist Association. Using this and Katayama's paper, *Labor World,* they continued and expanded their previous programs: selling the magazines and other publications and sending members on speaking tours. This went on with only minor harassment from the government for the next two years.

The inconsistency in the authorities' treatment of the socialists is difficult to follow, let alone to understand. It can only partly be explained by the slight variations of policy of the different cabinets which came and went every two years in this period. Kublin's interesting explanation for it is that the government was not concerned about the Socialist Association's long-term goals, but was very concerned about some of their immediate policies.[27] In the case

24. Notehelfer, 67.
25. Powles, 109. One point from it illustrates its nature very clearly: "Our theory is radical . . . but the means we will employ are absolutely peaceful. To achieve these desired ends, we will use political institutions."
26. Sakai, 118.   27. Kublin, 147.

of the Social Democratic Party, he maintains the government was not afraid of the party's long-term proposals for the equitable distribution of wealth, public ownership of land, and communications, and so on. These were too far from the political consensus to be of any possible danger. Furthermore, the socialists concentrated their propaganda on the industrial workers who at that time were without the vote, largely unorganized and with no sense of class consciousness, besides being a very small section of the population as a whole.[28] What the government really feared were the immediate aims of the socialists: general suffrage, and a reduction of the army. Here the socialists could find allies from other groups, like the radical wing of the liberals, and support from some merchants and landowners. It was because of this threat that the government suppressed the party.

Kublin says that this attitude helps explain the authorities' dealings with the socialists throughout the Meiji period. The later suppression of the Commoners' Press, ostensibly because it published a translation of the *Communist Manifesto,* would seem to throw doubt on his explanation. However, it is quite likely that the translation of the *Manifesto* gave an excuse to the government, which wanted to suppress it for its antimilitarism. Of course, this attitude of the government applied only to socialists and not to anarchists, and I feel that Kublin's theory, while interesting in relation to the case of the Social Democratic Party, cannot be the whole answer to the complicated problem of the government's inconsistency.

During these same years there was another group advocating some socialist ideas: the Idealist Band, a group with a much wider influence. The Band's ideal was typically socialist and very similar to the Chinese *datong:* "Therefore liberty, equality and fraternity, the breaking down of natural boundaries, common currency, the setting aside of armaments, the abolition of private property in land, the abolition of inheritance in wealth must all be among the Idealist Band's aspirations." [29] However, this was to be reached by a method that placed the Band clearly outside the socialist camp. As one of its leaders wrote, "the Idealist Band strives to reform society by a

28. According to figures published in 1905 the number of factory workers (no definition is given of the word factory) was 558,041, of whom 225,040 were women. This was out of a population of over 45 million; see *Chokugen* (4/16/05), 1.
29. Kosaka, 339.

special method: namely it desires first to reform itself." [30] This type of method, which one sees frequently in China, is more religious than political and in this case seems to have been based on a mixture of Buddhism and Christianity. [31]

The Band, consisting of journalists centered around *The Daily News,* was led by the paper's editor Kuroiwa Ruikō. In rather the same way as the American "muckrakers," Kuroiwa, with a brilliant team which included Kōtoku Shūsui and the unorthodox Christian socialist Uchimura Kanzō, built up one of the largest newspaper circulations in Tokyo.

Kōtoku's presence in this group does not mean that he had given up his support for more orthodox socialism. On the contrary, he developed it a great deal, as can be seen by the difference between two books he wrote, one in 1901 and the other in 1903. In 1901 he published *Imperalism,* in which he attacked the institution violently, but only from a humanist point of view. According to him, imperialism was a specter made up of patriotism and militarism—he did not mention its class or economic aspects. [32] The other book, *Essence of Socialism,* showed a much greater understanding of Marxism and social democratic theory. [33] In it he saw class conflict as the basis of history, the economic substructure determining the whole of society. Modern critics say that he still misunderstood some aspects of Marxism, when for instance he appealed to "patriots, men of good will and the revolutionary intelligentsia to work for the acquisition of parliamentary power by means of universal suffrage." [34] In fact, Kōtoku's ideas seem to reflect policies very much to the fore in contemporary socialism all over the world. To take the second point first, socialists in most European countries were active in, or led the movements for, adult suffrage. Their preoccupation with elections and members of parliament went far beyond the Marxist principle of using elections after the capitalist

30. Kosaka, 339.

31. Tatsuo Arima, "Uchimura Kanzo: A Study of the Post Meiji Japanese Intelligentsia," Harvard *Papers on Japan,* I, 130–189, esp. 146.

32. Kosaka, 342.

33. The title was very likely suggested by Schäffle's *Die Quintessenz des Sozialismus,* the book which according to Kōtoku converted him to socialism. For a more detailed description of his ideological development see Notehelfer, 61–87.

34. Kublin, 154.

revolution purely as a means to consolidate the working class. For all their talk about revolution, Bebel and Kautsky were basically parliamentarians. Bebel would have been, and Kautsky was, horrified by the revolution they had always advocated. It could be argued that here Kōtoku understood the social democratic movement better than its leaders themselves, and that he saw it for what it was rather than for what it claimed to be.

Kōtoku's call to patriots, men of good will, and the revolutionary intelligentsia, and his reluctance to see the unique role of the proletariat is more significant. It was a symptom of a feeling common among all socialists, but particularly among the Japanese and Chinese. It probably comes from a reluctance to divide society. If there was no alternative, they still tried to keep the bulk of society under one banner by separating only a small minority of the rich from the great majority of the poor. This is exactly the Marxist picture of capitalist society at the brink of revolution, with the petty bourgeoisie and the peasantry forced into the ranks of the proletariat. But no Western Marxist at that time dreamt of saying that this situation actually existed anywhere. They still thought that the proletariat was the only real source of revolutionary strength, even though it was not the overwhelming majority of society.

The most striking thing about *The Daily News* was its antimilitarism. During 1903 it was the only important voice of protest as the atmosphere built up for the Russo-Japanese war. Suddenly, in October, Kuroiwa turned about and decided to support the war.[35] This was too much for Kōtoku and Uchimura, and for Sakai Toshihiko, another journalist who like Kōtoku was a socialist of the liberal not the Christian tradition. They all resigned, and Kōtoku and Sakai decided that the fight against the war must go on. In November they started a new magazine called *The Commoners' Newspaper*. This magazine and its publishing company, the Commoners' Press, became the center of Japanese socialism for most of the war, which lasted from February 1904 till September 1905. The new company was quickly supported by Abe Isō, Nishikawa Kōjiro, Katayama Sen, and the other Christian members of the Socialist Association. However, the Commoners' Press was dominated by

35. Kublin, 160

Kōtoku and Sakai, and for the first time control of the main organ of the Japanese socialist movement went to men of the Japanese liberal school, which through men like Kōtoku's teacher, Nakae Chōmin, was itself connected to French rationalist thought. This does not mean that the Christian socialists were displaced; they were still very important and had a large influence on the movement. But from this point on, materialism, and mainly Marxist materialism, became the dominant line of Japanese socialist thought.[36]

To begin with, there was considerable quarrelling inside the new organization. At this stage it was not between the Christians and the materialists, but seems to have been along class lines—Katayama the peasant against the rest, all of whom came from Samurai families. In December 1903, to the relief of the others, Katayama left Japan for America and Europe to represent Japan at the Sixth Congress of the Socialist International. After his departure his magazine *Socialism*, the successor of *Labor World*, merged with *The Commoners' Newspaper*.[37]

Throughout the war the main concern of *The Commoners' Newspaper* was pacifism. But it was chiefly a socialist pacifism. In January 1904 when the last negotiations between the Russians and the Japanese broke down, an article in the newspaper said:

Formerly when the Franco-Prussian war started, the German Socialist Party opposed it with all its strength. When the Boer war started the English Socialist Party opposed it ferociously. Socialists know that modern international wars are the results of the clash of interests of capitalist classes, and that whoever wins, it is the working class that makes the sacrifices. Japanese socialists also know this, that is why we shout against the war.[38]

Kōtoku openly disapproved of bourgeois pacifism. In June 1904 he criticized *Bethink Yourselves,* Tolstoy's protest against the war: "Tolstoy ascribes the cause of war to the debasement of man, and accordingly desires to save him by teaching repentance. We socialists attribute the cause of war to economic competition. For this reason we are not completely in accord with Tolstoy."[39]

Not all the members of the Commoners' Press shared Kōtoku's views, and most of the Christians, while not quarrelling with

36. Powles, 111.   37. Powles, 111; and Kublin, 151.
38. Quoted in Sakai, 138.   39. Kublin, 172.

Kōtoku, still seemed to feel that their opposition to war was a moral part of their basically moral socialism.

In March 1904 the Japanese socialists gained great credit from socialists all over the world by their friendly letter to the leaders of the Russian Social Democratic Party. The letter condemned the capitalists on both sides saying, among other things, that "it is an unimportant question which government wins."[40] This credit was redoubled when later that year Katayama made his famous handshake with Plekhanov, representing the Russian Social Democratic Party, at the Congress of the International at Amsterdam.

These activities must have seemed the blackest treason to most Japanese during this period of patriotic fervor. The courage of the socialists in carrying on antiwar propaganda in Japan, "the land of the Samurai," in wartime is extraordinary. The public hostility against them must have been far greater than that against the pro-Boers in England or the opponents of the colonization of the Philippines in the United States. However, Meiji Japan was not Showa Japan, thirty years later. No socialist was assassinated, and they even seem to have had sympathetic audiences at their meetings.[41] What is more, government oppression was only sporadic and, to begin with, fairly ineffective. In April the police tried to close the magazine down, but the ban was reversed by the courts. Final disaster came after November 1904 when the Commoners' Press decided to tempt providence by planning a public celebration of its first anniversary, and by bringing out a special anniversary edition of *The Commoner's Newspaper* containing a complete translation of Marx's *Manifesto*. The police immediately banned the celebration, seized the special edition, and started actions which compelled the magazine to close two months later. Kōtoku and Nishikawa were each sentenced to several months' imprisonment which they served in 1905.[42]

Despite the war, for the year of its existence the Commoners' Press carried on full-scale socialist propaganda, with meetings, lecture tours in the country, and the sale and distribution of books and pamphlets. *The Communist Manifesto* was not the only transla-

40. Kublin, 171.   41. Kublin, 178.
42. *Chokugen,* No. 26 (7/28/05), 1; and Sakai, 151.

tion printed by the society. During that year Bellamy's *Looking Backward*, Bebel's *Woman Past, Present and Future*, Morris's *News from Nowhere*, and Tolstoy's *Bethink Yourselves* were all brought out, as well as several Japanese descriptions and interpretations of Western socialism.[43] The society also sold books in English which were less liable to government censorship. An advertisement in Commoners' Press lists Marx's *Capital* and Engel's *Socialism, Utopian and Scientific*, but most of the list consisted of the American general surveys.[44]

The group was subdued but not crushed by the police action at the end of 1904. Soon after the last issue of *The Commoners' Newspaper* they started a new magazine called *Straight Talk*, which came out every month. This magazine kept up its antimilitarism until the end of the war. *Straight Talk* also maintained its international contacts: in the thirtieth issue there was a letter to the Japanese antiwar movement from Tolstoy. He was delighted and full of praise for the stand against the war, but was very opposed to the group's socialism: "I must tell you," he wrote, "that I do not approve of socialism and am sorry to know that the most spiritually advanced part of your so clever and energetic nation has taken from Europe the very feeble illusory and fallacious theory of socialism which in Europe is beginning to be abandoned."[45] Five years before, a letter like that from a great European thinker might have destroyed the whole socialist movement in Japan. But by 1905 the Japanese socialists, both Christian and materialist, were sure enough of themselves to withstand Tolstoy's patronizing and violent attack.

The group's largest political effort came in May 1905 when one of its members, Kinoshita Naoe, was put up as a candidate for the diet from Tokyo.[46] The attempt was completely hopeless. A socialist

43. See Shioda.
44. *Heimin Shimbun*, II (11/22/03), 4. Apart from the books mentioned the list ran: Ely, *Socialism and Social Reform;* Schäffle, *Essence of Socialism;* Bliss, *A Handbook of Socialism;* and Bliss, *The Encyclopedia of Social Reforms.* In *Heimin Shimbun*, III (11/25/05), 4, there is another list containing the following: Ely, *French and German Socialism;* Wallace, *Land Nationalization;* and Henry George, *Progress and Poverty.*
45. *Chokugen*, Vol. II, No. 30 (8/27/05), 1.
46. Kinoshita's novels, *Hi no Hakira (Pillar of Fire)* and *Ryōjin no Sihaku (Confessions of a Husband)*, were probably the most effective media of socialist and feminist propaganda at the time. See Powles, 113; and Sakai, 6.

candidate, basing his campaign on opposition to the war, could have no possible chance of success, especially with an electorate from which the poor were totally excluded by the voting qualifications. Kinoshita received 32 votes out of a possible 16,000.[47] One motive behind this forlorn hope seems to have been to use the campaign to spread antiwar propaganda. This failed because the police prohibited their meetings and confiscated their leaflets. A more important factor was the desire to make the workers, who were still disqualified, accustomed to the ideas of a parliamentary Socialist Party. As the editors of *Straight Talk* stated: "When there are socialist votes in the election, however few, the Socialist Party can be said to have been established in reality. This is the aim of our movement in the coming election." [48] This is a clear example of the influence of the European Social Democrats and of the concept of gaining strength if not power by parliamentary means.

In fact, the limited suffrage probably saved the socialists' self-esteem. It is unlikely that any antiwar platform could have gained a much larger proportion of the votes, even if the poor had been allowed to vote.

During the war it was pacifism that kept the groups round *The Commoners' Newspaper* and *Straight Talk* united. After the war's end in September 1905 the personal and political tensions within the movement forced it to break up, and *Straight Talk* ceased publication in October. The division was more or less along religious lines. In November a group of the Christians founded a new magazine called *The New Age*, with Ishikawa Kyōkusan, as editor and Abe and Kinoshita as his assistants. *The New Age* tended to be more religious than political and to concentrate on Christian converts rather than on society as a whole.[49]

After his release from prison Kōtoku went to America, and Nishikawa and Sakai took over the more political or materialist wing of the movement. In December 1905 they started their own magazine *Light*, and Nishikawa became editor. It is clear from the fact that Nishikawa himself was a Christian that there was no absolute division between Christians and the rationalists. However, *Light* was much more concerned with both the introduction and application of materialist socialism than was *The New Age*.

47. *Chokugen*, Vol. II, No. 16 (6/14/05), 1.
48. *Chokugen*, Vol. II, No. 15 (5/14/05), 1.   49. Powles, 124.

The split was particularly unfortunate for the socialist movement because of the considerable popular unrest in the months after the end of the war. The unrest and rioting against the government was ostensibly caused by dissatisfaction with the terms of the Treaty of Portsmouth which was thought not to have given Japan her just rewards after all her magnificent victories. The riots were also caused by the very badly overstrained economy. These disturbances were the main cause for the overthrow of the Katsura government and its replacement by one led by Saionji in January 1906.[50] Saionji, who always preferred liberal policies, decided that one of the ways to get over the crisis was to relax the police laws. This relaxation allowed even socialists to organize parties. The opportunity was very quickly taken up by the *Light* group, and on February 24, 1906, they came to an agreement with some of the Christians to put aside their differences and unite. That day the Japanese Socalist Party was founded, under the leadership of Nishikawa and Sakai. The party was very conscious of its insecure position with the authorities and was determined to keep its legality. It included in the party program the phrase, "the party's aim is to advocate socialism within the limits of the law,"[51] a phrase that later destroyed the party's very superficial unity. But for a brief period the Japanese socialist movement had a legal organization.

During the period 1901–1905 it is the internal rather than the external successes of the socialist movement which were impressive. On the outside, it failed to reach the masses, *The Commoners' Newspaper* at its high point having a circulation of only 4,500. It failed to encourage the formation of trade unions, and it failed to influence the official elite or government in any way. But the socialist activists and the few faithful gained a confidence and a self-respect, particularly from their magnificent and uncompromising stand against the full force of virulent patriotism. At the same time they gained a much deeper understanding of Western socialism and especially of Marxism. By 1904 the non-Christian socialists like

50. Scalapino, *Democracy*, 128.
51. Sakai, 7. Most authors refer to this party as the Nihon Shakaitō. See Scalapino, *Democracy*, 318; and Kublin, 191. However, its members seem to have used the more nationalist pronunciation Nippon Shakaitō. See English column in *Hikari* (20/4/06), 1; reprint, 83.

Kōtoku and Sakai had practically become Marxists, or to be precise, Marxists of the school of Bebel and Kautsky. They accepted the Marxist analysis of capitalism, and with some modifications about the role of the proletariat, they also accepted the Marxist interpretation of history and belief in economic determinism. On the other hand the Christian socialists still believed that socialism was basically moral, not scientific. This view was strengthened by the fact that for most of this period the main issue was war which, despite Kōtoku's efforts to place it in the realm of economics, was more easily attacked on moral grounds.

Although understanding of "scientific socialism" increased, and rationalists came to the front of the socialist organizations, the Christians remained very important in the movement, and the picture originally painted by the American Christian sympathizers of socialism as a fundamentally moral force retained a considerable influence on Japanese socialism.

5 | Liang Qi-chao

There is no doubt that before the May 4 Movement of 1919 the most influential propagandist of Western ideas in China was Liang Qi-chao. Liang, like Kang You-wei and Sun Yat-sen, came from within fifty miles of Canton, the Chinese region under the most intense foreign pressure. A boy of extraordinary precocity, even by the high standards of the Chinese literati, he became a provincial graduate at the age of sixteen.[1] By this time he had already become interested in the West. The following year, 1890, he went to study under Kang You-wei, becoming his leading disciple. In 1895 he accompanied Kang to Peking to begin the agitation which led to the reform movement. In 1896 he went south to Shanghai where he edited *The Chinese Progress,* which became the Reformists' most important journal. The next spring he returned to Peking to help Kang with the reform movement there. Throughout this period Liang's ideas on the West, about which he wrote voluminously, came from three major sources: Kang, Timothy Richard (whom he knew personally) and *The Review of the Times,* and the Japanese. These influences were reflected in the vocabulary Liang used to translate Western terms. In his early writings this appears to have been drawn largely from the *Review,* although Japanese terms were retained in translations from that language in *The Chinese Progress.* This practice continued in the journals Liang published after his

1. For Liang's life and ideas see Joseph Levenson, *Liang Ch'i-ch'ao and the Mind of Modern China;* Hao Chang, *Liang Ch'i-ch'ao and the Intellectual Transition in China, 1890–1907* (Cambridge, Mass., 1971); and Zhang Peng-yuan, *Liang Qi-chao yu Qingji Geming* (Taipei, 1964).
2. As late as 1902 Liang felt obliged to gloss the word *Kexue* (science—*Kagaku* in Japanese), with the traditional term *Gezhi* used by the *Review.* See *Xinmin Congbao,* XVIII (10/6/02), 17 (hereafter referred to as *XMCB*).

flight to Japan—*Pure Criticism* (1898–1901) and *The Renovation of the People* (1902–1907)—until about 1903 when the terms were assimilated into Chinese.[2] Through this process, in which Liang was easily the most important single agent, Japanese terms superceded virtually all the neologisms coined by the missionaries and other writers like Yan Fu.

The vocabulary of socialism provides a good illustration of this transformation. The missionaries, having difficulties with the European suffix -"ism," tended to add the words "theory of" *(zhi shuo)*. This was replaced by *zhuyi*, the Chinese version of the Japanese *shugi*. "Society," which had been translated by the missionaries as *qun or renqun*, was replaced by *shehui*. Thus *renqun zhi shuo* socialism or *junchan zhishuo* communism became *shehuizhuyi* and *gongchanzhuyi* respectively.[3] The fact that these words, though comprehensible, sounded foreign gave them a sense of precision and scientific objectivity lacking in the more familiar and semantically blurred terms used in everyday speech. For example, the difference between *furen*, the word used in *The Review of the Times*, and *zibenjia* from the Japanese *shihonka* is very similar to that between their English equivalents "rich man" and "capitalist."

Socialism did not become a major concern of Liang's until 1906. This does not mean that he was ignorant of or uninterested in it. We know that he had read *Looking Backward* by 1896, and his journal, *The Chinese Progress*, contained a translation of a Japanese article on the Congress of the Second International held in London that year.[4] During the next two years there was a translated item on the execution of a socialist assassin in Spain, and the Socialist Party was mentioned in a survey of German political parties.[5] Liang's first writing on the subject came after his flight to Japan, in an editorial in *Pure Criticism*, entitled "On the Right of the Strongest." Ostensibly, this was based on some ideas of Katō Hiroyuki, but Liang

3. *Qun's* original meaning of "flock" must have helped the Christians' decision to use it. It has persisted in modern Chinese in *qunzhong* (masses) which had classical origins and does not appear to have been of Japanese origin. The word *tinggong* (strike) was replaced by the Japanese *bagong*.

4. See above and "Shehui dang kai wanguo dahui," translated from *Kokumin Shimpō (Shiwu Bao* in Chinese, hereafter referred to as *SWB*), VI (9/27/96), 28b.

5. "Cike jiu Xing," from the *Osaka Asahi*, SWB, XL (9/26/97), 23 and "Dequo Zheng Dong," *Osaka Asahi*, SWB, L (1/3/98), 25.

added many of his own, notably Kang You-wei's synthesis of Western evolutionary theory with the three epochs of the *Commentary of Gongyang*.

When human society was first established there was scarcely any difference between rulers and ruled . . . this was the epoch of "Chaos" *(juluan)*. After this, differences grew, and with them developed the rights of the nobility over the common people and men over women. This was the epoch of "Rising Peace" *(shengping)*. The world continued and knowledge developed and the common people and women who had previously been weak began to gain rights and attain equality. Thus savage rights became gentle rights. . . . This was the third epoch that of "Great Peace" *(taiping)*.[6]

Like all dialectical evolutionists after Hegel, Liang was concerned about the problem of the "negation of the negation": Was the process one of progress or merely one of alternation?

Some people say . . . how is the third epoch different from the first? This view is mistaken. In the first epoch no one has rights so they are equal. In the second epoch some have rights and some do not, therefore they are unequal. In the third epoch everyone has rights so you return to equality. . . . Have the rights of the Westerners reached the extreme of equality? Not yet. Today the classes *(jieji)* of capitalists *(zibenjia)* and workers *(laolizhe)* men and women have still not been eliminated. There are still great differences between them. Therefore two events are certain to happen in the future economic *(zisheng)* revolution and the women's rights revolution. Only after these two revolutions will all mankind have rights.[7]

For many Chinese as well as European radicals the connection between socialism and women's rights was obvious. Several men, like Jiang Kang-hu the future leader of the Chinese Socialist Party, were first attracted to socialism through feminism.[8]

Although Liang did not use the term *datong*, his "On the Right of

6. Liang, "Lun Qiang-quan," *Qingyi Bao,* XXXI (10/25/99), 4–7, esp. 6.

7. "Lun Qiang-quan," 6–7. The word *zisheng* has a note that "this is the Japanese *Keizai (jingji).*" Five years later Liang reiterated his belief in the inevitability of socialism in the world as a whole, saying, "It [socialism] is the general law of the world and will certainly come in the future." See "Waizi Shuru Wenti," XMCB, LVI (11/7/04), 13. For a study of Liang's use of Katō's concept of *Qiang quan,* see Hao Chang, 193–197.

8. Jiang was first drawn to socialism by reading the German socialist leader Bebel's *Die Frau und Sozialismus* in Kōtoku Shūsui's Japanese translation of 1904. See *The Masses* (Chicago, 1911–1917), VI, 1914, 18. See also Jiang, *Hongshuiji,* 15–17b.

the Strongest" was the first published attempt to link Kang You-wei's evolutionary schemes to socialism. As we have seen above, Liang did this even more specifically in his description of Kang's philosophy which appeared two years later in his biography of Kang in 1901. By the following year Liang had already formed a clear if rigid view of socialism. This is shown in an editorial in *The Renovation of the People* entitled "On Intervention and Laissez Faire" which appeared in October 1902. This was another of Liang's dialectical evolutionary schemes. It began with a passage, strikingly reminiscent of Bruce Wallace's letter to *The Review of the Times* three years earlier: [9] "From ancient to modern times there have only been two principles of government, intervention and laissez faire. . . . The history of the West over the past millennia has just been an alternation between these two principles."

He went on to describe the alternation from medieval intervention to eighteenth- and early nineteenth-century laissez faire. The second half of the nineteenth century he saw as a period of struggle between the two principles. Liang continued:

The twentieth century will be a period of the triumph of intervention. . . . with the tendency for free competition monopolies to flourish. The rich become richer and the poor become poorer so that socialism has emerged to replace it. The outside form of socialism is pure laissez faire. But in reality it is for intervention. It makes society like a machine and controls it as if with a switch. But it seeks equality in the midst of inequality. It is clear that socialism will reach everywhere in the twentieth century. That is why I maintain that the twentieth century will be the period of the triumph of intervention.[10]

This scheme was clearly influenced by Liang's reading of Kidd's *Social Evolution*. The latter's chapter on "Modern Socialism" also relies on the polarity of laissez faire and intervention.[11] We know

9. See above. Liang's outline was very common at the time. See for instance the translation of an essay by Katō Hiroyuki, "Shijiu Shiji Sixiang Bianqian Lun," published in *Qingyi Bao*, LII (7/26/1900), 4–5b.

10. XMCB, XVII (10/2/02), 63–64. This evolutionary scheme is similar to the development described by Marx in *The Poverty of Philosophy* by which Kidd appears to have been influenced either directly or indirectly. See *The Poverty of Philosophy*, English ed. (New York, 1971), 144–154.

11. *Social Evolution*, 193–242. I have not been able to find the date of the translation into Japanese.

that Liang was reading the book because the next issue of *The Renovation of the People* included his article on it. Just as *Social Evolution* had precipitated the first mention of Marx in *The Review of the Times* three years earlier, Liang's article on Kidd contained his first reference to "Marx—the polestar of German socialism." Marx's materialism and its role in the theory of the German Social Democratic Party was made clear, and as the champion of socialism he was contrasted with Nietzsche, the protaganist of individualism.[12]

The year 1903 saw an explosion of information on socialism available in Chinese, an expansion in which Liang and the organizations he had established played a leading role. Two years earlier he had collected money from some Chinese merchants in Japan to establish the Bookshop for the Diffusion of Knowledge in Shanghai. Its first books were translations from the Japanese, concerned with civil liberty, social Darwinism, and its critics.[13] In 1903, a year of great student activity, there was a surge of publications, and among other subjects the Bookshop for the Diffusion of Knowledge published three books on socialism.[14] All three were general surveys of European socialism written by Japanese socialists or socialist sympathizers and based as far as one can judge on the American "digests" mentioned above.

The first was *Modern Socialism,* written by Fukui Junzō in 1899 and translated by Zhao Bi-zhen.[15] The book contained four sections describing the history and contemporary situation of socialism. The second section, "German Socialism," described Marx and his socialism, placing him in the position he has retained. Before Marx, socialism, "was entirely idealistic sleep talking." Only Marx's socialism

12. Liang, "Jinhualun Gemingzhe Jide zhi Xueshuo," XMCB, XVIII (10/17/02), 17–28.

13. Zhang Jing-lu, I, 174.

14. For the increase, see the graph in Sanetō Keishō, 545. There is a list of these in Martin Bernal, "The Triumph of Anarchism over Marxism, 1906-1907," in Mary Wright, ed., *China in Revolution: The First Phase, 1900-1913* (New Haven, 1968), 97-142, esp. 100; and in Li Yu-ning, *The Introduction of Socialism into China* (New York, 1971), 13.

15. For *Jinshi zhi Shehuizhuyi,* see Li Zhu, "Lun Shehuizhuyi zai Zhongguo di Zhuanbo," in *Lishi Yanjiu* (1954), 3; and Rong Meng-yuan, 10. Zhao *zi* Ri-sheng was born in Changde in Hunan in 1883.

has used profound scholarship and detailed research to discover the economic base, and has seen what is and what ought to be. Therefore his socialism is easily grasped by the working people and receives the thunderous support of the majority, so it is easy to reach success. . . . And those who hate socialism have no leg to stand on against his scholarship.[16]

The second book published by the Bookshop for the Diffusion of Knowledge was *The Socialist Party,* originally written in 1901 by Nishikawa Kōjiro, one of the Christian founders of the Japanese Social Democratic Party. It was translated by Zhou Bai-gao. This too was a survey of modern European socialism, which it saw as divided into three schools: nihilism *(xuwu zhuyi),* Christian socialism *(Jitujiao schehuizhuyi),* "but the commonest is Marxism *(Makezhuyi)."* [17] The book gave detailed descriptions of social democratic parties and their leaders, including such figures as Plekhanov.[18] It also dealt with the differences between social democracy and state socialism. Despite its great detail it contained some points that would have been dubious to . many Western socialists; for example, New Zealand and Switzerland were described as "the ideal countries of socialism." [19] This attitude, however, was not so very different from that of the American writers. Bliss in his *Handbook of Socialism* stated that New Zealand was close to socialism because of the number of its labor members in parliament and its advanced labor laws.[20] In the case of Switzerland he wrote:

It must not be forgotten that the adoption of the referendum and of the initiative whereby all important questions may be . . . referred to a final vote of the people while all petitions signed . . . by enough citizens must be so referred *are themselves long long steps towards socialism* or the identification of the people with the government and of government with industrial life [my italics].[21]

This integral connection between political democracy and socialism in social democracy, felt strongly by American Christian Socialists, did not remain a strong strand in Chinese socialism. For

16. Rong Meng-yuan, 5.
17. There is a copy of *Shehui Dang,* by Nishikawa Kōjiro, trans. by Zhou Bai-gao (Shanghai, 1903), in the library of the University of California Berkeley.
18. *Shehui Dang,* 13.   19. *Shehui Dang,* pt. II, 1.
20. Bliss, 151.   21. Bliss, 127.

most Chinese socialists, economic problems and the need to achieve social equality were given primacy.

The third book was *Socialism,* written in 1899 by Murai Chishi. Murai was a professor of English at the Tokyo School of Foreign Languages. He was an American-trained Christian and was president of the Socialist Research Society, but he resigned in 1900 when the society decided to advocate socialism publicly.[22] The book, which was translated by Luo Da-wei, a returned student from Japan, was another general survey of socialism, but with sections on its ethics and aesthetics.[23] Interest in socialism by Chinese students at the time was sufficient to warrant the translation of *Socialism* by Hou Tai-wan for another publishing house, the Civilization Press, also in 1903.[24]

The same year yet another survey of socialism was published by a third publishing house. This was *A General Critique of Socialism,* written by Shimada Saburō in 1901.[25] Shimada, who had also been to America, was an active journalist for Katayama Sen's *Labor World* and played a leading part in labor agitation at the turn of the century. His book was a general history of socialism. It showed great respect for Lassalle and Marx, whom it described as the "only true socialists," and it gave a rough outline of the dialectical materialist interpretation of history.[26] He showed less respect for the anarchists, whom he distinguished from the nihilists only by the fact

22. Powles, 108.

23. Luo, born 1878, was from Wuling Hunan. He spent only a short time in Japan in 1902. For *shakaishugi,* see the description in Shioda, *Nihon Shakaishugi Bunken Kaisetsu,* 43.

24. Zhang Jing-lu, 1974. The Wenming Chubanshe was connected with the earlier *Yishu Huibian* (see below). Jiang Wei-qiao states that Wu Zhi-hui managed the Wenming Shuju before fleeing Shanghai because of the *Su Bao* affair in the summer of 1903; see Jiang, "Zhongguo Jiaoyu Hui Huiyi," *Xinhai Geming,* I, 485–496, esp. 488. The two presses are probably the same. However, Zhang Wen-bo does not mention any involvement by Wu in his *Wu Zhi-hui Xiansheng Zhuanji* (Taipei, 1960).

Wu Xiang-xiang refers to an advertisement in *Su Bao* (11/12/02) for Murai's book published by the Shanghai Zhina Fanyi Huishe; see Wu, *Song Jiao-ren* (Taipei, 1964), 77. It is probable that this was referring to the Wenming Chubanshe edition.

Tan Bi-an says that the book was translated by Zhang Ji; see Tan Bi-an, "Eguo Mincuizhuyi dui Tongmeng Hui di Yingxiang," *Lishi Yanjiu* (1959), I, 35–44, esp. 36. I can find no other evidence for this.

25. There is a copy of this book in the library of the University of California Berkeley.

26. *Shehuizhuyi Gaiping* (Shanghai, 1903), 9 and 14.

that the former existed internationally while the latter were confined to Russia.[27] The book ended with a description of contemporary socialist parties and laid great stress on their electoral successes.

It would appear odd that after this flood no more books on socialism were published until after 1911. However, this merely reflects a general trend in the number of translations from Japanese which fell from 187 in 1903, the highest annual total ever reached, to 17 in 1904.[28]

The situation for magazines was very different; people in China as elsewhere clearly preferred reading articles to books. The article was also a very convenient medium for writers who were students or politicians with very limited time. At least one article on socialism appeared in one of the magazines established by Chinese students in Japan well before 1903. *The Translation Magazine* began publication in January 1900. It consisted entirely of translations, most of them from, and the rest through, the Japanese.[29]

One of the works serialized from the first issue was Ariga Nagao's *History of Modern Politics,* the first section of which was devoted to Germany. The third chapter was concerned with Bismarck's suppression of the Socialist Party and the social policies he launched to undercut its appeal. In a note the translator gave the standard description of the rise of Western socialism and stated that it was the same as the Well-field system. The chapter's first section, which was entitled "The German Branch of the Workers' International," began:

Marx and Lassalle both proclaimed the principle of freedom/liberalism *(ziyou zhi shuo)* in 1848 and the two parties had great influence but their principles were not the same. Marx first started a newspaper in Cologne to proclaim communism *(junfu zhi shuo).* Later because he was not tolerated by the government he fled to London. In 1862 the workers' leaders from many countries met in London.[30]

It went on to describe Marx's involvement in the International and the organization's policy that

railways, mines and forests should be communally owned *(gongyou)* and divided equally. The products of the earth belonging to the state should be

27. *Shehuizhuyi Gaiping,* 30.   28. Sanetō Keishō, 545.

29. Incomplete copies of issues I, II, VII, and VIII have been republished (Taipei, 1966).

30. *Yishu Huibian* (Tokyo, 1900), I, 15.

sold equally. At the Boer (Basle?) Congress in 1869 they wanted to abolish completely the system of private ownership in land that is the so-called communism *(junchan zhi shuo)* of before 1848.[31]

For these reasons all governments were frightened of them and they were restricted in France and England. But the German Branch increased every day. This branch had been set up by Liebknecht, a disciple of Marx, and Bebel. The article then gave a summary of the 1869 Eisenach Program of the German Workers' Association. Its policies were directed toward limiting working hours and the employment of women and children as well as to the establishment of an inheritance tax "so that the nation will equalize the people's enjoyment of products and protect them."

This passage was followed by a section on Lassalle's party and his negotiations with Bismarck which "unfortunately Liebknecht and Bebel criticized as selling socialism to the government."[32]

It is also unfortunate that the subsequent numbers of *The Translation Magazine* are missing. It is almost certain that they contained a detailed history of the German social democratic movement written from a position sympathetic to Bismarck's "social policies," which granted a minimum level of social security, insurance, pensions, and so on to the workers while retaining or even strengthening authoritarian rule by the government. Nevertheless, the eighth issue of *The Translation Magazine* shows that considerable attention was paid to the German Socialist Party's electoral successes.[33]

The magazine also contained other passing references to socialists or socialism as well as to anarchism and Russian nihilism, with which it was to some extent confused.[34] Even before 1903 a number of Chinese students in Japan and Shanghai had some awareness of socialism, though vague and slight. The revolutionary veteran Zhang Shi-zhao, when describing Zou Rong the student writer of the famous anti-Manchu pamphlet *Revolutionary Army*, wrote: "I believe that when he was writing this book Zhang Ji was advocating anarchism and Tai-yen's [Zhang Bing-lin's] flowery phrases were

31. *Yishu Huibian*, II, 16.   32. *Yishu Huibian*, II, 18.
33. *Yishu Huibian*, VIII, 25.
34. *Yishu Huibian*, II, "Shijiushiji Ouzhou Zhengzhi lishi lun," 17. For references and articles on anarchism and nihilism, see "The Triumph of Anarchism," 116–118.

not able to counter him. [Zou] Rong promoted socialism in opposition. Tai-yan and I both recognize that Rong knew this."[35]

Zhang Shi-zhao wrote this to justify his thesis, that "Weiman," one of Zou's three great "Western thinkers," the other two being Rousseau and Washington, was in fact the English pioneer of socialism, Robert Owen.[36] Zhang Bing-lin, Zou Rong, Zhang Shi-zhao, and Zhang Ji formed the core of the student revolutionary movement in Shanghai in 1903.

Although only twenty years old in 1903 Zhang Ji had been in Japan since 1899, longer than almost any other student, and had absorbed many Japanese attitudes. His anarchism seems to have been more connected with his approval of violence in a "just" cause than with socialism as such.[37] It was probably in reference to him that a radical educator of the time wrote: "In 1902 and 1903 very few people knew about revolution, still less socialism, which had not been talked about. If there were one or two students who talked about it, they were bohemian and despised."[38]

By the end of 1903 the students knew considerably more about both revolution and socialism. During the summer of that year the student radical patriotic fervor against Russian encroachments in Manchuria culminated in violent and direct attacks against the Manchus in the Shanghai journal *Su Bao* and in the arrest by the foreign concession authorities of its two leading writers, Zhang Bing-lin and Zou Rong.

In this passionate and politicized atmosphere, interest in all kinds of radicalism flourished. As well as the books on socialism, more articles on it were published during this year. In October the Tokyo students' journal, *The Tides of Chekiang,* began a series on "the new

35. Zhang Shi-zhao, "Shu Huang-di Hun," in *Xinhai Geming Huiyilu,* 6 vols. (Peking, 1961), I, 217–304, esp. 247.

36. John Lust does not commit himself on the identity of Weiman. See his *The Revolutionary Army: A Chinese Nationalist Tract of 1903,* Introduction and Translation with Notes (Paris, 1968), 56–57.

37. For Zhang's anarchism, see "The Triumph of Anarchism," 116–117, and my *Chinese Nihilism before 1906,* forthcoming. For his life, see BDRC.

38. Jiang Wei-qiao, "Minguo Jiaoyu Zongzhang Cai Yuan-pei," in *Cai Yuanpei Xiansheng Quanji* (Taipei, 1968), 1339–1342, esp. 1341. Another man he was probably referring to was Su Man-shu, for whose life see BDRC, and Henry McAleavy, *Su Man-shu, 1884–1918: A Sino-Japanese Genius* (London, 1960).

social theory." Most of this series was devoted to socialism, which the author divided into two schools: communism *(gongchan zhuyi)* and extreme democracy *(jiduan minzhuzhuyi)*. Of communism, the author said, "This party was founded by the Frenchman Babeuf. Its later champion was the Jew, Marx; its present manifestation is the Workers' International." [39]

The author described communism's "principle" as the abolition of private property and its replacement by national ownership. This was justified because the owners of land and capital served no useful function and caused poverty and spiritual debasement. The author also outlined in simple form the theory of surplus value:

They (the communists) say that the products of labor are natural rewards. Today as the forces of production increase, the laborers reward should increase and the people be happier. Now the men who seize this profit are bandits and wages rise and fall with the market. This is worse than for animals.

They say . . . if land and capital were nationalized then living expenses would be calculated by time—6 hours a day would be enough. Today 12 or 13 hours are still not sufficient for their livelihood.[40]

The article then turned into an attack on the Manchus who were thought even worse than landlords and capitalists.

It is strange that the author did not employ the new Japanese word for anarchism, *Wuzhengfuzhuyi*,[41] because this was clearly what he meant by extreme democracy, about which he wrote that "this party was founded by the Frenchman Proudhon and the Russian Bakunin. . . . Its manifestation is today's Russian nihilists." [42]

The passage continued with a description of the "extreme" democrats' hostility to selfishness and authority as well as the "savage slave system of socialism." After distinguishing what were generally agreed at the time to be the two major strands of socialism, the next instalment of the article went on to describe

39. *Zhejiang Chao,* VIII (10/10/03), 17. The article was signed Dawo.
40. *Zhejiang Chao,* VIII, 18.
41. *Museifushugi,* though not as commonly used as *Kyōmushugi* (nihilism), was widely current in Japan at the time. Kemuyama Sentarō's *Kinsei Museifushugi,* published in Tokyo, 1902, was extremely influential. See Chapter 8 below, 202–3, and also for the blurring of distinctions between anarchists and nihilists.
42. *Zheijiang Chao,* VIII, 18.

governmental social policies with which the author had greater sympathy.[43] Thus the readers of *The Tides of Chekiang* could gain some knowledge of Western socialism even though greatly filtered.

What were the circulation and readership of this and similar journals? The Chinese authorities tried to censor press criticism of the government or the Manchus, but the power of the foreigners made this impossible. They were unable to prohibit the publication of Chinese-language newspapers abroad or even in the foreign concessions in China. In 1903, although they succeeded in suppressing *Su Bao*, the difficulties and humiliations suffered by Chinese officials in the affair made them very cautious in their dealings with the concession authorities on this subject. Later that year the Chinese authorities tried to strangle *Su Bao's* successor, *The China National Gazette*, by asking the post office to seize all copies sent through the mail. Post office officials claimed that this was impracticable and shifted responsibility by suggesting that it might be easier to stop them at source.[44]

It is even more surprising that radical journals could be sold in the interior. There is little doubt that in many places magistrates tried to prevent this, but in many others they could or would not prevent their sale. It is known for instance that *The Tides of Chekiang* was openly sold in at least twenty-eight cities and towns in China. However, the number of copies sold in most outlets was very low, almost always less than ten and often just one or two.[45] Thus it is unlikely that more than five hundred copies were sold in China of any one issue, and most of these were sold in Shanghai, Tientsin, Wuchang, and lesser treaty ports. More copies must have been brought in by students returning from Japan and south east Asia.

43. *Zhejiang Chao,* IX, 9–11.

44. See the official exchanges quoted by Ge Gong-zhen in *Zhongguo Baoxueshi* (reprinted, Hong Kong, 1964), 155. See also Yan Du-hou "Xinhai Geming Shiqi Shanghai Xinwenjie Dongtai" in *Zinhai Geming Huiyilu,* IV, 78–85, esp. 79. For Zhang Zhi-dong's attempts to stop the publication of subversive magazines in 1902, see XMCB, XXVII (3/13/03), 84.

45. See the figures given for sales in Changshu, Hangzhou, Chefoo, Wuhan, Zhenjiang, Hangkow, Quzhou, and Nanking in *Guomin Riribao* (9/22, 9/30 and 10/2) as well as in *Jingzhong Ribao* (11/17, 12/1 [or 11/31], 12/8, 12/10/04 and 1/2 and 1/18/05). Wuhan, where 40 copies of *Zhejiang Chao* were reported sold, had five outlets. As the number of journals sold was a sign of "enlightenment," these figures are, if anything, overestimated.

The readership was made up of students or "new students," that is, the sons of gentry and rich merchants studying for the traditional examinations or at the new Western-style schools.[46] In the Yangtze valley, at least, the older generation of officials, landowners, and merchants were also becoming newspaper readers, and their reformist and conservative journals had a much greater circulation than the radical ones.[47] Naturally, peasants and laborers were not able to read the journals' literary and Japanese style. The vernacular press, much of which was radical, was only just beginning to make some headway.[48]

Liang's journal, *The Renovation of the People,* had approximately the same type of outlet and readership as *The Tides of Chekiang* but a somewhat larger circulation. In 1907 Liang talked about printing 3,000 copies of the journal, but it is probable that most were sold in Japan and only about 1,000 in China.[49] It is possible that as Liang claimed there were reprints in China, and there is no doubt that each copy was read by tens if not hundreds of readers.[50] Nevertheless, even if the total readership reached twenty or thirty thousand this was a minute proportion of the population of 400,-000,000 or even of the gentry class of approximately seven million.[51] However, these twenty thousand were disproportionately significant. This group of educated nonconformists constituted an important segment of the Kuomintang ruling elite, as well as becoming the teachers of the communist leaders.

The Renovation of the People also published articles on socialism in 1903. There was an item on state socialism in Australia, and Liang's colleague Ma Jun-wu wrote on John Stuart Mill's cham-

46. See the descriptions in the surveys noted above.

47. The three largest papers *Xinwen Bao, Zhong Wai Ribao,* and *Shen Bao* had circulations approximately ten times that of *Zhejiang Chao.*

48. According to these figures Chen Du-xiu's *Anhui Subao* sold only 20 copies in Wuhan, 40 in Nanking, and 10 in Zhenjiang. However, the *Hangzhou Baihuabao* claimed to sell approximately 1,000 copies in that city.

49. Letter to Xu Fo-su quoted in Ding Wen-jiang, *Liang Nianpu,* I, 227. This would correspond to the statement that *Min Bao* sold 3,000 copies: 2,000 in Japan and 1,000 in China. See Tang Leang-li, *The Inner History of the Chinese Revolution* (London, 1930), 54.

50. Writing in the 1920s, Liang claimed that there were ten editions of each issue. See Hsü, *Intellectual Trends of the Ch'ing Period,* 102.

51. For estimates of gentry numbers see Chung-li Chang, *The Chinese Gentry: Studies on Their Role in Nineteenth Century Chinese Society* (Seattle, 1955), 113.

pionship of female emancipation and its relationship to socialism. Ma also wrote a detailed description of the lives and theories of the French founders of socialism and anarchism, Saint Simon and Fourier.[52]

Liang himself was away during 1903. He set out for Canada and the United States in February and did not return to Japan until November. Liang wrote extensively on his experiences and impressions, and among other incidents he described was a meeting in New York with the American socialist Helisun (Harrison?), a correspondent of the *New York Call*.[53]

In America I have been visited by socialists four times. . . . Their reason for coming so often is to persuade me that if China is to reform she should follow socialism. I stated that regrettably one needed several stages in progress and could not reach it in one step. They all said that in reform one must war with old society. This is always difficult but it takes about the same amount of effort to have a small reform as a big one. . . . Because they knew so little of China's circumstances I could not talk deeply with them.[54]

This tone of condescension and Liang's disdain for missionaries of all sorts pervaded his description.

The socialists I saw were sincere, concerned and deserving respect. . . . Their attitude toward the works of Marx (the polestar of German socialism) is like the respect Christians have for the Bible. Their evangelism is also similar. Now socialism is a sort of superstition. But the power of superstition is the strongest in the world and the spread of socialism in the world is easy.[55]

It is clear that Liang had absorbed many Western bourgeois attitudes toward socialism. In fact, his not being a Christian gave his opposition a consistency theirs lacked. Nevertheless, Liang was not

52. "Guojia shehuizhuyi shixing yu Aotali," XMCB, XXV (1/13/03), 83; "Mile Yohan zhi Xueshuo," XMCB, XXX (4/26/03), 9–14; and "Shengximen zhi Shenghuo jiqi Xueshuo," XMCB, XXXI (5/10/03), 9–21.

Ma Jun-wu *zi* Xing (1881–1940) came from Kweilin in Kwangsi. He was a major translator from Japanese. He was particularly interested in Mill and translated sections of *On Liberty* as well as Spencer on women's rights. He later became a member of the Revolutionary Alliance and was for a time Sun Yat-sen's secretary. See Zhu Xue-hao, "Ma Jun-wu Zhuan," in *Guoshiquan Guankan*, I, 3 (8/1948), 120–122.

53. I have been unable to identify Helisun.

54. Liang, in *Xin Dalu Youji*, supplement to XMCB, 60–61.

55. *Xin Dalu Youji*, 61–62.

categorically opposed to socialism. His sympathy for state socialism made this impossible. Even before his trip to America he was convinced that at least some aspects of state socialism should be applied in reforming China. In the conclusion to his essay on "Intervention and Laissez faire" he wrote, "Which of these two principles should be selected in China today? . . . I estimate that in today's China we should use seven parts of intervention to three of laissez faire." [56]

Here intervention meant some form of state socialism. This was spelled out in his description of the meeting with Helisun.

Roughly speaking "extreme socialism" can not be practiced today in China or in Europe and America, the evils resulting from it could not be described. But the ideas of so-called "state socialism" are daily becoming stronger and China can use many of them. This would be even easier than in Europe and America. For state socialism uses extremely authoritarian organization to practice an extremely egalitarian spirit. It tallies in an extraordinary way with China's historic nature.[57]

Liang reiterated this in an article on China's socialism published the following month in which he cited two traditional equivalents to Western socialism: the reforms of Wang Mang and those of the eleventh century A.D., both of which attempted to strengthen central power as well as relieve the sufferings of the peasants.[58] In an article that appeared in the autumn of 1904 Liang spelled out the way in which he thought elements of state socialism could be applied to China.

My idea is that when the new government is established (through reforms) we should obtain one large loan from abroad to provide money for the nationalization of capital so that every industry can be controlled. This is simply a policy of state socialism like that which is beginning to spring up in Germany and Austria. Then after some years we will not suffer greatly from the labor problem and our productive system would probably reach that of other countries. However, this is very far off and is like talking about the West River to a desiccated fish.[59]

Thus Liang's position emphasized caution but recommended a slow progress to state socialism on the German model. In this he was very different from Sun Yat-sen who clearly preferred social

56. "Ganshe yü fangren," XMCB, XVII, 65.   57. Xin Dalu Youji, 61.
58. "Zhongguo zhi shehuizhuyi," XMCB, XLVI–XLVIII (2/14/04), 302–303.
59. "Waizi Shuru Wenti," 4th instalment, XMCB, LVI (11/7/04) 13.

democracy. Indeed, Hu Han-min specifically attacked the use of socialist policies by nondemocratic countries: "Governments sometimes use these policies. However, in a constitutional country which has not yet forgotten autocracy, profit to the state is not entirely profit to the people. They even use them to check the roots of social revolution and in secret to protect their class system." [60]

Hu's targets can only have been Prussia or possibly Japan. Thus Sun Yat-sen's position was in some ways similar to that of Marx in that he supported bourgeois democracy against autocracy, seeing this struggle as essentially linked to any genuine socialism. Liang's position was closer to that of Lassalle in that he saw the possibility of a coalition between a centralized government of the old ruling class and the industrial workers. The comparison is of course inexact, if only because Liang would have seen himself as Bismarck rather than as Lassalle.

What is the significance of the differences on socialism between Sun and Liang, and where did they originate? One difference came from the sources of their knowledge of socialism. Both men learned from Japan, England, and America, but with Liang the Japanese component was much greater and, therefore, the Japanese special affinity for Germany affected him more than it did Sun. Modern scholars have shown the growth of Liang's misgivings about Western democracy, particularly during his trip to North America.[61] These, together with his admiration for the effectiveness of the strongly authoritarian Meiji oligarchy, meant that his preferences were clear by 1904 when he first formulated his ideas on socialism.

At a psychological level, Liang's matching attitude was one of pessimism about human nature. For him, structure and continuity were essential to keep men's darker passions under control. Sun, as a revolutionary, was more hopeful. Although he became sufficiently cautious to believe in the necessity of a period of tutelage to guide the people, he was profoundly optimistic about human nature and was prepared to work with the poorest strata of society in ways that horrified Liang.

The differences between the two men over socialism had a social aspect which I believe to be the determining one. Despite his

60. Hu, "*Min Bao* zhi Liu da Zhuyi," 13.
61. Hao Chang, 238–271; and Zhang Peng-yuan, 163–201.

dependence on overseas Chinese merchants between 1899 and 1907, Liang always was, and felt himself to be, a member of the upper gentry—the ruling class. Admitting the existence of social and economic problems which could endanger the position of that class, he urged their solution, but slowly, so as not to upset the precarious social structure. As a member of the Chinese official class he had at this stage no objections to official management of industries. This was a traditional arrangement in China which had, furthermore, been practiced by Germany and Japan, whose economic and political development he approved. Indeed for him as for many traditional and conservative Chinese, official management was more natural and even perhaps more profitable than private ownership. However, the Chinese ruling class had another attitude toward land ownership.[62] As a member of this class, Liang was fiercely opposed to any nationalization of land, and said, "It is absolutely impermissible for land to be nationalized. But for every sort of large enterprise, railways, mines, manufactures, most of these could be nationalized." [63]

Sun's priorities were the reverse: "Not all collectivists' theories can be applied to China at her present stage, only land nationalization. . . ." [64]

As a spokesman for the bourgeoisie in the coastal cities he could call for the nationlization of land without hazarding his position. He had to be much more careful when talking about plans for the nationalization of other enterprises. As Sun's constituency grew to include students of gentry origin, the position of his social program became more complicated.

62. See Chung-li Chang, *The Income of the Chinese Gentry* (Seattle, 1962), esp. 127–147. Chang plays down the amount of gentry income received from land. For a more balanced view see Barrington Moore, Jr., *Social Origins of Dictatorship and Democracy* (London, 1967), 165–174.

63. *Xin Dalu Youji,* 61.   64. See above ch. 3, note 62.

6 | The Socialism of *The People's Journal*, 1905–1906

At the same time that Sun was introducing his principles of *Minshengzhuyi* and Equal Land Rights there was a linked and parallel interest in European socialism among the revolutionary students in Tokyo, and especially among the inner core of the Revolutionary Alliance around *The People's Journal*. The period from November 1905 to June 1906, in which Zhang Ji and Hu Han-min edited the magazine, can be considered the highest point of interest in orthodox Marxist socialism among Chinese intellectuals until the 1920s.[1] In the first five issues of *The People's Journal* four writers wrote or translated over ten articles on European socialism, treating it either as an independent entity or in relation to Sun's principles. Although the political ideas expressed in these articles were more or less similar to Sun's, there were some significant divergences of opinion, both about European socialism and about its application to China.

In December 1905, Feng Zi-you, one of the very few members of the Society to Restore China's Prosperity to hold even a minor position in the Revolutionary Alliance, wrote an article called "Socialism and the Future of China's Political Revolution" which was published in the Hong Kong revolutionary *Chinese Daily*.[2] In April 1906 it was reprinted in the fourth issue of *The People's Journal*, "because," as the editors said, "what is developed in the article fits the principles of our magazine." [3] Feng was born and brought up

1. This period coincided with the one in which Zhang Ji was the nominal and Hu Han-min the actual editor of *Min Bao*. (See Hu, "Hu Han-min Zizhuan," 16).

2. See Feng Zi-you, *Zhonghua Minguo Kaiguoqian Gemingshi* (referred to hereafter as *Kaiguo shi*), 2 vols. (Taipei ed., 1954), I, 171–185.

3. *Min Bao*, IV, 97. See also Feng, *Shehuizhuyi yu Zhongguo* (Hong Kong, 1920), 4.

in Japan. He could read Japanese fluently and had clearly been subject to the same Japanese influences in favor of German state socialism as Liang Qi-chao. On the other hand he came from an overseas Chinese merchant family and was a revolutionary and a long-time associate of Sun.[4] In many ways his article can be seen as an attempt to synthesize the Japanese views expressed by Liang with the policies of the Revolutionary Alliance, although it is clear that he was closer to the former.

The article started with a rather jumbled description of the vast and fast-growing power of the world socialist movement. In very much the same way as the authors of the Japanese books and their Anglo-Saxon models, he ranged from France to Australia to demonstrate the growth of successful socialist parties, although without giving any historical background.[5] Feng described the horrific conditions under European and American capitalism, pointing out that conditions in China were not nearly so bad as yet. He then went on to describe the Chinese tradition of socialism. Although making such minor concessions as "the Well-field system only includes the meaning of 'Equal Land Rights,' it is not large enough to cover the whole of socialism," Feng's decision, after listing many examples, was that "socialism is an indigenous product of China, several thousand years old. We can truly re-light its hidden flame. How can we yield it to the West, and consider it a newly discovered Western theory?"[6] He then discussed the timing of the social revolution, deciding that it would be easier to have it before capitalism became established, and that it would be best to have it simultaneously with the political revolution. "If this were done," he said, "China would become a model to the world."[7]

Feng believed that state socialism *(guojia minshengzhuyi),* would be the best form of socialism at present. But he specified: "What is the main principle of state socialism? It is (the solution of) the land question."[8] Here he supported Sun's preference for Henry George, wanting all rent to go to the state.[9] Feng showed all the benefits that

4. For Feng's biography see BDRC.

5. Feng, "Minshengzhuyi yu Zhongguo Zhengzhi Geming zhi Qiantu" (referred to hereafter as "Minshengzhuyi"), *Min Bao,* IV, 97–122, esp. 98.

6. Feng, "Minshengzhuyi," 106.   7. Feng, "Minshengzhuyi," 109.

8. Feng, "Minshengzhuyi," 109.   9. Feng, "Minshengzhuyi," 110.

would come from the single-tax system and the abolition of taxes on trade and industry. He pointed out that "socialists of every type have theories wanting to tax everything. Therefore they have many clashes with Mr. George's theory of single tax." [10] Feng then described the enormous profits made by landlords in the West in general and in Great Britain in particular. He ended by summing up his own views and the party line, with the call, "I deeply want our party to study socialism's theory of land nationalization. I deeply want our party to study the theory of land nationalization's theory of single tax." [11]

Feng went further than Sun in his conception of state socialism. At this stage Sun had not stated publicly, as Feng did, that "postal services, land electricity, railways, banks, steamship lines, tobacco and sugar, all rights affecting the public interest, should be nationalized." [12]

Feng's view of the world scene differed from Sun's. Feng praised Bebel and the Social Democratic Party for their power in the Reichstag and their stand against Germany's foreign policy. But unlike Sun he had no reservations in his support for the German government's internal policies:

Today all Germany's internal policies are based on socialism, and the rate of its industrial and commercial expansion is much greater than those of England or America. When travelers in Europe talk about government, they all praise Berlin as much the best for the good order of its houses and the arrangement of everything. Are these not the achievements of socialism? [13]

Feng's attitude toward the Japanese socialists and their oppressor, the Japanese government, was exactly the same. Later, in the article in which he said that China should choose state socialism, he said: "The German government uses it completely for their internal policies and their achievements are evident. The Japanese government in recent years has shown a great tendency toward this principle." [14] Feng had none of the reservations expressed by Hu about social reforms practiced by "countries which have not yet forgotten autocracy."

10. Feng, "Minshengzhuyi," 118.   11. Feng, "Minshengzhuyi," 123.
12. Feng, "Minshengzhuyi," 109.   13. Feng, "Minshengzhuyi," 98.
14. Fen, "Minshengzhuyi," 109.

One of Hu's purposes in drawing this distinction was to avoid giving support to the Manchu government's official control of industries, and to allow the Revolutionary Alliance to join the merchants' protests against this. Feng made it logically more difficult to oppose the Manchu government's efforts to maintain or extend official control, by saying that the Chinese government's control over so many of China's natural resources was yet another advantage which would make it "easier to have land nationalization in China than in any other country." [15]

Feng's lack of concern about authoritarianism was demonstrated in another difference between him and Sun. One of Feng's main reasons for wanting the social revolution to be applied at the same time as the political revolution, was that

China must apply this principle with a military government. If you wait until a republican government has been set up . . . not only will it rouse the opposition of the capitalists, but its administration will not be able to avoid hindrances. . . . Whenever there are political revolutions, there must be militarism, and a military government will be temporarily set up. [16]

The idea that the social revolution could be forced through by military force was implicit in the combination of two of Sun's proposals: one that a military government be set up immediately after the revolution; the other that the social revolution be carried out at the same time. However, Sun did not connect the two, at least in public. He was too smooth a politician to suggest that his form of social revolution would encounter serious opposition or cause real administrative difficulties.

The precise Japanese sources of Feng's ideas on socialism are unknown. In some other cases the situation is clearer. The Hunanese revolutionary, Song Jiao-ren, arrived in Japan at the end of 1904. He lived among the radical students, editing one magazine and writing for others. [17] Some of Song's knowledge of socialism came through personal contact; for instance, the entry in his diary for New Year's Day 1906 reads:

15. Feng, "Minshengzhuyi," 114.   16. Feng, "Minshengzhuyi," 108.
17. Song, *Wo zhi Lishi* (Taipei reprint, 1962). For his life, see BDRC and K. S. Liew, *Struggle for Democracy: Sung Chiao-ren and the 1911 Revolution* (Berkeley, 1971).

Fine; got up early and drank with Zhang Ji, He Xiao-liu, and Tian Zi-qin. At ten we all went to Miyazaki Tōten's [Torazō's] house to wish him a happy new year. Saw Tōten's elder brother Miyazaki Tamizō, the Japanese socialist. We talked for a long time and left at one.[18]

Song's diary records several more meetings and discussions with the Miyazakis about socialism, and it is clear that most of the inner group of the Revolutionary Alliance knew the brothers quite well. The connection is also shown by the printing of the constitution for Tamizō's Society for the Restoration of Land Rights in the *People's Journal,* number II, and the publication in the fourth issue of a piece written by him.[19] This article, which was translated by "a society member," was entitled "Forms and Criticisms of the Western Social Revolutionary Movement." The introduction dealt with the development of industry and the growing gap between rich and poor. This had led to the rise of "men of spirit and kindness" who wanted to save society through basic reform. He divided their ideas into three groups: socialism, anarchism, and equal land ownership *(tudi junyou)*.[20]

The section on socialism began by describing its general principles "which are in making land and capital public and making the state control them."[21] It mentioned Marx and Engels and divided their followers into the extremists (the communists) and the Christian socialists (the moderates), who aimed at achieving parliamentary majorities. Tamizō ended the section with a violent attack on Bismarck and the state socialists. The section on anarchism was rather longer, dealing with the anarchist emphasis on the individual and hostility to all authority. He divided them up into the "Philosophical," "Christian," and "Destructive" schools, putting most stress on the last group and their three activities—propaganda, secret organization, and assassination.

The final section on equal landownership gave all the usual

18. *Wo zhi Lishi,* 89.

19. Miyazaki Tamizō used the pen name of Junkō. In the article he refers to his work *"Tochi kinkō" Jinrui no Taiken.* This has been reprinted in *Meiji Bunka Zenshū,* XXI, 199–229.

20. Miyazaki, "Ou Mei Shehui Geming Yundong zhi Zhonglei ji Pinglun" (referred to hereafter as "Shehui Geming"), *Min Bao,* IV (5/1/06), 123–133, esp. 124.

21. Miyazaki, "Shehui Geming," 124.

arguments and divided its proponents into two schools: single tax and land nationalization. The critique at the end stressed the basic unity among the three major principles and the great and unselfish principles shared by them.[22] Tamizō gave examples of various arguments between the socialists and the anarchists. He then brought in the question of landownership, and suggested that state or social ownership of property created by the individual would infringe on his rights. Therefore, he supported a land policy. He hesitated to choose between the two different land policies, but in the end came out in favor of Wallace and against Henry George, because under single tax "the individual would not have direct rights to enjoy and use land."[23]

The Miyazakis were outside the mainstream of Japanese socialism, and there is no reason to suppose that because they had relations with Chinese revolutionaries the students knew many other Japanese students personally.[24] In May 1906 *Light*, the new organ of the Japanese Socialist Party, welcomed the foundation of *The People's Journal*.[25] Perhaps this recognition was due to Song Jiao-ren, who noted in his diary for April 15:

> Wrote a letter to the Commoners' Press, the organ of the Japanese Socialist Party, asking whether they had *The Commoners' Newspaper* or *Straight Talk* and whether they would like to exchange them for *The People's Journal*.[26]

Song's request illustrates both his interest in the Japanese socialists and his lack of direct contact with them. At the time he wrote, *The Commoners' Newspaper* had been closed for seventeen months, and *Straight Talk* had been banned the previous October.

However, Song quite often bought socialist magazines or independent ones containing articles on socialism.[27] For example, on

22. Miyazaki, "Shehui Geming," 130.

23. Miyazaki, "Shehui Geming," 132. For the Japanese socialist view of Miyazaki Tamizō as a heroic eccentric, see Sakai Toshihiko, "Tochi Fukkensetsu," in *Shakaishugi Kenkyū*, II (4/15/06), 53.

24. The following year 1907 the situation changed when Kōtoku Shūsui came to Zhang Ji, Liu Shi-pei, and other Chinese anarchists. See Robert Scalapino and George Yü, *The Chinese Anarchist Movement* (Berkeley, 1961), 31; and Bernal, "The Triumph of Anarchism," 141; see also Chapter 8 below.

25. "Welcome to Minpo," international column of *Hikari*, XII (5/5/06).

26. *Wo zhi Lishi*, 141.   27. See, for instance, *Wo zhi Lishi*, 67.

April 4 he bought a copy of *The Study of Socialism*, edited by Sakai Toshihiko. A few days later Song became interested in one of the articles in it, written by Osugi Sakai and entitled "Brief History of the Socialist International."[28] Song translated it into Chinese and published it with some alterations in *The People's Journal.*

The article had a short introduction on the world-wide division into *fushen* (bourgeois—French in the original) and *pingmin* (proletarians—English in the original). It then quoted Proudhon's famous phrase that "property is theft" and the last few sentences of the *Communist Manifesto.*[29] After this preamble the article gave a history of the Second International from the meeting of unification at Ghent in 1877 to the Sixth Congress of the International in Amsterdam in 1904. There was a section on each congress, listing the number of delegates from each country, mentioning the chief topics and speakers and printing short synopses of the main resolutions passed by each. Near the end of the article there was a section on the "split between the hard and soft schools of socialism." This dealt with the divisions in the French party over the Dreyfus affair and the revisionist quarrels in Germany. But it ended on a more cheerful note:

Now the fierce struggle between the hard and the soft schools makes it appear that there is internal confusion in the socialist party. This calamity would indeed cause everybody to be unhappy, but since the resolution of "one state, one party" was passed unanimously, it is still evident that the socialists' morality is perfect and their force for unity is strong.[30]

The article was purely descriptive, and there was very little discussion of socialist theory, and none at all of the application of socialism to Japan. The only mention of the Japanese party came in the context of Katayama's attendance at the Amsterdam congress and the International's resolution against the Russo-Japanese War.[31]

Although at this time the vast bulk of the information in Chinese on socialism came from Japanese sources, a small amount came

28. Osugi, 1885–1923, later became a famous anarchist. See Robert Scalapino, *The Japanese Communist Movement, 1920–1966* (Berkeley, 1967), 3–12; and *Geming di Xianqu* (Shanghai, 1928), 403–448.

29. Song, "Wanguo Shehui Dang Dahui Lueshi" (referred to hereafter as "Shehui Dang"), *Min Bao*, V (6/26/06), 79–106. For the Japanese version, see *Shakaishugi Kenkyū*, I, 58–73.

30. Song, "Shehui Dang," 104.   31. Song, "Shehui Dang," 98.

directly from Western languages. In the first issue of *The People's Journal* there was a translation of a short piece of Henry George's *Progress and Poverty*. The translator was Liao Zhong-kai, who had been born and brought up in the United States and was about the only Alliance member at that time, apart from Sun himself, who claimed to read English. We know that Sun tried to persuade Liao to translate the whole of George's book, but that Liao gave it up after publishing this very short fragment.[32] This did not mean that Liao had lost interest in socialist theories. In number VII of *The People's Journal,* which was published on September 5, there is a long letter from him on the subject. The letter, which was the only piece published on European socialism under Zhang Bing-lin's editorship, was entitled "General Outline of Socialist History." [33]

At the beginning of the letter Liao stated that it was a chapter from W. D. P. Bliss, *A Handbook of Socialism.* He omitted to mention that this chapter had been translated into Japanese by Sakai Toshihiko only two months before. He continued: "Mr. Bliss is a Christian socialist, and therefore has a few differences in his point of view from Mr. Marx and Mr. Engels." [34] But Liao thought Bliss was useful as an introduction to socialism.

The letter was a translation of the fourth chapter of the book.[35] It began with a section on premodern socialism, ranging from John Ball to the Essenes, and the Russian *Mir* to Sir Thomas More. Then there was a section about the unselfishness and spiritual nature of even the most hardened self-professed materialist socialists, like Marx and Bakunin.[36] The next passage dealt with the parallel development of industry, misery, and socialism in the nineteenth century. Finally, there was a schematic division of socialist history into five periods. The last two divisions of this dealt with the struggles between the socialists and the anarchists in the Inter-

---

32. Feng, *Geming Yishi,* III, 216. Liao used the radical pen name of Tufu ("butcher the rich"); see his "Shehuizhuyi Shi Dagang" (referred to hereafter as "Shehui Shi"), *Min Bao,* VII (9/5/06), 101–130.

33. This time Liao used the milder pen name of Yuanshi. The title of the article is not as listed at the front of the journal where it is given as "Shehuizhuyi *Si* Dagang." The mistake proves that the printers were southerners.

34. Liao, "Shehui Shi," 101. The Japanese translation was by Sakai Toshihiko, in *Shakaishugi Kenkyū,* II (4/15/06), 33–39.

35. Bliss, 39–49.   36. See above.

national. In the description of these struggles, Bliss took up a very partisan position for Marx and against Bakunin. To some extent Liao followed Bliss, saying that "Bakunin . . . led the International into the whirlpool of anarchism and almost wrecked what Marx had tried so hard to build."[37] However, Liao's only major deviation from Bliss's and Sakai's text came when he cut out the latter's purple passage: "Marx in the greatest deed of his life drove out the anarchists . . . and saved socialism from the scourge that anarchism has since proved to modern Europe."[38] But Liao was faithful to Bliss's final note, which was to praise the genuine internationalism of modern socialism.

Although Liao had forwarned his readers, Bliss's great stress on the religious and moral aspects of socialism and his attribution of its violent elements to anarchism gave a rather one-sided impression of the whole. The distortion, however, was a common one. These aspects were emphasized by most socialists and by all socialist sympathizers at the turn of the century.

Liao was as cosmopolitan and bourgeois in the classic sense as Sun himself. In this he was atypical; most of Sun's immediate entourage from 1905 to 1907 and beyond were gentry students from Kwangtung who provided a bridge between Sun, the Cantonese, and the other gentry students. These men, like Hu Han-min and Wang Jing-wei, were also marginal in another sense: their families were *muyou* or private secretaries who, though originally from central China, became attached to officials in Kwangtung.[39] Thus although members of the *literati* and thoroughly educated in the classics, they had no rural roots and could look at traditional Chinese society—and landholding—with some detachment.

Wang Jing-wei's brilliant nephew, Zhu Zhi-xin, was one of the most prolific writers for *The People's Journal*.[40] He wrote five full-length articles in its first five issues. The first, which was called "Biographies of German Social Revolutionaries," came out in two parts in issues II and III. Zhu justified writing the article by saying:

37. Liao, "Shehui Shi," 110.   38. Bliss, 46 and Sakai, 38.
39. For Wang Jing-wei, who later became the Japanese puppet ruler of Eastern China, see BDRC.
40. For Zhu Zhi-xin, see BDRC; and Zhu Zhi-ru, "Zhu Zhi-xin Geming Shiji Shulue," *Xinhai Geming Huiyilu*, II, 422–429.

"I want to introduce socialism to my brothers. . . . I hope that the theories and actions of these gentlemen can be spread to the minds of our countrymen so that it may be some help to the social revolution." [41] The article began by referring to the recent growth of socialism, particularly in Germany. The victory of socialism was inevitable, because "political power cannot change social power," and social power and the current of history was with the social revolutionaries. Zhu used this idea to account for something that must have been very puzzling to all Chinese: the question of why the Western governments tolerated these movements dedicated to their overthrow.

Although government oppression can cause worry . . . the social revolutionary movement need not consider it a disaster. In Germany between 1878 and 1890 there were orders repressing the Socialist Party, but the party grew in strength, and its growth was faster then than either before or since. [42]

Zhu's conclusion was that it was not in the government's interest to repress the Socialist Party. As for the socialists themselves "they do not separate from the government, but are content to seek toleration. Their purpose is to avoid having many enemies. Therefore, if they order their organizations not to interfere with social organizations, they are tolerated." [43]

The next few pages were taken up with a short life of Marx. Extremely favorable to him, the biography contained several references to, and quotations from, the *Communist Manifesto,* including the first translation into Chinese of the *Manifesto*'s ten points. One of the most interesting aspects of Zhu's interpretation of Marx was his attitude toward Marx's belief in violence. On the whole he seemed to value both sides of Marx's feelings on the subject: "Marx definitely hated war; however (he thought that), if it could not be avoided to eliminate inequality, use of it should not be ruled out." [44] On the other hand, in his selection of quotations and sometimes in the translations themselves, Zhu seemed to be stress-

41. Zhu, "Deyizhi Shehui Geming jia Xiaozhuan" (hereafter referred to as "De jia zhuan"), *Min Bao,* II, 4.

42. Zhu, "De jia zhuan," *Min Bao,* II, 2.

43. Zhu, "De jia zhuan," *Min Bao,* II, 10.

44. Zhu, "De jia zhuan," *Min Bao,* II, 10.

ing Marx's more peaceful aspects. The reason why he quoted Marx's ten points was probably an attempt to get at the nub of Marx's political ideas. But the effect of quoting them out of context was to give a disproportionately moderate impression, especially as Zhu paid particular attention to point number 2, "a heavy progressive income tax," and point number 3, "abolition of all rights of inheritance."

Zhu's free translation of the final words of the *Manifesto* is also extremely interesting in this respect. The standard English version reads:

The communists disdain to conceal their views and their aims. They openly declare that their ends can be attained only by the forcible overthrow of all existing social conditions. Let the ruling classes tremble at a communistic revolution. The proletarians have nothing to lose but their chains; they have a world to win. Working men of all countries unite.[45]

Zhu's version read:

All communist scholars know that it is disloyal and shameful to conceal their aims and their views. When they publicly announce their activity to eliminate all the unjust organization of society and to replace it, their goals will not take long to reach. Then the groups who oppress and despise us will be terrified into surrender by our bold advance. Then the world will be for the common people, proletarians *(pingmin),* and the sounds of happiness will reach the deepest springs. Ah! Come! people of every land, how can you not be roused![46]

It is difficult to know how much significance can be attached to the many fascinating discrepancies between the two versions, but some of them, such as the difference between *pingmin* and "proletariat," will be discussed below. Generally, Zhu's version sounds much less violent than Marx's. It is interesting that the word "forcible" in the phrase "forcible overthrow" was also missing from Sakai's and Kōtoku's otherwise much more accurate version of this passage which Song Jiao-ren translated into Chinese a few months later.[47]

Zhu then gave a description of Marx's version of the labor theory of value, and his theory of surplus value, in both of which he firmly

45. *Selected Works,* I, 65.   46. Zhu, "De jia zhuan," *Min Bao,* II, 6.
47. See above, n. 29.

believed. He concluded: "All sociologists respect this theory of Marx's, and up to now it has not fallen." [48]

The last section of Zhu's article consisted of his own comments on Marxism. First he criticized Marx's view that "all capital comes from plunder." He agreed wholeheartedly that at present all capital came from plundering the workers according to the theory of surplus value. But he said that there must have been a time when men lived independently and saved the fruits of their own labor to form capital. Thus "Marx's theories on the origins of capital are somewhat excessive, but his description of today's capitalism is absolutely correct." [49] This criticism was probably connected with the general view that serious class differences did not exist in China and, by making it, Zhu left the door open to excuse at least small businessmen in China.

Zhu finally took up an argument with the theory that the exchange of work for wages was a simple contract and that profit from employing labor was the same as interest on a loan and was therefore justifiable. Zhu argued very powerfully with all manner of precedents from Roman and English law to prove that an agreement to work for wages was made under "undue influence" from the employer and was therefore not a valid contract. [50]

The second part of Zhu's article, which came out in the third issue of *The People's Journal* was concerned with Lassalle. Most of it was devoted to the latter's flamboyant life, about which it gave a good deal of information. It dealt very thoroughly with Lassalle's trial, and his defense of his right to speak, giving several very eloquent quotations. [51] Zhu described Lassalle's activities in the Progressive Party and his later struggles with the leader of the cooperative movement, Schulze-Delitzsch. Zhu also gave a very clear definition of Lassalle's main ideological weapon in the struggle: his "iron law of wages."

This considers that the wages earned by the worker will not rise above the level of subsistence. If they do rise temporarily, they will fall again. If they

48. Zhu, "De jia zhuan," *Min Bao,* II, 13.
49. Zhu, "De jia zhuan," *Min Bao,* II, 15.
50. Zhu, "De jia zhuan," *Min Bao,* II, 16–17.
51. Zhu, "De jia zhuan," *Min Bao,* III, 9.

fall too far, they will rise again. If wages are high, life becomes prosperous and the people become numerous. If they are numerous, the number of workers increases, and according to the law of supply and demand, wages will decrease. If they decrease too much, the workers' source of livelihood will not continue and they will starve to death: thus there will be a shortage and wages will rise.[52]

Lassalle believed that the only way to destroy the law was to destroy the existing economic structure and set up producer cooperatives, a system which would make the worker and the capitalist the same man. Zhu also described Lassalle's hope that the state would provide the capital necessary to these cooperatives, and his belief that the way to make the state do this was for the workers to devote themselves to organizing a political party, which under general suffrage would send representatives to the Reichstag to protect their true interests.

Zhu continued Lassalle's biography up to the latter's death in a duel over a woman, an event to which Zhu devoted little attention at this point but to which he returned in the section containing his own comments at the end of the article. This section began: "Lassalle's proclamation of social revolution was not perfect like that of Marx, but he had many achievements in propaganda and action."[53] Zhu criticized Lassalle for his lack of internationalism. He had mentioned that Bebel and the present Social Democratic Party followed Marx in this respect.[54] He also criticized Lassalle's ambiguous relationship with Bismarck. The end of the section and of the article was devoted to Lassalle's romantic and untimely death. Unlike a contemporary group of Japanese aesthetes, who particularly admired this aspect of Lassalle's life story, Zhu deplored it.[55] He admitted, however, that although "later generations are in his debt, Lassalle . . . died without fulfilling his life. . . . If Lassalle had not died for another three or four years, his power would have grown, and perhaps Bismarck's laws oppressing the socialists would never have been applied."[56] Zhu, for all his interest in socialism and economics, made his final point a purely moral one:

52. Zhu, "De jia zhuan," *Min Bao*, III, 17.
53. Zhu, "De jia zhuan," *Min Bao*, III, 19.
54. Zhu, "De jia zhuan," *Min Bao*, III, 18.
55. Kosaka, 334.   56. Zhu, "De jia zhuan," *Min Bao*, III, 19.

Today there are many men of spirit who are immature, do not know Chinese culture, and have never devoted themselves to an academic discipline. They use European culture as an excuse to break all barriers. They are licentious and sacrifice everything to pursue their lusts. What can they say when they look at Lassalle? [57]

In the same issue of *The People's Journal* Zhu also wrote a short piece called "Progress of the Labor Party in the New General Elections." The article dealt with the increase in the number of labor members of parliament from one to forty-nine in the election of 1905–1906. Zhu discussed the previous reluctance of the English workers to form a political party, surprising because of the strength of their labor organizations. He said that political parties were necessary for class conflict and that the English workers could learn from the German Social Democratic Party in this respect. In other matters he thought that the English workers had the advantage. He believed that social revolution might be more easily carried out in England than in other countries, mainly because of the lack of bitterness in class relationships. The rich might make concessions before involving themselves in a struggle: "Obstinate defense is a rare phenomenon in England, so that the obstacles in the workers' way might be slightly less." [58] This advantage might, he thought, be offset by British natural conservatism. But Zhu ended on a cheerful note: "If the advance of the English workers' political movement goes on at this rate, who knows but within twenty years they might capture the majority and reach their goal. I pray for it all the time." [59]

Zhu's other two articles dealt largely with the application of socialism to China, but also helped to throw some light on his general attitudes toward it. The first of these was "The Nationalization of Railways from a Socialist Point of View and Official and Private Management of China's Railways." The introduction to this said:

Recently there has been a struggle in Kwangtung over the private or the official management of the Canton-Hankow railway. This has been a discussion between the merchants and the officials, so that in common opinion

57. Zhu, "De jia zhuan," *Min Bao*, III, 19.
58. Zhu, "Yingguo Xin Zongxuanju Laodong Dang zhi Jinbu," *Min Bao*, III, *Shiping* section, 6–11, esp. 10.
59. Zhu, "Ying Laodong Dang," 11.

there has been doubt about the principle of railway nationalization. Now railway nationalization is not the same thing as the official management talked about at present, as is extremely evident. But private management clashes with the basic principle of railroad nationalization and no one can defend it. Are the evil results of private management really limitless? What methods can remedy them? This should be studied.

We first give a summary of what our group proposes:

1) Railway nationalization is a policy to control exclusive private management of a natural monopoly, so as to develop our social aims, with the rights of railway management going to the state and public bodies.

2) The management of this by the state or public bodies is to be a public utility as compared with the nature of an official enterprise.

3) Official management of railways is a method of raising taxes: This is what financial experts call a regulation of the public economy. This is not the same thing as railway nationalization.

4) A privately managed railway is against the spirit of railway nationalization, but if there is no alternative, we should apply the strictest public supervision while it is being practiced, to wipe out its exclusive rights.[60]

Zhu made an analysis of various of the points raised by this statement. "What is a natural monopoly? What are exclusive rights?" and so on. He went on to investigate methods of controlling these exclusive rights, quoting the German "Socialist of the Chair," Wagner, as his authority to prove the superiority of government ownership. He gave a short history of railway nationalization, pointing out the differences between Anglo-Saxon laissez-faire and continental nationalization. He ended with a rhapsody on the benefits that would come from nationalization. The interesting thing about the article is that, apart from the two statements at the beginning, there is no further discussion of the differences between nationalization and official management. The promise that nationalized railways would not be extortionate would hardly have been enough to satisfy the would-be shareholders in profitable railways. It is surprising that Zhu came out so strongly against merchant ownership, when it might have meant antagonizing the merchants' Railway Rights movement, one of the most important forces against the Manchu government.

60. Zhu, "Cong Shehuizhuyi Lun Tiedao Guoyou ji Zhongguo Tiedao Guanban Siban" (hereafter referred to as "Tiedao Guoyou", *Min Bao,* IV, 45–56.

The clearest exposition of Zhu's views came in his article, "That the Social Revolution Should Be Carried Out with the Political Revolution." This article was part of the literary battle between *The People's Journal* and Liang Qi-chao (which will be treated in the next chapter). But the article was concerned not only with China. It was extremely wide-ranging and showed what Zhu thought about socialism in general and about which form of its thought was the "true" one:

Formerly there were people who rejected socialism, but what they rejected was not modern socialism but pure communism. When people like this say that this cannot be practiced today, I cannot contradict them. Now since Marx, all the theories have changed and no scholar can absolutely denounce what is generally known as "scientific socialism" [English in the original]. . . . Only our opponents do not know this. What our group proposes is state socialism, a principle not at all difficult to practice.[61]

The first section of the main part of the article was concerned with "the causes of the social revolution." According to Zhu these were in "the imperfections of social and economic organizations." The worst imperfection was of course the gulf between rich and poor, and this was going to be the cause of the future social revolution in Europe. Unlike most of his colleagues, Zhu admitted: "China today is not without a division between the rich and the poor," but, he went on, "one cannot call it a gulf, because the inequalities are not as great as in Europe and America." [62] Zhu maintained that it was the imperfections of social and economic organization that had caused the gulf in the West and would cause it in China. Therefore the social revolution was against the "imperfections." It was not against the rich, as the reformers claimed. Zhu pointed this out, trying, incidentally, to show the party's moderation.

Now social revolution is not saying, "Rob the rich people's property and divide it among the poor." [63] Even if you did do that . . . after you had leveled everything, if you restored competition as before, everything would

61. Zhu, "Lun Shehui Geming dang yu Zhengzhi Geming Bingxing" (hereafter referred to as "Geming Bingxing"), *Min Bao*, V (6/26/06), 43–66, esp. 45. This article is very well summarized by Schiffrin and Scalapino, 329–334.

62. Zhu, "Geming Bingxing," 49.

63. This was a quote from Liang Qi-chao in "Lun Kaiming Zhuanzhi Shiyong yu Jinri zhi Zhongguo" (hereafter referred to as "Kaiming Zhuanzhi lun"), *Xinmin Cong-bao*, LXXV (2/23/06), 11–48, esp. 20.

go in the same rut. Thus the makers of the revolution change the system which causes inequality. So toward existing inequality they use laws to reach equality gradually: this is their true meaning. Thus if the shape of inequality has not arisen, but the system which causes it is there, then removal of the system must be called social revolution. Hence we can deduce that in China's future, this cannot be neglected.[64]

Having established that a social revolution was necessary in China, Zhu went on to set up a typology of revolutions. First, he touched on cases where a political revolution was necessary but a social one was not. Because many of his opponents felt that this was China's situation, Zhu considered that dangerous ground and left it as quickly as he could, admitting that "there are many examples of this which I will not raise." [65] He paid more attention to cases where a social revolution was necessary but a political one was not.

The European countries today are mostly in this position. In France, if there were a social revolution, it would not be necessary to change the Republican constitution. Or Germany: if there were a social revolution there, it would not be necessary to change the federated monarchies.

There would have to be political reform but not revolution: "If the roots are not changed, but the branches move, it would simply be a reform and not a revolution." [66] Zhu then dealt with cases where he thought the causes for both revolutions existed together. For this he developed a more complicated scheme, according to the subjects *(zhuti)* and objects *(keti)* of a revolution. Before he could start, he had to define his terms: "The subject of any political revolution is the common people *(pingmin)*, its object is the government in the broad sense. The subject of the social revolution is the *ximin* ["proletarians"—English in the original]: its object is the *haoyou* ["bourgeois"—French in the original]" [67] Zhu justified the use of the new terms by saying that *haoyou* had a wider meaning than the Japanese *shihonka*, which simply meant "capitalist" and was too narrow. It was also more suitable than the other standard Japanese translation for bourgeois, *shinshi batsu*, which he thought had different connotations in Chinese. Zhu was against the standard Japanese translation for proletarian, *heimin*, which he himself had used in this sense five months earlier, because he wanted to use its

64. Zhu, "Geming Bingxing," 49–50.   65. Zhu, "Geming Bingxing," 51.
66. Zhu, "Geming Bingxing," 51.   67. Zhu, "Geming Bingxing," 52.

Chinese form, *pingmin,* in opposition to the government. His reason for not using the other standard Japanese translation *rodosha* (worker), was that "the concept of worker has always been extremely restricted in China. It does not include the peasants, therefore one cannot say it is suitable."[68]

Having settled the problem of correct names, Zhu drew up his new typology.

There are two positions for the objects of the revolutions: "A" when the objects of the political and social revolutions are in the same position; "B" when the object of the political revolution is in a different position from the object of the social revolution.

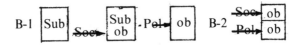

In situation "A," it was obvious that both revolutions had to be carried out together. If either were not carried out the status quo could be restored. Zhu's example of this was Russia, where he thought the feudal regime held the economic power.

He divided situation "B" into two: "B-1" was "when the subject of the political revolution is the object of the social revolution; 'B-2' when this is not the case."[69]

B-1 — B-2

In situation "B-1," in which the subject/object is always the bourgeoisie, the two revolutions could not be carried out simultaneously. Because in cases where the bourgeoisie provide the main support for the political revolution, the proletariat has not enough strength to create a successful social revolution. This had been the situation in all the political revolutions in Europe.[70]

China's situation fitted situation "B-2." The objects of both revolutions were different. Zhu says that "now the corrupt government has indeed stored every kind of wealth, but it does not have an

68. Zhu, "Geming Bingxing," 53.   69. Zhu, "Geming Bingxing," 53–54.
70. Zhu, "Geming Bingxing," 56.

inseparable relationship with the wealthy families."[71] It was also clear to him that the object of the social revolution was not the subject of the political one:

Since Nanking fell . . . and all China has been thrown to the stinking barbarians, the secret societies of the south and east have united, gathered their strength, and bided their time for 260 years. Everybody must know what sort of men are in these organizations. The future revolution will not rely entirely on the secret societies. However, its strength will definitely not come from the bourgeoisie, but rather from the proletariat.

This is a remarkable parallel to the old Marxist argument that in certain Eastern countries, Germany, and Russia, the bourgeoisie is incapable of carrying out its own revolution, a theory later developed by Trotsky and Lenin.[72]

In situation "B-2," Zhu thought the two revolutions should be carried out simultaneously. One reason was that in this situation the subject of the political revolution would presumably have enough strength to carry out a social one. Another was the following:

During a political revolution people's ideas are unsettled and they do not covet wealth. . . . and theories of public peace and security enter their minds easily. Once times are settled they become concerned with their own families and are not satisfied with their condition and start wanting to surpass others. . . . Thus practicing social revolution at the same time as the political revolution means that there will be fewer difficulties.[73]

Zhu's argument here was close to Feng's, but in its lack of emphasis on the force needed to carry out the social revolution it was nearer to Sun's optimistic view of his theories.

Zhu went on to give the two reasons for China having the social revolution quickly and easily, which had been raised by Sun and all of his supporters: one, to have it before the gulf between rich and poor became too great, and two, because the tradition of policies

71. Zhu, "Geming Bingxing," 57.
72. Zhu, "Geming Bingxing," 58–59. See the reference to the relative strength of the proletariat in Germany, at the end of the *Communist Manifesto, Selected Works*, I, 65. When Zhu was writing, Trotsky was formulating his theory of "permanent revolution" which stressed the inability of the Russian bourgeoisie to carry out its own revolution and as a consequence of this the immedate beginning of the socialist one. See I. Deutscher, *The Prophet Armed: Trotsky, 1879–1921* (London, 1954), 153–159.
73. Zhu, "Geming Bingxing," 56.

which oppressed the rich and favored the poor had always been respected in China. "Therefore having a fundamental reform cannot be said to be unsuitable to social psychology."[74]

Zhu was afraid that an easy social revolution in China might lead people into another error: "We definitely cannot take a short cut there by avoiding a political revolution. Because to practice it you must use political power and without a political revolution the common people will not hold this power."[75] Zhu then devoted a short section to giving precedents in Chinese history for land nationalization.

From this series of articles, Zhu Zhi-xin's political ideas came out clearly. He was easily the most original of the writers on socialism, particularly in his typology of revolutions, for which I can find no parallel in China or the West. The two most important influences on his political thinking seem to have been Marx (through various filters) and Sun Yat-sen. One of the revolutionaries writing twenty-five years later said that by 1905 Zhu was a Marxist, and Zhu certainly considered himself a Marxist or a "scientific socialist."[76] He had many of the necessary qualifications. He firmly believed in surplus value, even though he disagreed about the accumulation of capital; he believed in economic or at least "social" determinism: "political power cannot change social power."[77] He quoted Marx with approval when he wrote, "the history of all hitherto existing society is the history of class struggle,"[78] and he agreed with Marx that this would end after the coming social revolution. Zhu, like many contemporary socialists, was non-Marxist in his use of the terms "social revolution" and "political revolution," but he made it clear that he used the terms only for convenience and that he was aware that the political revolutions were also social ones.[79]

Zhu was definitely a socialist of the Second International, and a moderate one at that. Marx himself was vague about the forms the socialist revolution took in different countries, and he probably would not have disagreed with Zhu's belief that socialism could be

74. Zhu, "Geming Bingxing," 63.   75. Zhu, "Geming Bingxing," 63.
76. Tang Leang-li, *Inner History,* 54.
77. Zhu, "De jia zhuan," *Min Bao,* II, 13.
78. Zhu, "De jia zhuan," *Min Bao,* II, 6.
79. Zhu, "De jia zhuan," *Min Bao,* III, 50.

achieved in Britain by parliamentary means. But even the revisionist Bernstein might have balked at Zhu's idea that the social revolution would not fundamentally affect the political structure of the German Federation.

Zhu's moderation did not make his attitude the same as that of Feng Zi-you or Liang Qi-chao, that is, in favor of Prussian state socialism. It is true that he quoted A. Wagner with approval, and praised railway nationalization and other aspects of the German government's internal policies.[80] On the whole, however, he was hostile to Bismarck's social policies, commenting: "Thus they often claimed the title of social reform, and protection of labor, to entrap those of spirit, secretly trying to cut the stem of social revolution. Their policies are just like the Manchus' daily talk of constitutions."[81] Zhu claimed, and probably believed, that he was in the mainstream of revolutionary socialist thought: "As for methods to bring it (the social revolution) about, each scholar has a different proposal. To sum them up, they all want the most ordered and peaceful methods to stop the accumulation of riches."[82]

Although the political ideas expressed in Zhu's articles were more or less similar to Sun's, there were some significant differences between the two, both about European socialism and about its application to China. The main difference in Zhu's and Sun's attitude to European affairs was that Sun repeatedly stressed the violence of the coming social revolution in the West, while Zhu, on the whole, seems to have thought that this would be a peaceful transition. The difference between them over policies in China was that while Zhu accepted Sun's policy of land nationalization, he did not stress it. In "That the Social Revolution Should Be Carried Out with the Political Revolution," he mentioned land nationalization at the very end of the article, almost as an afterthought. He seems to have been more interested in the nationalization of capital, or at least capital in the category of "natural monopolies," which according to Zhu included railways, water supplies, electricity, trains, and natural products such as coal and oil.[83]

Feng's state socialism and Zhu's social democracy were both divergences from Sun's policies, and the fact that they were printed

80. Zhu, "Tiedao Guoyou," 9.   81. Zhu, "De jia zhuan," *Min Bao,* II, 2.
82. Zhu, "Geming Bingxing," 60.   83. Zhu, "Tiedao Guoyou," 5.

in *The People's Journal* with favorable introductions by the editors shows that the distinctions cannot have been considered of great significance. Nevertheless, the variety must have made it difficult for the reader to find out the precise social policies of *The People's Journal* and of the Revolutionary Alliance, even though the general bias was quite clear. On the other hand, the articles, together with the translations, increased the reader's knowledge about the world socialist movement. For some of the student readers, the articles must have repeated material they had already read in other Chinese journals or in Japanese. But the first five issues of *The People's Journal* provided a great deal of information for the high proportion of Chinese students who had difficulty in reading Japanese, especially the thousands who by 1906 were pouring into Tokyo.

7 | The Controversy on Social Policies between Liang Qi-chao and the Revolutionary Alliance

By 1906 there were approximately 13,000 Chinese students in Japan. Twelve years before, there had been none. The Chinese government had sent small numbers of students to the West since the 1870s. But it was only in 1896 after the Japanese victory in the Sino-Japanese War that the first few students accompanied the Chinese ambassador to study in Tokyo.[1] In 1898 there were over 70. Of these about one half were army officers studying at military colleges, and most appear to have been sent on scholarships given by the "modernizing" governors general.[2] Four years later in 1902 there were more than 650 students in Japan, over one half of whom were providing their own funds.[3] This figure was already greater than the total number of Chinese students studying elsewhere in the world.

The main reasons for Japan's popularity with both officials and students were simply cheapness and convenience. Not only were fares to Japan far lower than to any Western country, but living expenses were also much less, and the language was relatively easy for Chinese to read and write if not to speak. There were other important but less tangible factors, such as the relevance to China of Japan's recent rise to world-power status and the possibility for

1. For the numbers of Chinese students in Japan see Roger F. Hackett, "Chinese Students in Japan, 1900–1910," Harvard, *Papers on China,* III (1949), 134–169. Hackett did not have available the other sources quoted here. For a general study of Chinese students abroad before 1911, see Y. C. Wang, *Chinese Intellectuals and the West, 1872–1949* (Chapel Hill, 1966), 41–98.

2. "Lun liuxue Riben zhi Xianzhuang," ROT, CCVII (4/1906), 3–7, esp. 4, states that there were 68. However, over 70 are listed in Fang Zhao-ying, *Qingmo Minchu Yangxue Xuesheng Timinglu chuji* (Taipei, 1962), 1–53.

3. Fang Zhao-ying, 1–45.

Chinese to "pass" in Japan in a way that was out of the question in the West.

During 1903 and 1904 the numbers more than doubled.[4] But the greatest increase took place during 1905 and 1906 with the abolition of the imperial examination system.[5] The disappearance of this system meant that for China as for the rest of the world—with the possible exceptions of England, France, and Germany—study abroad became a vital source of status. For the upper ranks of the ruling class, study abroad had all the advantages of the traditional system. It required large sums of money to provide for the preparation and expenses, not to mention the delay in the beginning of earning. After its completion it gave the student possession of skills that were supposed to be unavailable to those who had studied at home. Furthermore, it gave the returned student possession or apparent possession of an esoteric language which in many ways served the same elitist function as classical Chinese had for the traditional literati or as Latin had in the West.

The change from classical to Western studies, however, meant a narrowing of the recruitment base for the elite both economically and geographically. In traditional China the main expense of education was in obtaining leisure. Some level of traditional instruction was available relatively cheaply throughout the empire. Although modern schools were established in great numbers during the first decade of the twentieth century, they were much more expensive than classical tutors, and they existed only in the larger cities. Those able to prepare seriously for study in Japan came from a very narrow social base. Study in Japan was in fact less expensive than many students supposed.[6] But the reputation was more important than the reality; for the vast majority of the Chinese gentry, study abroad, even in Japan, was out of the question. The precise economic position of the students in Japan is unknown, but the pattern of

4. Fang Zhao-ying's list has 663 names. An article in *Jingzhong Ribao* (6/13/04) refers to 1,199. Another, four months later, mentions "more than two thousand" (10/25/04). ROT, CCVII (4/15/06), 4, states that there were 2,406 (presumably at the end of the year).

5. See Hackett, and ROT, CCVII, 5, which say that at the end of 1905 there were 8,620.

6. See for instance Wu Yu-chang, *The Revolution of 1911.*

their geographic origin is clearer.[7] Well over half of them came from two regions: the lower and middle Yangtze, including the provinces of Kiangsu, Chekiang, Hupeh and Hunan, which contained less than a third of the total population of China.[8]

The flood of students in 1905–1906 meant that many were without adequate preparation. During these years relatively few of the students attended university courses. Some were studying at university preparatory schools, and more were registered at irregular schools of dubious academic standing. Even before then, the number of graduates was always considerably lower than that of students.

Youth (*qingnian,* in Chinese) has always had rebellious tendencies. The concept has of course connotations of wealth and class as well as of age. Most men and women go straight from childhood to work. In nearly all societies it is only youth that has the leisure for an intermediate stage and a different style of adult life. Students are the quintessential youth; away from immediate economic and family pressures and forming their own subgroups they are particularly likely to be radical, and the most radical of all are likely to be those most cut off from home and dependent on each other—students abroad.

Nationalism is usefully distinguished from xenophobia by its admission of some kind of equivalence between one's own and other nations. In China with its traditional dichotomy between men and barbarians the first nationalists were overseas Chinese aware of their common Chineseness in the foreign context but forced to recognize not only the power—this had occurred before with nomad

7. The figures for up to 1902 in Fang Zhao-ying are Kiangsu and Chekiang, 260 (36%) and Hupeh and Hunan 171 (18%). In *Jingzhong Ribao* for 1904 the figures are 246 (27%) and 499 (41%), respectively, and in 1905, 20% and 31%. According to official figures for the post-Taiping period Kiangsu and Chekiang contained 9% of the total population of China and Hupeh/Hunan 16%. See Chung-li Chang, *The Chinese Gentry,* 102. However, Ho Ping-ti thinks that the estimate of the lower Yangtze provinces is too low. See his *Studies on the Population of China, 1368–1953* (Cambridge, Mass., 1959), 70. Interestingly, the proportion from Kwangtung was roughly proportionate, the number of students being 11% up to 1902, and 7% in 1904 and 1905. The population was 8% of the total. Under the Kuomintang the proportion of students from Kwangtung rose strikingly. See Y. C. Wang, 160.

8. In 1905 the proportion from these four provinces was reported to be 44%.

rulers—but also the different but in some ways equivalent culture of the whites. However, nationalism has always had a special link with students abroad. It is probable that the concept of one's own "nation" originated in the medieval University of Paris where students from different parts of Europe tended to group according to their local dialects and customs in student houses or *nationes*. Their concept of themselves as members of a "nation" came from emersion in a foreign environment and the presence of other equivalent groups.[9]

Thus the Chinese students in Japan were almost inevitably nationalist and radical. They were also young; in 1902 the average age was 22, and although rich by Chinese standards they were relatively poor in urban Japan.[10] There seems to have been a certain amount of feeling against the Chinese students in Tokyo, and certainly they felt themselves to be despised. At a national level their direct contact with Japan made them acutely conscious of Japan's progress and of China's stagnation and weakness in the face of the West. There was a natural reluctance to accept the view held by many Westerners that sluggishness was the result of the fundamental conservatism and corruption of the Chinese people. This forced them to put the blame on the Chinese government even though they themselves were often closely connected with it.

There were student radicals in Japan almost as soon as there were students. Men from Hupeh and Hunan who had studied in Tokyo formed the core of Tang Cai-chang's abortive rising in the summer of 1900. This attempt. which took place at the same time as the Boxer movement in North China and Sun Yat-sen's rising in Kwangtung, was, in name at least, reformist. Its student leaders were promised financial aid by Liang Qi-chao. Liang's arrangements were hopelessly bungled, and the survivors of the rising— several student teachers having been executed—returned to Japan extremely embittered against Liang and the reform movement

9. *Natio nationis* is a classical word, but it refers to *others,* or to other strange or foreign peoples. A Roman would never speak of his own *natio*. See Cicero, "Omnes *nationes* servitutem ferre sunt. Nostra *civitas* non potest," in *Philippics* 10.10.20. I am indebted to Dr. Anthony Bulloch for help on this point.

10. One major difference between Chinese students in this period and almost all other students was that most of the former were married. Virtually all left their wives behind. The proportion of women students was minuscule. The figures given in *Jingzhong Ribao* report that out of 1,199 only 20 were women.

to form among the students a revolutionary nucleus of a few dozen.[11]

In 1903, as in Shanghai, a large number of students were brought into the revolutionary movement through the anti-Russian movement.[12] The Manchu government was aware of the dangers of radicalization of the elite and tried to control the radical students directly through their embassy in Tokyo and indirectly through the Japanese authorities.[13] These attempts backfired and were used by the student militants to generate more nationalist and radical feeling. By the autumn of 1904 a significant number of the 2,000-odd students were committed anti-Manchu revolutionaries. A contemporary radical journalist estimated that they constituted roughly four or five out of every ten students. According to him there were very few who were openly in favor of the Manchus, the majority being "centrists" who followed the wind, "telling Revolutionaries that they are revolutionary, and Reformists that they are reformist." Thus as in so many countries the spectrum of student politics barely overlapped with that of the country, or rather the ruling class of the country, as a whole.[14]

The foundation of the Revolutionary Alliance and the establishment of *The People's Journal* in 1905 provided the revolutionaries with central organizations and increased their numbers. However, it is likely that the flood of new younger and less politicized students resulted in a decline in their relative strength. Nevertheless, the revolutionaries maintained their self-confidence and ideological initiative.

11. For Tang's rising, see Joan E. Smythe "The Tzu-li hui: Some Chinese and Their Rebellion," Harvard *Papers on China*, XII (1958), 51–67; and Feng Zi-you, *Kaiguo shi*, I, 73–89, and 111–117. For contemporary estimate of the number of students involved, see *Jingzhong Ribao* (3/29/04).

12. See Wu Yu-zhang's own involvement, 57–59; and Schiffrin, *Sun Yat-sen*, 257–262.

13. See Feng, *Kaiguo shi*, I, 56–57.

14. *Jingzhong Ribao* (10/25/04). Ernest Young points out that the line between the two groups was anything but hard and fast at this time. See his "Problems of a Late Ch'ing Revolutionary: Chen Tien-hua," in *Revolutionary Leaders of Modern China*, ed. Chun-tu Hsueh (London, 1971), 210–247, esp. 227–233. However, the article in *Jingzhong Ribao* shows the strength and extent of revolutionary feeling among the students *before* the foundation of the Tongmeng Hui. This goes against Scalapino's statement that the balance shifted after its establishment. See his "Prelude to Marxism: The Chinese Student Movement in Japan, 1900–1910," in *Approaches to Modern Chinese History*, ed. Feuerwerker et al. (Berkeley, 1967).

The only significant force to oppose them was Liang Qi-chao, whose reputation as the introducer of Western thought was still enormous. From the first issue of *The People's Journal* in November 1905 to the last issue of *The Renovation of the People* in October 1907 a literary battle raged between the journals as Liang tried to check the revolutionary advance among the students. In the early rounds of the struggle the arguments were mainly concerned with the racial and political policies of the Revolutionary Alliance, but its social policy became an increasingly important element, until by the end it had become the dominant issue. During the struggle both sides developed and modified their attitudes toward socialism and its application to China. The two sides were influenced in their ideas by the changing political scene in China and the world. But the changes seem to have come largely from the argument itself and from the research both sides found it necessary to make to answer the other. From this argument and research the revolutionaries were able to build a relatively logical and coherent structure on the basis of Sun's earlier policies and statements.

For convenience, all the articles concerned with the social policies of the Revolutionary Alliance will be listed here. First, those written by Liang Qi-chao in *The Renovation of the People:*

I. "Discussion on the Advantages and Disadvantages of Racial and Political Revolution," 76 (4th year IV) April 1906.

II. "Discussion of the Suitability of Enlightened Despotism in China Today" (eighth and last section of a series, "Discussion of Enlightened Despotism," in 2 pts), 75 (4th year III) Feb–March 1906, and 77 (4th year V) April 1906.

III. "Reply to the Attack on Our Journal in the 4th Issue of a Certain Journal," 79 (4th year VII) May–June 1906. (Liang takes Supplement to *The People's Journal* III as the 4th Issue.)

IV. "Is Social Revolution Really Necessary in China Today," 86 (4th year 14) December 1906.

V. By Wu Zhong-yao, "Discussion of Socialism" with an introduction by Liang, 89 (4th year 17) Feb. or March 1907.

VI. "Another Attack on a Certain Paper's Theory of Land Nationalization," 90, 91, and 92 (4th year 18, 19, 20) April–May–June 1907.

The articles written by members of the Alliance for *The People's Journal* were the following:

1. Sun Yat-sen, "Introduction to *The People's Journal,*" I, Nov. 1905.

2. Hu Han-min, using the pen-name Han-min, "Six Great Principles of *The People's Journal,*" III, April 1906.

3. "Twelve Points of Contention," Supplement to III, April 1906.

4. Zhu Zhi-xin, pen-name Xian-jie, "That the Social Revolution Should Be Carried Out with the Political Revolution," V, June 1906.

5. Hu Han-min, pen-name Bian-jian, "Against the Lies of *The Renovation of the People,*" V, June 1906.

6. Sun Yat-sen, "Words of a Lecture Given on the Anniversary of *The People's Journal,* X, December 1906.

7. Hu Han-min, pen-name Min-yi, "To the Denouncers of *Minshengzhuyi,*" XII, March 1907.

8. Zhu Zhi-xin, pen-name Xian-jie, "Land Nationalization and Finance," 2 pts., XV and XVI, July and September 1907.

9. Tai Qiu, "Denunciation of the Errors of *The Renovation of the People*'s Attack on Land Nationalization, XVII, October 1907.[15] The attacks and counterattacks went as follows:

The People's Journal   *The Renovation of the People*

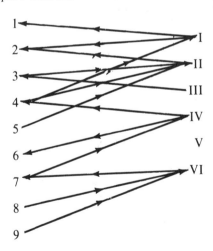

15. The dates on the cover of *Min Bao* and given by Tang Zeng-bi (Man-hua, in "Tongmeng Hui Shidai *Min Bao* Shimo ji," reprinted in *Xinhai Geming,* II,

Liang first mentioned the Alliance's social policies in his two earliest attacks on *The People's Journal,* in "Discussion on the Advantages and Disadvantages of Racial and Political Revolution" and the eighth section of the "Discussion of Enlightened Despotism."

Liang wrote:

I have heard that their group's proposals, as well as racialism and nationalism, include what they call *minshengzhuyi.* They have brushed up the old idealistic nonsense of Proudhon, St. Simon, and Marx, etc. They want to steal the property of the rich and divide it among the poor. This is the "land nationalization," one of six principles shown in their organ. Now because Western society is deeply divided into classes of rich and poor, this principle can agitate the lower classes. All scholars, not only I, know that this is obvious, and that this principle cannot be practiced in reality or reached in the next two millennia. Their leader has glimpsed the West and has dabbled in Western history, and he has seen that agitators have often had success using this principle.[16]

Liang continued by saying that one of the main reasons for the failure of the Taiping Revolt was that political and religious revolutions had occurred simultaneously, and that many of the upper classes who might have been sympathetic to the first aspect had been antagonized by the second. He suggested that the same thing might happen if a political and social revolution were practiced at the same time. Liang then mentioned a related point, saying that if *minshengzhuyi* were practiced, the members of parliament would be poor and ignorant, and it would be difficult to form a new government.[17] This section of Liang's argument was the main provocation for Zhu Zhi-xin's article, "That the Social Revolution Should Be Carried Out with the Political Revolution" (which appeared a month or so later). As we have seen, Zhu's chief purpose was to prove that a social revolution at the same time as a political revolution was not only possible but necessary, thus trying to dis-

---

452–454), are confirmed by Song Jiao-ren's diary. The dates given in *Xinmin Cong-bao* in the reprint and by Zhang Nan and Wang Ren-zhi in their *Xinhai Geming qian Shinianjian Shilun Xuanji,* 2 vols., with 2 sections each (Peking, 1963), are shown by internal evidence to be consistently too early. I have therefore given approximate dates on the basis of their references to *Min Bao.*

16. "Kaiming Zhuanzhi lun," XMCB, LXXV, 20.
17. "Kaiming Zhuanzhi lun," 20.

prove Liang's contention that the Alliance was using the idea of social revolution only to agitate the lower classes. Zhu also dealt with two of Liang's specific points. First, his charge that land nationalization meant robbing the rich: Zhu's reply to this was that they wanted to attack the system, not the individual rich men. Zhu also answered Liang's next attack, which he restated, changing Liang's idea of reforming the government to his own thoughts on political revolution: "If there were *minshengzhuyi,* all the members of the local assemblies would be poor and ignorant. His [Liang's] meaning is that if the rich fled and the poor became dictators, the social revolution would prevent the political one."[18]

Zhu attacked this position in four ways. First, he denied that the rich would flee, because he said, "what rich men want is to preserve their present riches; it is not their hope of future gains. What rich men lose through social revolution is their chance of future gains; it is not the riches they have already accumulated."[19] Second, he disclaimed the reliability and importance of the rich in the political revolution, saying "most rich families are in two minds about the political revolution. If they think the government will win, they will follow it. If the revolution reaches success, they will follow the revolutionary army."[20] Third, he thought the poor were perfectly fit to govern, insisting that "today all the European countries have many members of parliament who originated from the poor people." Finally, he denied the possibility of an unjust dictatorship of the poor:

You must understand that the poor are the great majority and are not like the rich, who are only a small minority. If those in the minority want to benefit themselves, they can turn their backs on justice and make the wrong decisions. But the decisions of the representatives of the majority would not be selfish.[21]

Liang's next attack in his "Discussion of Enlightened Despotism" was to refer to the argument he claimed to have had with Sun some time before.

18. Zhu, "Geming Bingxing," MB, V, 58.   19. "Geming Bingxing," 61.
20. "Geming Bingxing," 61.
21. "Geming Bingxing," 61–62. This raises the fundamental political problems surrounding the concept of "general will." See below.

I asked him why the social revolution should be carried out at the same time. He said, "If we delay, we cannot succeed. After the great revolution, about half, or at least a quarter, of our 400,000,000 people will be lost, the catastrophe will level things, and 70 or 80 per cent of the land will not be owned. Thus we will be able to take it in one step. That is why I advocate great bloodshed: it is the only way to reach our goal." When I heard him say this, I hated his inhumanity and pitied his ignorance. Now he is still proclaiming this doctrine to the world, shamelessly tricking the intellectually immature.[22]

Zhu indignantly denied that this was what Sun had said:

He also quoted Mr. Sun Yat-sen's words about practicing the social and political revolutions at the same time; [saying that he had said] that when people would be killed, it would be easy to practice a social revolution. [Liang's] intention is to frighten people and cunningly gain sympathy. When Sun was talking, all that he said was that during the political revolution, many people would leave their villages, and they would have less sense of property, so that it would be easy to practice [social revolution].[23]

The argument about the two versions of Sun's statement continued throughout the verbal battle.

Near the end of "Discussion of Enlightened Despotism," Liang returned to his attack on the revolutionaries' advocacy of social revolution.

If you want to talk about a social revolution, you are deceiving yourselves that you can discover a new theory which Marx never reached. It would be an extraordinary achievement if a civilized society chose it [socialism] after several hundred years. Now if you want to use savage force to kill half 400,-000,000 men and seize their land, this is not only savage and inhuman, but it is also a theory which the pioneers of socialism have not heard of. Marx said that landlords and capitalists are robbers, but if the state used these means to seize [the land], it would be the chief robber. The knowledgable smile; they have never heard of righteous coercion. You want to raise this together with the common revolution, using it to gain the sympathy of the lower classes of society, hoping that gamblers, swindlers, bandits, burglars, beggars, layabouts and gaol-birds can all be used. I am afraid that the Red Eyebrows and Yellow Turbans will be aroused.[24]

22. "Kaiming Zhuanzhi lun," 21–22.   23. "Geming Bingxing," 51.
24. "Kaiming Zhuanzhi lun," 45. The Red Eyebrows were peasant rebels at the end of the reign of Wang Mang, circa 20 A.D. The Yellow Turbans were a Taoist sect which rebelled against the Han dynasty at the end of the second century A.D.

Liang reinforced his attack with an argument, from the conservative German scholar, Gustave Bornhak, saying,

to begin with, power is seized by the propertyless class; after that there are repeated reactions, which always follow the track described by Mr. Bornhak. Finally a great despot may appear. Although the people do not gain freedom, order can be restored, and the country can be saved. If the man is not there, the country will be destroyed forever. Even if there is such a man, but he appears too late, foreign power will have encroached upon the center, there will be nowhere for him to stand and the country can never be restored. Even if there were a dagger stabbed in my breast, I would still cry out in a loud voice, "He who dares to practice social revolution and the other sorts of revolution, is a traitor to the Yellow Emperor and a criminal against China. He should be executed by 400,000,000 men together." [25]

This passionate denunciation was directed against all kinds of revolution and not only social revolution. In it, Liang used patriotism, the most common and most effective of all weapons against revolution. Liang used patriotism and xenophobia repeatedly against the Alliance, and there is no reason to doubt his sincerity in this. Although a Westernizer for many years, Liang was not nearly as cosmopolitan as Sun, nor as many of the latter's supporters. He was much more aware than the revolutionaries of the menace of imperialism, and he did not share Sun's faith in the rational and enlightened self-interest of the West and Japan. Liang was genuinely appalled at the idea of China's being disunited in the face of imperialism.[26] His pain was made even more acute by his belief in the concept of *qun* (society). This belief, which he shared with his teacher Kang You-wei, was based on the analogy between the community and the human body, in which each organ has its own function and is dependent on all the others. For Liang it was bad enough that the different parts could not communicate with each other, or coordinate action.[27] He believed that this was the reason for China's

25. "Kaiming Zhuanzhi lun," 45. For Liang's response to the antirepublican statism of Gustav Bornhak, see Hao Chang, 248–271. For the revolutionaries' reactions to him, see Michael Gasster, *Chinese Intellectuals and the Revolution of 1911: The Birth of Modern Chinese Radicalism* (Seattle 1969), 109–124.

26. See for instance his "Guafen Weiyen," *Qingyi Bao* (1899), XV–XVIII.

27. See Hao Chang, 95–110. Although Hao Chang shows that Liang extended his concept of *qun* into the inanimate physical world and therefore translates it as "group" or "grouping," he admits that Liang concentrated on its sociopolitical aspects, 97. I would maintain that in many ways Liang simply used *qun* as a transla-

paralysis in the face of the West. But for Liang it was inconceivably immoral to suggest that one section of society should attack another.

Zhu dismissed Liang's argument that the Alliance was merely using socialism for agitation, and used his socialism to combat Bornhak's theory that after the social revolution the different social classes would succeed each other in power, thus causing chaos and disaster. According to Zhu, the theory

was based on the French revolution, which had no element of a social revolution in it. . . . Only before the social revolution can there be a theory that the rich and poor succeed each other in holding power. The social revolution uses class conflict as its means, but after it has been achieved there will no longer be any economic classes. . . . One definitely cannot say that one class holds political power, still less can one say that this class removes that class.[28]

It is quite clear that, despite the passion involved, *minshengzhuyi* and land nationalization were relatively minor elements in the general struggle at this stage. Liang's arguments, mentioned above, take up only a small portion of his writings before 1907. The issue was no more important to the revolutionaries. Only the very last of the "Twelve Points of Contention" listed in the special supplement to *The People's Journal*, III, was concerned with socialism, where it was said that "*The People's Journal*, looking at the future of the world, knows that the social problem must be solved, therefore we advocate socialism. *The Renovation of the People* thinks it is only a tool for 'agitating beggars and scoundrels'" [29] Several writers at the time and later have maintained that Liang's use of this phrase represented a sharp change in his attitude. It was stated that he had

tion for the Western "society." As shown above, it was used in this sense by the missionaries, being replaced later by the Japanese *shehui*. For discussion of the organic analogy for society in Europe and China, see Schwartz, *Yen-Fu*, 57–60.

28. "Geming Bingxing," 64–65.

29. Supplement to *Min Bao*, III. The supplement must have come out with later editions. "Kaiming Zhuanzhi lun," which contains criticisms of Hu's article in *Min Bao*, III, is itself referred to. Article 10 of the supplement also had some bearing on socialism: "*Xinmin Congbao* slanders revolution but praises nihilists. *Min Bao* considers that all nihilists have revolution as a principle; they do not merely kill people." For more on what seems to be a fair description of Liang's approval of nihilists, see Bernal, "Triumph of Anarchism," 117–118.

previously "used all his strength to promote socialism in China" but that after the third issue of *The People's Journal* he had opposed it.[30] Liang claimed with justification that his position had been consistent on the issue, and he stated his views on it:

I recognize socialism as a high and pure principle. Moreover, in my advocacy of enlightened despotism and in establishing enterprises after a political revolution there should be the spirit of state socialism to prevent the disaster of a future social revolution. The extreme type of socialism, the principle of land nationalization, is not acceptable to me. I do not believe it is necessary today to use social revolution to rouse our people. For savage men to urge extreme principles of social revolution at the same time as racial and political revolution, this I see as inciting beggars and scoundrels.[31]

At this stage Liang still supported state socialism while retaining his hatred of radicalism in general and threats to landed property in particular. The change after the third issue of *The People's Journal* was that what he saw as dangerous ideas, which had previously merely been advocated by the eccentric Sun Yat-sen, had now become the official policy of the dominant group among the students in Japan, the cream of Chinese youth.

In late December 1906 or early January 1907, when Liang resumed the controversy, he made a much stronger and more detailed attack on the social policies of the Alliance. This appeared in "Is Social Revolution Really Necessary in China Today?" The article was divided into three sections: one general, one in reply to points made on the social revolution in Sun's speech of December 2, and one in reply to Zhu's article on the need for a simultaneous social revolution.

Liang began with a short paragraph on the differences between evolution and revolution. The former was described as natural and creative, and the latter as unnatural and destructive.[32] The passage was in fact a word-for-word translation from Yamanouchi Masaakira's Japanese translation of Ely's *Outlines of Economics,* a book on which Liang and his opponents relied heavily. Liang had

30. See Hu, "Gao fei," *Min Bao,* XII, 46, quoted by Rong Meng-yuan, 8.
31. "Da Moubao Disihao Duiyu Benbao zhi Bolun," XMCB, LXXIX, 65.
32. Liang, "Shehui Geming guo wei Jinri Zhongguo suo biyao hu?" (referred to hereafter as "Geming biyao hu"), XMCB, LXXXVI, 5–7, 5th part of *Zada Moubao.*

referred to Ely at another point, but was attacked for not giving this citation by Min-yi (a pseudonym for Hu Han-min) in his reply to Liang's article, "To the Denouncers of *Minshengzhuyi*." [33] The article, which was published in March 1907, went over Liang's article in great detail and at enormous length.

Hu's reply to Liang's first point was that revolutions were often natural and were not necessarily destructive. He gave as an example the "revolutionary" change in Kwangtung from human portage to railway portage. [34] Liang's argument, which was the fundamental one between the Reformists and the Revolutionaries, might have come in any part of his attack, but the rest of Liang's article was specifically against *minshengzhuyi* and land nationalization. The first section introduced the two main themes of the article, which seem to have underlain all Liang's theories on the subject. First, that while he thought Europe and America needed a social revolution, he was certain that China did not; second that China's over-riding need was to be able to compete with the West economically as well as politically.

Liang gave the reasons why he thought the two situations were qualitatively different. The revolutionaries had claimed that the terrible state of Western society resulted from political and industrial revolutions, both of which were an inevitable part of human progress. Liang maintained that "the imperfections of European social and economic organization at present came from the imperfection of European social and economic organization before the industrial revolution." [35] And, further, that "in every country in Europe . . . the minority of nobles were the landlords, and the majority of commoners had no place to stand an awl [no land at all]. . . . The nobles were also the rich men." [36] In China, he said, the situation was completely different: "In China since the Qin the nobles have been destroyed and although they have sometimes been restored later, they have never been able to survive for long." [37]

---

33. Min-yi was a pseudonym used by both Wang Jing-wei and Hu Han-min. It is almost certain that Hu alone wrote this article. Hu stated in his autobiography that Wang concentrated on questions of constitution and race while he explained *minshengzhuyi*. See Hu, "Hu Han-min Zizhuan," 389. For Wang's part in the controversy, see Gasster, 71–150.

34. Hu, "Gao Fei," 49.   35. Liang, "Geming biyao hu," 13–14.

36. Liang, "Geming biyao hu," 11.   37. Liang, "Geming biyao hu," 11.

According to Liang, China had had two further advantages: no primogeniture to consolidate the estates of the rich men, and light taxation, unlike the terrible burden imposed on the French peasants before the revolution. Without the clear-cut class divisions of feudal Europe, China should be able to avoid both the industrial and social revolutions.

In China the problems of production and distribution—for both of which revolution was a drastic remedy—could be solved gradually. The way for China to concentrate the capital necessary for industrial development was to raise it from the large numbers of a middle class which existed in China but had no counterpart in feudal Europe. New companies would be formed with vast numbers of shareholders, as was already happening with the provincial railway companies. This would be very similar to the idea of a cooperative factory put forward by Ely. With this type of industrial organization, China would avoid having the capitalists and trusts which so oppressed the West.[38] The government would also have to play a part in this development, and once more Liang attacked Adam Smith and laissez faire.

The Chinese government would have to play a positive part in society. It should have two specific aims: to encourage capital and to protect labor.[39]

Hu's reply to this argument was to ask why Liang had begun by referring to the desperate state of European and American society, but when he came to analyze its origins he had talked only about Europe and not America. Hu quoted Ely to show that American industry had emerged smoothly, and that before industrialization America had had no nobility and as a consequence no heavy taxes on the people. What is more, America had had plenty of land.

Liang wildly says that our economic and social organization is better than Europe's was at that time. Thus he says we can avoid the future disaster of social revolution. But American economic and social organization was better than ours: what is the result now? . . . [There is] the tyranny of the trusts, all the industry of the country is monopolized, there are the miseries of high rent and unemployment. The problem of social revolution came later than in Europe, but is now more serious there.[40]

38. Liang, "Geming biyao hu," 10.   39. Liang, "Geming biyao hu," 16–17.
40. Hu, "Gao Fei," 58.

Hu then attacked Liang's picture of a Chinese industry made up of large numbers of shareholders. According to Hu, small shareholders were very quickly squeezed out: shares "always fall into the hands of a few men." [41] This was what had happened all over the world and would happen in China. He quoted Ely on the happy state of England before the industrial revolution. Ely's description of a period in which there were many independent craftsmen and farmers sounded exactly like Liang's picture of China. According to Hu Han-min, in some respects England had been better off. Ely said at that time there were no beggars in England. Liang had accused the revolutionaries of trying to gain the sympathy of gamblers, swindlers, bandits, burglars, beggars, layabouts, and gaol-birds. "Are these good phenomena in a society?" Even so, Hu admitted that on the whole China's society was better than Europe's had been, but it was worse than America's.

He agreed with Liang that China should "look at the evils of the last hundred years [in the West], deeply examine them and apply curative methods." This was, he said, exactly what Sun had proposed. He also agreed that "the things that brought about the present evil phenomena in Europe were (1) given birth to by the old society, and (2) reared by the governments' mistakenly using the theory of license." [42] America proved that the evil could not have come from the existence of a nobility.

Thus it was the recognition of a system of private landownership, and the encouragement of the capitalists, together with the land being in the hands of a few, who could seize the capital of society, which caused the calamities of today. Thus we know that the land problem is the origin of the social problem. If one cannot solve the land problem, it is because one cannot understand the origins of the sickness of Western society. [43]

Liang turned to the question of economic imperialism. He restated his version of Hobson's theory: "Economists all say that if rent and wages are high, profit is low, and that if rent and wages are low, profit is high." [44] According to Liang, after the industrial

41. Hu, "Gao Fei," 62.   42. Hu, "Gao Fei," 64.   43. Hu, "Gao Fei," 65.
44. Liang had written about this before in "Waizi Shuru Wenti." See Schiffrin, *Sun Yat-sen,* 286–288. For parallels and differences between the views of Hobson and those of Kōtoku Shūsui in his *Teikokushugi (nijuseiki no-kaibutsu),* see Notehelfer, 82–84.

revolution land and labor had become increasingly expensive in Europe. At first the capitalists went to America and Australia, where land was plentiful and where by bringing in Chinese labor, wages could be kept down. "But after a few decades, America and Australia, which had been the back of beyond, [have now] stood up for themselves and are concerned about excess of capital."[45]

The capitalists turned to Japan, and the same thing happened there. Then they looked around the world for new places and found none so suitable as China, with its vast areas of land and cheap labor force. According to Liang, this situation had great potential for everyone:

If our people at this time could collect capital and use Western techniques to seek profit from our cheap labor, the national wealth would rush ahead, and after a decade no one in the world could withstand us. Otherwise, if the capital stays immobilized as it is at present, without the possibility of devoting it to large enterprises, all Western and Eastern countries will be compelled by the economic principle to take their excess capital and supervise us. . . . How will we be able to withstand it?[46]

Liang then described the actual scene with the foreigners competing with each other to invest in China. If this went on "China's economic sphere would be divided into two great classes: those who enjoyed the benefits of civilization—the foreigners; and those who suffered from its evils—the Chinese. At that time, one would have to summon the whole country and proclaim a social revolution."[47] Meanwhile, there was only one thing to do to avoid this calamity:

Today, if we in China want to solve this extremely dangerous problem, we can only encourage the capitalists so that they can use their savings and unite them, using the new Western methods of production discovered in the last hundred years for production . . . so that the enterprises can develop and oppose the foreigners. . . . Although for the first few years this may slightly prejudice the interests of the other sections of the population, for the sake of the national economy this is not to be shirked.[48]

Liang restated this by saying the immediate problem was that of production: how to help the capitalists; not the problem of distribution: how to help the people.

45. Liang, "Geming biyao hu," 17.
46. Liang, "Geming biyao hu," 18.   47. Liang, "Geming biyao hu," 19.
48. Liang, "Geming biyao hu," 19. The word translated as prejudice is *xixing* (literally, sacrifice).

The problem of production is a problem of international struggle; the problem of distribution is a problem of internal struggle. . . . The survival of the country depends on the solution of the problem of production. If we do not solve the problem of production there will be no problem of distribution for us to solve.[49]

Hu came out clearly against Liang's views on economic imperialism:

Is this worth considering a disaster? We welcome it. Why? Because, as Liang himself says, not many decades ago America and Australia were the back of beyond to the old world, but now they themselves have stood up and are worried about surplus capital. Thus if capitalists of every country rush toward us and pour in their capital . . . after a few decades we will be the America and Australia of today and will be worried about our own excess of capital.[50]

He thought that Liang had made the mistake of confusing military and economic competition. In trade it was not necessary for one side to win and the other to lose: "Those who trade in our country to gain profit, generally do profit from us, but they do not rob us to fatten themselves." [51] If it were like that no one would trade, whereas in fact all economists believe in it. He admitted that "in our country in the last century the people's life has become more difficult, and there has been no improvement or progress in methods of economic production and distribution. This is because of the faults in society. It is ignorant to blame it on the introduction of foreign capital." [52] The amount of trade always increased as a country became civilized.

Hu tried to show how the investment of foreign capital in China could help China develop her own industry. He quoted Ely on the nature of capital: "Capital is the result of production, less the amount needed for expenses. If the surplus is used in production or saved for production, it forms capital." [53] He drew a chart showing the benefits of foreign investment, how it increased the amount of production and lessened its expenses, thus increasing capital. He

---

49. Liang, "Geming biyao hu," 20.   50. Hu, "Gao Fei," 70.
51. This follows Ukita Kazuomi's theory that there were two kinds of imperialism, one aggressive and military, the other natural, benign, and economic. Ukita's book *Teikokushugi* had been translated into Chinese. See Schiffrin, *Sun Yat-sen*, 283–284.
52. Hu, "Gao Fei," 70.   53. Hu, "Gao Fei," 80.

drew from Ely again to show the classical division of the results of production into rent, wages, interest, and profit. If money were invested in China, the interest would definitely go abroad; the profit might or might not, depending on whether the entrepreneur were Chinese. In any case, wages and rent, two of the former parts, went to China, and she was sure to receive these, whether the enterprise succeeded or failed, because it was the entreprenuer who took the risks.

Hu's support for foreign investment did not mean that he was opposed to the movements to "restore rights" of railways, and so on, but these, he said, were questions of national sovereignty. He accused Liang of confusing economics and politics.

Hu then attacked Liang's scheme for Chinese capitalists to oppose the foreigners from another point of view. If the Chinese capitalists stood against the whole world, they would be doomed to failure. He quoted from Yan Fu with approval.

I have heard some students abroad say, "Rather than allow foreigners to export to our country and make a profit, China's railways should not be built nor her mines opened." How is this different from the minister Xu Dong-hai (Shi-chang) saying:" 'If we attacked the barbarians, it would be the greatest glory even if we sat in a ruined country.'" [54]

According to Hu, Liang's half-hearted attempts at state socialism would not be any more successful than the capitalists' attempts. What was needed was land nationalization. Hu talked about the annual value of land rent in China, which was, he said, about 8,000,-000,000 (taels?).

This figure, which was later to cause a great deal of controversy, was arrived at in the following way:

In China, land tax is a twentieth of rent. Now the amount that is taken from the people and that reaches the central government is 40,000,000 per annum. We do not know how much of this is embezzled. The Englishman, Hart, once said that without adding to taxation China could raise 400,000,-000 a year. Hence the total amount of rent is 8,000,000,000 annually, which would probably be enough for development. If it were not, the state would have sufficient credit to borrow from abroad; there would be no need to

54. Hu, "Gao Fei," 72. For Xu see BDRC.

wait for capitalists to emerge. The only result of encouraging them would be to create a class system in China.[55]

According to Hu, Liang's plans would be exactly the same as the Western governments' mistake of encouraging laissez-faire.

Hu also attacked Liang's sharp distinction between production and distribution. Ely had said that they were not really distinct. According to Hu, there could be no solution to the problem of production if the problems of rent, wages, and profits were not solved first. Besides, if the problem of individual property were not solved, there would be no advantage in producing a great deal.[56]

Liang attacked the revolutionaries for not being proper socialists:

If one wants a social revolution, unless one has it complete one cannot gain its benefits. If even the West, after a century, will still not necessarily be able to practice it, how much less could China today. . . . They do not understand what socialism is. The most complete social revolutionary theory has as its main principle the nationalization of all the means of production. The reason why land must be nationalized is that it is an important factor of production. But apart from land there is another important factor of production, namely, capital. If one investigates the fundamental causes of the inequalities of distribution in Western society and weighs them up, capital is the most important.[57]

The argument that partial or piecemeal reforms were useless and should be delayed until complete reform could be undertaken is of course a standard conservative delaying tactic. According to Liang, land had been controlled by a minority before the industrial revolution, and there was no social problem then; the problem must have other causes. The land problem was only an appendage to the capital problem. He praised the justice of complete socialism, and made his customary obeisance to it as a theory. He then used the arguments of "Western opponents of this principle" against its immediate practice, and indeed he produced all the old chestnuts. If there were no competition, there would be no progress; if rewards were equal, there would be no incentive; and if the state were to run everything in China today, there would be all sorts of abuses. "Clearly," he said, "the revolutionaries must know that their

55. Hu, "Gao Fei," 7–5. For Sir Robert Hart, see Stanley F. Wright, *Hart and the Chinese Customs* (Belfast, 1950).
56. Hu, "Gao Fei," 78–9.   57. Liang, "Geming biyao hu," 21–22.

schemes are impracticable and they must simply be rabble-rousers."

Hu replied to Liang's statement that if civilized countries could not practice socialism, China surely could not, by saying: "All modern scholars of socialism recognize that the possibility of a country practicing socialism varies inversely with the degree of its civilization."

That this was not an example of the influence of Russian populist thought on the Chinese revolutionaries, or of early Maoism, emerges from the example Hu went on to give: "New Zealand is a savage island in the South Seas, and it may at any moment become a socialist paradise." [58] Thus the West's inability to create socialism did not rule out the possibility in China. Hu also said that Liang had exaggerated, and that the Alliance had never said that it was only going to nationalize land. As for Liang's thinking capital was more important than land, this was clearly ridiculous. Hu gave a good George-like reply: "Land united with labor produces capital; that is why all economists see land as the source of wealth. Liang says that capital is the chief force: we believe that land is the original force behind capital." [59] When Liang had talked about a minority holding the land before the industrial revolution, he was admitting that the land problem should come before that of capital.

Hu denied Liang's statement that to be a complete socialist one had to nationalize all the means of production. "According to this all people holding a principle would have to go to the extreme, before they could be called complete." According to Hu, even "extreme socialism" was not as extreme as its enemies made it out to be.

Now the people who most terrify the world today with their theory of capital *(Das Kapital)* are Marx and Engels. But these two gentlemen not only recognize the private ownership of personal belongings for one's own use, but even the private ownership of capital by farmers and artisans. The Japanese scholar Kawakami has said that socialists often exaggerate, saying that all capital will be publicly owned and private property prohibited; that is why people fear socialism. . . . He also said that when Abe Isō and Kōtoku Shusui use the words entirely *(shitsu)*, or all *(subete)*, in their discussions of the nationalization of capital, they are not in fact using them correctly. Thus even for the most extreme socialism one cannot say that all capital will be nationalized. [60]

58. Hu, "Gao Fei," 90.   59. Hu, "Gao Fei," 100   60. Hu, "Gao Fei," 100.

Having described foreign socialism as he saw it, Hu said, "Our socialism *(shehuizhuyi)* is not the same." He went on to describe the party's own beliefs, which later in the article he was to call *minshengzhuyi,* or "demosology," for the first time making official the break between Western-style *shehuizhuyi* and Chinese *minshengzhuyi.*[61] Hu said that the party's proposals were

the nationalization of land and the nationalization of large capital. When there is land nationalization, the state will be the only landlord, with the revenue from rent. At the same time, it will become a capitalist because it will manage all natural monopolies. However, it will not be mean about the private ownership of productive enterprises.[62]

This appears to contradict the other argument put forward by Alliance spokesmen and Hu Han-min himself, that "Not all collectivist theories can be applied to China at her present stage of development. Only land nationalization. . . ."[63]

Sun's attitude toward the nationalization of capital is not altogether clear. One writer has stated categorically that he did not mention the nationalization of capital of any sort before 1911.[64] But another reports that at the foundation of the Revolutionary Alliance Sun referred to "Equal Land Rights and Control of Capital."[65] The position is somewhat clarified by Hu's statement here on state management of natural monopolies.

Thus it seems that although Sun's major concern was with land values, he foresaw eventual public control of other natural monopolies. He had no intention, however, of threatening the capital of the small-scale merchants and entrepreneurs who formed his original financial and political base. It was mainly for this reason that his policies of nationalization of capital of any kind were played down by Alliance spokesman. The other important consideration was the fear of offending the merchant and gentry leaders who were agitating against the Qing government's nationalization of the railways.

Many radical non-socialists and land nationalizers took similar positions on the question of natural monopolies. Ely was a firm supporter of their nationalization, and Henry George himself, after

61. Hu, "Gao Fei," 126.   62. Hu, "Gao Fei," 100.
63. Hu, *"Min Bao* zhi Liu da Zhuyi," 12.   64. Tang Leang-li, 172.
65. He Xiang-ning, "Wodi Huiyi," in *Xinhai Geming Huiyilu,* I, 12–60, esp. 17.

1887, was forced by socialist argument to advocate the nationalization of railways and other natural monopolies.[66]

Hu Han-min gave the reasons why the Alliance concentrated on land and not capital:

In our future China, there will be nationalization of land and large capital. The nationalization of land will be by legally making it the state's. The nationalization of capital, when land is state property, will naturally become state property. Why do we talk about land and not capital? Because land is at present in the hands of private individuals, while capitalists have not yet appeared. Why should land but not capital be nationalized by making it legally belong to the state? Because land is a natural monopoly and capital is not.[67]

Hu listed six reasons why society would become more equal after land nationalization was carried out:

1. Since there will be no private ownership of land, there will be no landlords able to use the profit from land to obtain superior positions in production.

2. The capitalists will not be able to use both weapons (land and capital) to control the lives of the workers.

3. Without a system of private land ownership, all capital will be used in productive enterprises, not in consumer ones; thus the capital of society will increase daily, and there will be no disasters of supply not meeting demand. (Speculation in land is nonproductive and is of no benefit to society.)

4. Land is the biggest of natural monopolies. After land is nationalized, the other monopolies will follow it. Enterprises which can be competitive will still be managed privately. Since there will be no other checks, profit will be entirely according to business ability, and there will be no feelings of inequality in society.

5. As the workers will have land to till, they will not be excessively worried about their industrial wages; thus the capitalists will still less be able to control the lives of the workers.

6. The small people have always liked working their own land, and hated laboring (for others). Therefore, wages cannot possibly be less than the amount a peasant would receive, and the benefits of other workers will come up to this standard.[68]

66. Cole, *History of Socialist Thought*, II, 374.
67. Hu, "Gao Fei," 103.   68. Hu, "Gao Fei," 101.

The Kuomintang scholar Wang De-zhao thinks that this list is inconsistent in that points 2, 5, and 6 are related to Miyazaki's theory of land nationalization and not to what he sees as Sun's policy that the profit of the land should benefit society as a whole. I would maintain that Sun's policy at the time did include eventual land nationalization and its availability to the population as a whole.[69]

Hu answered Liang's antisocialist arguments, that without competition there would be no progress, with an argument that seemed dangerously near to Western liberalism and laissez-faire. What the party advocated, he said, was not mathematical equality, but psychological equality, by which he meant equality of opportunity.

There will be no unequal classes. Each individual will stand in an equal position; what is more, in a constitutional country there will not be classes like a nobility. After that, each man will receive according to his ability and intelligence. There will be differences, but they will not be inequalities. This is the essence of our theory of social revolution.[70]

In the section of Liang's "Is Social Revolution Really Necessary . . ." devoted to Sun's speech, Liang quoted passages from it and then gave answers to the points raised. Some of these answers simply repeated arguments Liang had put forward earlier; others developed previous arguments, or put forward new ones.

The most interesting part of Liang's attack came after his quotation of the section of Sun's speech dealing with the actual land policy to be followed, where Sun suggested fixing land prices and compensating landowners, with the profits from land price increases going to the state. Liang seems to have had the same difficulty as later scholars in finding out Sun's exact meaning. "Ha ha," he says, "this then is Sun Wen's newly discovered policy of social revolution. I have been over it hundreds of times and I still do not see what he calls 'going into it point by point.'"[71]

Liang tried to deal with all the possible permutations and combinations allowed by Sun's statement:

We do not know whether the government will buy (the land) immediately after land prices have been fixed, or if it will only buy it slowly after some time. If it buys it immediately after fixing land prices, it will naturally allow

69. Wang De-zhao, 167. For the Alliance policy in detail, see below.
70. Hu, "Gao Fei," 102.   71. Liang, "Geming biyao hu," 29.

no more trade (in land). Now economists are generally agreed that if goods cannot be exchanged, they cannot have any value. If land were not saleable, it would be false to say that land which was first bought for 1,000 was worth 1,000 or that land which was bought for 2,000 was worth 2,000, so how can you have the theory that 8,000 of the future increase of 10,000 will go the the state. If you wait and only buy it after a time, why must you fix the price beforehand? The reason is the fear that before the land is bought land prices would rise through the bustle of trade, and the expense of the government buying it would be greater. They do not realize that after prices are fixed, trade will stop immediately. A has land valued at 2,000 and because of the development of communications B buys it from A for 4,000. But when the government buys it from B, it still only pays the original price of 2,000. Who then would want to be B? . . . Once land prices are fixed, land ceases to have any value. Therefore it is quite definite that there is no reason for the price to go up to 10,000 and the profit of 8,000 to go to the state. Thus the state has no reason for thinking that this can be the principal source of financial revenue.[72]

Liang then turned to another difficulty in the application of the scheme. "The state as landlord will charge rent to the people." How was the amount of this rent to be assessed? According to Liang, it was quite easy in most countries, because land tax was assessed on the basis of the fluctuating price of land in a free market. This would be impossible after land nationalization. In this situation Liang saw two possible methods. The first was for the officials to make their own assessment. "But could not the officials use this as a malpractice to oppress the people? Would the people submit to the values estimated by the officials?" The second method was for the government to rent the land to the highest bidder. But in that case "only the big capitalists would be able to rent large or rich sections of land, and those with small capital would only be able to crouch in corners. If it were like this, how would they be able to avoid the trend for the rich to get richer and the poor to get poorer?"[73] According to Liang, both methods could provide the government with a great deal of money, but neither would have anything to do with socialism.

Liang suggested that Sun might have yet another plan. He referred to the conversation he had had with Sun seven years before,

72. Liang, "Geming biyao hu," 29–30.   73. Liang, "Geming biyao hu," 30.

in which Sun had said: "After land nationalization, to receive land one must till it and pay rent to the state directly."[74] Liang understood this to mean that all who could till land could receive it. He attacked the scheme violently. Who was to allocate land to the peasants? How much should they be allowed to have? Should it be the amount they could plow by hand or should it be as much as they could cultivate by machine? If it were the former, the government would in effect be banning machinery. If it were the latter, there would not be enough land to satisfy all the claims. If it were both, it would favor those using machinery.

Liang then returned to his attack on the lines that Sun's policy was not socialist. If the state owned land, the capitalists owned capital, and the workers owned labor, one would still have to retain the existing system for dividing the rewards of production, that is, rent, wages, and profit. Thus a state monopoly of land would replace the landlords' monopoly, and it would not fundamentally alter the situation. The state would simply behave like a selfish individual. Thus single tax might be satisfactory financially, but it would not stop the rich getting richer, and so on.[75]

In his reply to Liang's first point, Hu started by saying that Liang must have been very stupid not to understand Sun's theories, which he had stated very clearly. Hu continued, "To say that if one cannot exchange, one cannot talk of value, is not to say that if one cannot buy and sell one cannot talk of value."[76] Rent was a type of exchange. After land nationalization and price fixing, land could not be sold, but it could be rented. Thus one could talk about land value. If rents rose, one could talk about prices rising and the state receiving the profit. It would also be perfectly easy to assess the value of a piece of land by looking at its rent.

Hu said that Liang had misinterpreted Sun's statement about the peasants receiving land. Sun had not said that all who could till must receive land, or that all men must be made to receive land and till it. What he had said was that to receive land one must till it—his purpose was to avoid wasting land. He went on: "It is right to say that this method agrees with *jingtian,* but it is a mistake to say this method is *jingtian.*"[77] *Jingtian* meant mathematical equality; the

74. See above.   75. Liang, "Geming biyao hu," 32–36.
76. Hu, "Gao Fei," 113.   77. Hu, "Gao Fei," 123.

Alliance's social policies meant psychological equality. Under the party's system, land would be rented to the highest bidder, and land prices would increase by the laws of supply and demand.

As for Liang's charge that only those with capital could rent land, Hu admitted that those with absolutely no capital, "men without farm implements or axes," would have to work for others. But those with implements could ask the government for land. They would not have to pay immediately; the government would only cancel the agreement if they failed to pay after two or more years. Hence, even the poorest tenant would not be worried about being without land.

In answer to Liang's point that the capitalists would rent vast areas of good land, Hu started by describing Ricardo's theory of differential rent. But he said that after land nationalization all rent would go the the state, and advantages gained by good position and high fertility would be canceled out so that there would be fair competition. Under these conditions, a special characteristic of agriculture became important. "Agriculturalists say that agriculture is different from other things, in that it is profitable to have it divided up." [78] Large-scale mechanized farming did not produce as good a yield per unit area as small-scale peasant cultivation.

After land nationalization we must seek full value from the land. If we take as our standard the small-scale cultivator receiving four parts, half or a third will be taken as rent. The large farmer, using machinery only, receives one part for every *mou*. As it is not his private property, he must pay this amount as rent; thus not only is it not profitable, but it is harmful. Thus after the system of (land) nationalization is practiced, we need not fear that the capitalists will monopolize agriculture. [79]

Hu disagreed with Liang that if the state took over the land it would make no difference to the people. This might be true, he admitted, under a despotic government, but it would not be true under the future Chinese Constitutional Republic *(Zhonghua Lixian Minguo)*. With such a government owning the land, the revenue from rent would be used to benefit the people, and the manifold evils of landlordism would disappear.

Liang attacked one of Sun's clear-cut distinctions between China and the West. Sun had said that in the West, land prices had risen to

78. Hu, "Gao Fei," 118.
79. Hu, "Gao Fei," 120–121, with a misprint of *ziben* for *tudi* in the original.

such an extent that it was too late to nationalize it, because prices would not go any higher. In China, on the other hand, except for Shanghai and some of the other ports, land prices had remained stationary for thousands of years. Liang said that when he had been in the West he had seen that land prices were still rising in the cities. Moreover, land prices in China had risen considerably throughout Chinese history, particularly in the last twenty years. If one said that since land prices were cheaper in China it would be easier to nationalize land there, one could also say that Western countries had much more money available to buy land.

Liang concluded this argument by saying, "The reason why Sun says that it would be easier to practice a social revolution in China than in Europe, is his theory, 'After the great chaos the people will be scattered, the fields will be wild and not cultivated, to take it,' etc. etc." [80] This abbreviation of Sun's words showed that Liang had considerably modified his original description of Sun's statement. There was no longer any mention of killing half of 400,000,000 people. However, Liang was indignant that anyone could doubt his word, and gave a highly colored background to the conversation to gain verisimilitude:

You said this some time in the seventh month (8/7–9/4/99) in 1899. I was living at (Ike Kyōkichi's [house]) and I was in my bedclothes; it was about midnight. The Green-eyed Tiger (you must remember this nickname) was there, and knows the circumstances. How can you forget? [81]

Hu did not notice the modification of Liang's report of the conversation. He quoted something Sun had said on the subject, presumably after Liang had first raised the matter.

Six years ago, when I talked with Liang, he did not know a word about socialism. After the failure of 1898, he was full of resentment, and thought that revolution was gaining revenge by killing people. . . . Today, when he hears our method of fixing land prices and buying [land], he cannot argue with it, so he attaches his own fantasies on to others in the hope of confusing people. His vileness is extreme. [82]

    80. Liang, "Geming biyao hu," 36.
    81. Liang, "Geming biyao hu," 36. *Kittei*, in the original, appears to be a misprint for *Kyokichi*, the personal name of Ike, one of Sun's Japanese supporters. See Feng, *Kaiguo shi*, I, 304.
    82. Hu, "Gao Fei," 146.

He denied that Sun had meant that land prices all over the West had reached the extreme point. (That is exactly what Sun had said.) According to Hu, what Sun had meant was that in places like south New York (Manhattan) or central London, land prices were at their zenith. Hu quoted Ely to the effect that in the centers of some cities land prices had not only stopped rising but had sometimes actually fallen. Hu restated the case for the Chinese government buying land which was bound to increase in value. Then, avoiding the issue completely, he said that if a government bought land in New York or London, it would make no profit and might have a loss. According to him, the difference between China, where land prices were bound to rise, and Europe, where this was not so, was one of principle, and it was ridiculous to consider the relative amounts of money available to the different governments.[83]

Liang's final attack on Sun's speech was against the latter's statement that after land nationalization, prices would fall. Liang, who had read his Ely, said prices came from comparison; they were really only ratios. It was impossible for them all to fall together unless the prices of gold and silver went up. He then looked at it from another angle: "Prices vary in proportion to demand and production costs."[84] According to Liang, as civilization advanced, demand increased, and because wages went up, production costs rose. That is why there was a general pattern of rising prices wherever civilization was advancing. He cited the difference in prices between the civilized coast of China and the backward interior.

If Sun wanted complete socialism, Liang said, the question would not arise. In that case there would simply be tickets issued for labor done, which people would spend at public stores. It would then be impossible to talk about prices rising or falling. However, Sun's socialism was not complete. The only way to make cash prices fall would be to make civilization go backwards. "When I look at it, I suspect Sun Wen's theory of social revolution can only mean a retreat to the old period of the *jingtian*." Liang thought this was like Confucius saying, "Do not fear poverty; but fear inequality." He was certain that this method could not work. If there were no industry, and each peasant owned an equal patch of land, the patches

83. Hu, "Gao Fei," 127–130.   84. Liang, "Geming biyao hu," 43.

would become impossibly small as the population increased. Liang ended in slight confusion by suggesting that the only other method Sun could use to make prices fall would be to close all the gold and silver mines in the world.[85]

Hu denied Liang's premise, and came out firmly in favor of the labor theory of value. "The standard of value must vary in proportion to labor and not in proportion to gold and silver." The only value that mattered was the ratio of prices to wages. Civilization sometimes brought cheaper goods. Use of machines meant that less was spent on wages; thus goods could be produced more cheaply. For instance, wages were higher in America than in Shantung, but American flour cost less than that grown in Shantung.[86]

The last section of Liang's article was an answer to Zhu Zhi-xin. He repeated his arguments on the inconsistency of wanting to nationalize land while leaving capital untouched. The capitalists did not need to own land to be able to exploit others and, before complete socialism, the state as a landlord would act at least as oppressively as the previous landowners.

Liang attacked Zhu's description of the socialism he believed in and defined the two great schools of socialism:

1. The school of social reform, which recognizes present social organization and corrects it. What Wagner, Schmoller, and Brentano proclaimed and what Bismarck supported belong to this.

2. The school of social revolution, which does not recognize present social organization but wants to destroy it and create a new one. What Marx and Bebel proclaimed belongs to this. The two are easy to confuse, but their natures are very different. I find it difficult to see to which school the doctrines of Sun and his followers belong. They say they are not like school A or school B. They want to unite the two schools and select from them [both]. They do not know that they are incompatible. . . . In fact they have simply never known what socialism is.[87]

Having challenged the revolutionaries to define their position, Liang stated his own. In reply to the Alliance's repeated charge that he had previously said that a social revolution was inevitable and that he had now changed his mind, he declared: "My [saying] an economic revolution was inevitable applied to the West. Today have

85. Liang, "Geming Biyao hu," 42–44.
86. Hu, "Gao Fei," 142–143.   87. Liang, "Geming biyao hu," 46–47.

I ever said it can be avoided?" Having said this, he clarified his statement in such a way as to alter his position somewhat: "I show absolute sympathy toward social reformism and I have always praised social revolutionism. But I have said that it cannot be practiced; or, if it can, only after a millennium." [88]

This statement summed up Liang's attitude toward socialism—from the time he knew about the difference between social reform and social revolution. Liang did not see any incompatibility between his social reformism and his growing belief in the necessity of supporting capitalism in order to face the West. In the description of the type of socialism he believed in, he showed that he believed capitalism should be somewhat limited.

This sort of socialism which is "social reformism" has many different articles, and I cannot write them all, but roughly speaking it is that things like railways, streets, electric lights, trams, gas light and water supplies should all belong to the state or the municipality. Factory regulations, laws for all types of production, associations, and compulsory insurance, should all be enacted, and every sort of savings organ should be established. There should be progressive income tax and death duties. Railways should be publicly owned, because they are a monopoly, and their profits should not be monopolized by a minority. There should be laws for production associations so that small capitalists and people without capital can devote themselves to production, etc., etc.[89]

A theme which linked the seemingly contradictory elements in Liang's ideas was his belief in Japan as a model for China's modernization. The Meiji oligarchy suspected foreign capital and supported native capitalists, more than "somewhat at the expense of other sections of the population." At the same time during the last decade of the Meiji era the Japanese government seemed to be beginning to apply state socialism: the railways were nationalized and factory regulations were passed. This combination appeared to be strikingly successful, and it is not at all surprising that Liang should advocate both of these aspects.

Liang replied to Zhu's argument, that in times of political revolution people are not concerned about prosperity and merely want security, and that therefore it would be the best time to practice a

88. Liang, "Geming biyao hu," 48.   89. Liang, "Geming biyao hu," 49–50.

social revolution. He said that this was only another version of
Sun's theory that it would be easy to take the land after chaos. They
were both similarly evil. "I do not know what the difference is
between killing a man with a stick or a knife." Once more Liang
denounced the revolutionaries for trying to incite the lower orders,
and he ended his article with an appeal to patriotism: "Today, if we
want to save our country, we should only proclaim 'nationalism'
(guojiazhuyi); 'racialism' *(minzuzhuyi)* and 'socialism' should be
subordinated to nationalism." [90]

Hu Han-min did not reply to any of these points, perhaps because
he wanted to avoid Liang's challenge to the revolutionaries to
declare whether they were social reformists or social revolutionaries.
This was a dilemma which none of the Alliance theoreticians was
ever able to solve.

In *The Renovation of the People,* No. 89, which appeared early in
1907, there was an article by one of Liang's supporters, Wu Zhong-
yao, called "Discussion on Socialism," for which Liang himself
wrote an introduction. In this, Liang began by stressing the importance of the economic problem and the problem of socialism in the
West: "Although one cannot say that socialism is the only problem
in the world, one could roughly say that among the many problems
of the world it has the most important position." [91] Then, in a
manner very reminiscent of Sun, he mentioned the parallel development of civilization and the social problem, and his belief that as
China developed this problem would become extremely urgent.
Moreover, Liang said, socialism, the answer to the problem, was
very complicated and, "no one can really understand its meaning.
. . . Even though there is an enormous number of books on this
from every country, our countrymen might as well not have seen
them." [92] Liang then launched into an attack on the Alliance:
"Recently one or two savage-minded people have falsely wanted to
use this as a tool for agitation . . . but they do not know anything
about its nature and profit from the confusion of our countrymen." [93]

90. Liang, "Geming biyao hu," 52.
91. Liang "Shehuizhuyi Lun yu," XMCB, LXXXIX, 35.
92. Liang, "Shehuizhuyi Lun yu," 36.   93. Liang, "Shehuizhuyi Lun yu," 36.

Only the first part of Wu Zhong-yao's article was published. Others were promised but never appeared.[94] Wu's arguments seem to have supported Liang's. The main part of his article was devoted to a classification of the different branches of socialism. His general division was into two categories, broad and narrow socialism, which became very important later. These terms seem to have been exactly the same as Liang's social reformism and social revolutionism. According to Wu, narrow socialism was noble, idealistic, and impracticable, while broad socialism was moderate and realistic. Narrow socialism could not possibly be applied to China in the foreseeable future, but broad socialism was essential for her.

Liang's reply to "To the Denouncers of *Minshengzhuyi*" did not appear until April 1907, when the first of a series of three articles appeared in *The Renovation of the People*. These were the first articles devoted especially to the Revolutionary Alliance's social policies, and it may very well have been as Zhu Zhi-Xin charged: "As *The Renovation of the People* was not successful in attacking our anti-Manchu theory, it has withdrawn in a plot to attack our weak points, thinking to damage our theory of land nationalization." [95] There is every reason to suppose that Liang was in fact attacking the weakest and least popular point in the policies of the Revolutionary Alliance.

At the beginning of his article, Liang announced that it would contain three sections, "to correct the mistakes of the theory of land nationalization": "from the point of view of finance, from the point of view of economics, and from the point of view of the social problem." The two later points were to be dealt with in the succeeding articles.

The main part of the first section was concerned with the problem of whether or not the single tax system could provide enough money for government expenditure. Liang began by saying that only a few Swiss cantons used single tax, while the whole of the rest of the world used multiple taxes. He then claimed to quote from W. H.

94. See Schiffrin and Scalapino, 338.
95. Zhu, "Tudi Guoyou yu Zaizheng," 2 pts., *Min Bao,* XV, I, and XVI, II, 67 (referred to hereafter as "Tudi Guoyou").

Mallock, a prolific and violently antisocialist and land nationalist writer.[96]

According to Liang, Mallock has said that the total land rent in Great Britain was £49,000,000, while government expenditure was £68,000,000. Thus, even if all land rent were to be confiscated, it would clearly be insufficient to meet the government's needs. Liang conceded that Britain had less land than China, but he said rent was much higher in a developed country like England, so that the amount of rent would be more or less the same in both countries. What was more, the Chinese government would require a much larger expenditure, because the expense of administration varied in proportion to the size of the country. Thus it would be quite impossible for a Chinese government to rely completely on a single tax on land.[97]

Zhu Zhi-xin, using his pen-name of Xian-jie, wrote the Alliance's reply to the section of Liang's attacks dealing with finance. His article, "Land Nationalization and Finance," appeared in two parts, in July and September 1907.

The beginning of the first part was concerned with refuting Liang. According to Zhu, Mallock had been unfair to take the agricultural land rent of Britain as an example; not only was Britain extremely small, but it also had a very small proportion of arable land. What was more, Mallock had taken his figures from the late 1880s, a time when rent in Britain had been very low; it had been higher before that, and it was now rising again. Mallock had also failed to include rent from houses; this, according to Zhu's figures, was £149,000,000. Two-thirds of this was ground rent, which meant that one could add approximately £100,000,000 to the total. This was very important, as Zhu said: "The main aim of our policy is that built-up land should be taxed."[98]

Mallock had also not included the amount taken in local taxes, or the rates for local government, most of which were paid out of rent. Zhu attacked Liang's own statement that although China's land

96. For William Mallock, who was also a good poet, see his *Memoirs of Life and Literature* (London, 1920). I am indebted to Dr. Joseph Needham for this identification.

97. Liang, "Zaibo Moubao zhi Tudi Guoyou Lun" (referred to hereafter as "Bo Tudi Guoyou"), 3 pts., XMCB, 90, 91, and 92, I, 4–5.

98. Zhu, "Tudi Guoyou," I, 72–75.

area was eleven times that of Britain, British rents were ten times those of China. According to Zhu, rents were, if anything, higher in China. Zhu then attacked Liang for having said that government expenditure was proportionate to land area. He pointed out that 40 per cent of the British budget went for military purposes to defend her colonies. Thus government expenditure was not in proportion to land area. Zhu summed up by saying: "Thus with Mr. Mallock's theories one can oppose the theory of single tax on arable land in England, but one cannot oppose single tax on land in England. Still less can one oppose the theory of single tax on land." [99]

Liang then attacked Hu Han-min and his source of information, Sir Robert Hart. Hu had referred to Hart's having said that without increasing taxes the Chinese government could, by eliminating graft and using efficient methods, raise its revenue from 40,000,000 *taels* to 400,000,000. Liang said that Hart had been arbitrary when he had said that revenue could be increased tenfold. In any case, Hart had not used the figure 40,000,000 but one nearer 30,000,000. This amount could, with other taxes, be raised to 60,000,000 which with improvements might be doubled to 120,000,000. This was still very far from the revolutionaries' total of 400,000,000. Sun had said that land tax was one-twentieth of the product. Liang disagreed; according to him, land tax in Kwangtung was one-tenth, and with extortions this could rise to a fifth, and the rate was probably higher in other provinces. Thus, if the total tax was 30,000,000 *taels,* the total rent would be 300,000,000; or, if one added the rent coming outside the eighteen provinces of China proper, the total might possibly reach 600,000,000. How could they possibly talk about 8,000,000,-000 *taels?* [100]

In his reply to this argument, Zhu told a direct lie: "We first talked about land tax being 40,000,000, then we quoted Hart's words. It was absolutely clear that they had no connection." [101] Zhu more or less admitted that Hart had said that *tianfu,* the tax on arable land, was only 30,000,000 *taels.* But it was not *dishui,* land tax. *Dishui* included several other taxes, among them taxes on forests, mines, and built-up areas. Hart could not have studied these other taxes. Zhu then produced a mass of figures, to show that if you included

99. Zhu, "Tudi Guoyou," I, 78–79.
100. Liang, "Bo Tudi Guoyou," I, 4–5.   101. Zhu, "Tudi Guoyou," I, 83.

the sums from all the taxes which could come under the heading of land tax, the total would be just under 60,000,000 *taels.* Zhu listed four ways in which the bureaucracy cheated the Chinese government and people: (1) excessive levying of taxes; (2) officials gaining from land which had been newly cleared and was not on the tax register; (3) officials levying taxes which the government had remitted because of natural disasters; (4) extortionate loans levied by the officials. If these abuses were "corrected," that is, if the money taken by the officials were handed over to the government, a further 210,000,000 *taels* would be added making a total of 270,000,000. Zhu then added house tax, which at present was 60,000,000 or 70,-000,000, but which, even before China was developed, could be doubled to 120,000,000 if abuses were done away with. Thus Zhu had forced the grand total up to 390,000,000, almost the amount set. This, as he said, "was not far below 400,000,000 and was really close to Hart's figure. . . . So Liang's figure of 60 or 70 or 120 million has absolutely no foundation." [102]

According to Zhu, not only had Liang made a mistake in his first figure of 30,000,000 for land tax, but he had also gone wrong in his estimate that the ratio of rent to tax was ten to one. Liang in his calculations had taken the mean instead of the average: cases where the rate of taxation was high were very rare, but cases where the rate was low were very common. According to Zhu, the average *mou* of arable land in Kwangtung had a rent of 2.5 *taels,* while it was taxed at 0.159 of a *tael,* a ratio of about 16 to 1. But in forest and lake areas the tax was only a hundredth of the rent, and house tax was only a twentieth. Thus, over all, the ratio was 17 or 18 to 1. Although this was not 20 to 1, which according to Zhu had been only a rough estimate, it was much larger than the ratio of 10 to 1 claimed by Liang. Therefore, although the total rent was not the 8,-000,000,000 originally claimed, it was not far off. Zhu concluded the first part of his article, by saying, "this proves our theories were not mistaken." [103]

Liang attacked the unreliability of single tax on land as a source of government revenue. Every type of single tax fluctuated, but a single tax on land was more liable to fluctuation than any of the others because of the differences between harvests. Under the

102. Zhu, "Tudi Guoyou," I, 93–94.   103. Zhu, "Tudi Guoyou," I, 99.

system proposed by the revolutionaries, the fluctuation would be still greater, because it would depend entirely on the varying amounts people were prepared to pay to rent land. How could a system like this provide the state with regular funds, let alone the special funds necessary for emergencies like war?

Liang then supplied an answer he thought the revolutionaries might give. They would say that, as well as being the great landlord, the state could also be a great capitalist, and it could use the profits of its industries to supplement the amount gained from land tax. Liang said, as he had stated before, that he was in favor of some state control of industry. However, he believed that one had to be very careful about it: "If one practices it in country A, there will be more good than bad; if one practices it in country B, there will be more bad than good." [104] Liang then quoted from Wagner, whom he called "the leader of state socialists." Wagner had said that the state should rely on tax and use the income from state enterprises only as a supplement, and in general the state should not interfere in the private sphere for economic, political, and financial reasons. According to Liang, Wagner was in favor of long-term planning in the nationalization of industries. This was what the Japanese government had done with the railways. It had first entrusted them to private ownership, and had only taken them over after three conditions had been fulfilled: first, that there were enough technically trained men to take over; second, that national education and morality were sufficiently advanced to avoid corruption; and third, that laws were perfected, and the officials and people were used to them, so that malpractices could be regulated:

As for what that paper proposes, they [say] that when the new government is first set up, it should immediately buy the land, and at the same time the government should become a great capitalist, so that it could monopolize all big productive enterprises. I think that this method cannot be successful. [105]

Liang also objected because, if the state became a large capitalist, the large capitalists who were essential to China's survival would not appear.

Liang said that it was quite clear that the revolutionaries would

104. Liang, "Bo Tudi Guoyou," I, 13–15.
105. Liang, "Bo Tudi Guoyou," I, 16.

have to compensate the landowners for the land taken from them. For the time being, Liang accepted his opponents' figure of 8,000,-000,000 *taels,* for the total of rent, in order to calculate the total value of land in China. He also accepted their statement that land rent was six per cent of value; from this he calculated a total of 130,-000,000,000 dollars.[106]

Liang continued by saying that unless the revolutionaries had the secret of alchemy, it would be impossible for them to raise such a huge amount of compensation. The revolutionaries had said that they would pay with interest-bearing government bonds which would later be bought back, in the same way that the Japanese government had managed to nationalize the railways. But Liang asked how could a newly set-up government take on a national debt ten times as large as that of France, a rich country with a well-established government? If the revolutionaries accepted Liang's own estimate, the value of land would be only 10,000,000,000 dollars. In this case, the revolutionary government would have a slightly smaller national debt than France, but a larger one than any of the other great powers. Whatever the size of the debt, it would be necessary to pay five per cent interest, while revenue from rent would only be six per cent. Thus the state's total income would have to come from only one-sixth of rent.

Liang then attacked the theory that all land prices would rise enormously. He believed that only a minute area of land would rapidly increase in value. Although some land prices would fall, he thought that most would rise, but only slowly. He estimated that they would double in twenty years, but even for this rate of growth government help would be needed to increase the people's prosperity. Of course, if the revolutionaries practiced land nationalization,

106. Liang, "Bo Tudi Guoyou," I, 16. Liang slipped casually from *taels* to dollars, presumably because it was useful in comparison with European figures given in dollars. The customs *tael* was worth 3s 3d (sterling) according to Wright in *Hart and the Chinese Customs,* 892. The American dollar was 5s. The situation is made more complicated by the fact that local dollars were often worth less than the *tael.* The ease with which Liang slipped from currency to currency gives an air of unreality to the controversy.

I have seen no figures for the ratio of rent to value in Kwangtung. However, in 1905 rent was approximately 4.5% of value in Nandong in Kiangsu. See the table given in "Lun Qingmo Geming Dang ren Guanyu Tudi Wenti Sixiang," by Xia Dong-yuan in *Xinhai Geming Wushi Zhounian Lunwenji,* I, 304.

prosperity would decrease, and land prices would fall. If this happened, the regime would not be able to pay the interest on the national debt, its credit would collapse, and the country would be destroyed.

For the sake of argument, Liang conceded that land value might double in ten years; even so, what would remain after interest had been paid would not be able to support a stable economy. The revolutionaries, Liang said, claimed that the new government would be able to raise money from abroad. This was ridiculous; with their sort of policy, their credit would be extremely bad. They would not be able to attract capital from abroad. This difficulty would be compounded because the government would have to use all its resources to pay the interest, and therefore would not be able to begin repayment.[107]

Liang then returned to his earlier argument that, because of her size and population, China needed a larger budget than any of the Western powers and one at least the size of Russia's. This meant a total of more than 2,000,000,000; the government would not be able to raise even 70,000,000 (currency unspecified),[108] which was only about one-thirtieth of what was needed.

Once again, Liang tried to pin his opponents down about their exact policy. He pointed out a contradiction in Hu Han-min's article. At one point, Hu had said that "landlords will receive their original rent, but the increase will go to the state." At another, he had talked about the state distributing land to the peasants who could cultivate it. If the revolutionaries meant to leave rights of ownership with the landlords after their so-called legal fixing of prices, they would avoid creating a monstrous national debt. On the other hand, as the government would have no other taxes, it would not have enough revenue. Liang responded: "Now the increase in land prices will not be fast, as I have said before. Thus the government will have a period of several years without revenue; it would be a miracle if it got a few million. The first year the government practiced this system, it could not have a single cash."[109] Because the

107. Liang, "Bo Tudi Guoyou," I, 23.
108. Liang, "Bo Tudi Guoyou," I, 24. It is impossible to see how Liang arrived at this figure; he had conceded that annual rent could be 600,000,000. If interest were 5% of land value, this would still leave 100,000,000.
109. Liang, "Bo Tudi Guoyou," 25.

rents of that year would be the basis, there could be no increment to go to the government. Liang also suggested that under this system tax evasion would be very easy, because landlords and tenants could split the increases in real rent between them. According to Liang, the revolutionaries' whole scheme was disastrous.

This onslaught forced Zhu to make the clearest and most concrete description of the Alliance's social policies ever made.[110] The argument of the second part of Zhu's article began with an answer to what Zhu described as Liang's mistaken assumption that the revolutionaries would pay for land nationalization with a public debt. Zhu started with a rather curious admission: "In our previous statements about land nationalization, we have never discussed what methods we will use for the nationalization." He went on:

It is true that in the nationalization of other things the method of buying has often been used, but the value of land is too great, and we cannot consider the method of buying it at once as satisfactory. This fact could be understood by anyone who thought about it a little.[111]

He restated the old argument about the increase of land prices, and continued:

It would better to take the future increase to compensate the losses of the present landholders and for the additional profit from this land to go to the state, than to buy it all at once recklessly. Therefore two complementary methods appear: (1) to give state bonds which will later be bought back; (2) to fix prices with all the increase going to the state, later buying [the land] at the original price. Both of these methods can be practiced together without any contradiction, but the second is more convenient. Why is this? At present, very little land belongs to large landlords. During the next few decades, there must be exchange. If [land] prices have been fixed, there will be still more vigorous exchange. This exchange must be carried out officially without any hidden trickery. In exchange after prices have been fixed, the fixed price will go to the seller, and the increase to the state. In this way, without spending a single cash, the government could receive the profit from the increase; this profit could be used to buy [land].

Zhu gave the following reason for his belief that exchange in land would increase after prices had been fixed:

110. This point is brought out by Hatano Yoshihiro in "Shoki ni Okeru Son Bun no 'Keikei Chigen ni tsuite,'" *Shakai Keizai Shigaku,* XXI, 5.6.7.
111. Zhu, "Tudi Guoyou," II, 36.

Landlords are reluctant to sell their land, firstly because they fear loss, and secondly because they hope for profit. When land prices are fixed, they will not be afraid that they will not be able to receive the original price, nor will they be able to hope for extraordinary profits. If there were somebody who wanted to buy, although the might of the state could be used to compel him, the original owner, (to sell), if he did not want to sell, he would be allowed to pay in the additional price. . . . The landlords will not oppose this method, not because they will be coerced, but because it will be in their interest.[112]

Even if Liang had been correct, and the revolutionaries were planning to have a national debt of 130,000,000,000 *taels,* Zhu thought it would not have been at all dangerous. According to him, public debts were only dangerous if they were used for nonproductive purposes, such as wars, but debts incurred to increase production would help, not harm, the people. According to Zhu, Liang's statement that it would be impossible to raise money from abroad, because the government would not be able to make repayment in a short time, was quite wrong. He said that it was generally best to have long-term loans with distant or unfixed repayment dates. If the French government planned to repay its national debt over seventy years, the Chinese government could certainly repay a larger debt over a hundred years, which meant that repayment could be made at a rate of only one per cent per annum. The possession of the land itself would ensure the government's credit.

Zhu said that Liang's argument, that the interest on and the repayment of the loan would harm the state's finances, was wrong. The interest would be paid from the land and would not affect finance.[113] The basis for Zhu's statement appeared later in the article, when he made another important clarification of the party's policies. According to him, Liang was very mistaken when he thought that the revolutionaries advocated the cessation of all other taxes immediately after land nationalization began.

Mr. Sun's words about private individuals never needing to pay tax, were only concerned with the period after nationalization is completed. He did not say that immediately after a policy of nationalization had been decided upon, all other taxes would be abolished.[114]

112. Zhu, "Tudi Guoyou," II, 35–36.
113. Zhu, "Tudi Guoyou," II, 38–39.   114. Zhu, "Tudi Guoyou," II, 42.

When the party had said that land prices would double in ten years, this did not mean that land nationalization would be completed in that period. Most previous examples of nationalization in other countries had taken a long time; he cited the cases of the French and the Japanese railway systems. Land nationalization was much more difficult, and would take even longer. During this long process, taxes would remain the same:

The wherewithal for land nationalization will come from the profits produced by nature's bounty. When nationalization is completed, taxation will be reduced and abolished, and the burden on the people will be lightened. However, before it is completed, on the one hand nationalization will go forward and on the other there will still be the old taxes. This is not [to say] that the burden on the people will increase.[115]

Zhu said that after prices had been fixed, the new government would compensate the very few landowners whose land had fallen in price. He then repeated Hu's earlier statement that after land prices had been fixed, all the rights to land would remain with the landowner, except for the right of concession. He qualified this by saying: "From a legal point of view, the right of possession will belong to the state, and the people will only have the other rights. But at this time the government will not have enough for a suitable price, so it will not be able to practice its right of possession."[116] This, Zhu said, explained why the party had said: "Fix [land] prices and transfer it to the state"—the statement which Liang and many others found so difficult to understand.

Zhu then turned to the attack and again launched into Liang's theory that the expenditure of a nation depended directly on its size and population.[117] If China had more than ten times the area of Britain and had more than ten times the population, according to Liang her expenditure ought to be more or less ten times that of Britain. He had reckoned the total to be something in the order of 2,-000,000,000 dollars. Zhu thought that this was far beyond the reach of China: "Land nationalization, which we propose, would never cause any anxiety that the Chinese government might become bankrupt. But this policy of ten times the expense for the Chinese

115. Zhu, "Tudi Guoyou," II, 43–44.   116. Zhu, "Tudi Guoyou," II, 45.
117. Both Liang and Zhu said that this theory came from the Japanese professor Kobayashi Ushisaburō. See Zhu, "Tudi Guoyou," II, 49.

government would really force the Chinese government to have no other course but bankruptcy." [118]

According to Zhu, Liang's theory that costs of administration went up in a linear progression, with area and population, was completely wrong; the relationship was much more complicated.[119] On the other hand, Zhu admitted that Liang's statement that China should have more or less the same annual expenditure as Russia, which had a larger area but smaller population, contained some sense. Liang, however, had made a mistake in basing his estimate of Russia's expenditure on the abnormal years of the Russo-Japanese War. Zhu made various calculations and came out with the figure of 860,000,-000 *taels* for Russia's normal expenditure in peace time. He then calculated the amount of revenue received by the central and provincial governments of China, and arrived at a total of 260,000,-000 to 270,000,000 *taels*.[120] This, he said, was already three-tenths of the Russian total. However, as Zhu had said before, the Chinese people paid in several times the amount received by the government. If one reckoned that the ratio was three to one (Zhu had earlier estimated a ratio of seven to one), China would have almost the same amount as Russia and this would be enough for her normal needs.

Zhu then challenged Liang to show how he would raise the 2,000,-000,000 dollars he thought necessary. The amount the revolutionaries proposed was 270,000,000 *taels* which came to less than 400,000,000 dollars. How did Liang intend to increase taxation fivefold? The people, who were already in such misery, would not be able to bear it. Even the Manchus would not dare such a thing. Liang's policy was to protect native capitalists and oppose foreign capital. Because there would be no foreigners and there would not be enough native capitalists to employ the workers, wages would fall; then on top of this there would be these heavy taxes; and as a result the situation would be quite unbearable.

The last section of the article was devoted to showing how such revenue could be raised by single tax after China had become developed. Zhu did this by drawing deductions from the present

118. Zhu, "Tudi Guoyou," II, 51.
119. Zhu used his mathematical knowledge to draw up an impressive formula expressing the ratio between the two.
120. Zhu, "Tudi Guoyou," II, 55.

positions of various foreign countries. He divided the sources of revenue under six headings:

A. *Revenue from agricultural land.* This would not be the total amount of revenue, but it would be an important element of it. According to Zhu, the value of food produced in the United States was enormous, even though food prices there were very low. However, in Japan during her period of development the price of rice had doubled, and this would probably happen in China. Thus there would be a great amount of revenue from this source.[121]

B. *Revenue from built-up land.* In the United States a third of the population lived in towns of over 10,000 people. In these towns each person spent an average of $60.00 in rent every year. Half of this was ground rent and could go to the state. If a third of the Chinese population lived in towns, the total rent would be enormous. On top of this, a great deal of rent would be paid for factories and other industrial enterprises, roughly one-tenth of which was ground rent. In the future, China would have five times the amount America had at the time.

Zhu then speculated as to how long it would take China to reach America's level of development. If America had taken one hundred years, China, by learning from her successes and avoiding her mistakes, should be able to do it in about thirty years. After about ten years, China should have reached the standards of Japan and Hongkong. Zhu said that this level would provide the state with a considerable sum even before China became fully developed.[122]

C. *Revenue from mountains and forests.* According to Zhu, China was the richest country in the world in minerals. Already in China mineral rights belonged to the state, the landlords usually receiving just over twenty per cent of the value. In the United States hundreds of millions of dollars' worth of minerals were produced every year. China, with a larger area and more mines, would be able to produce more.

He saw two types of forestry, protective and productive. Protective forestry, which is to help the climate, prevent erosion, and so on, had to be managed by the government, while productive forestry was too long-term for private management, and should also be run

121. Zhu, "Tudi Guoyou," II, 59–61.   122. Zhu, "Tudi Guoyou," II, 61/66.

by the state. That was why the Japanese government owned 68 per cent of all forests, from which it gained an increasingly large amount of revenue. China, with twenty-six times the land area, should do much better.[123]

D. *Revenue from lakes, rivers, and the sea coast.* In China, salt and fish traditionally belonged to the state. Although students of finance were generally against a salt tax, it would be quite fair to tax the land on which salt was made. As well as this, harbors and canals could raise money for the state.[124]

E. *Revenue from hydroelectric power.* There were large profits to be made from this new discovery, and China had many suitable places for building barrages cheaply. The government could make 66 per cent profit from this.

F. *Revenue from railways.* In the United States great profits were made from railways, but the United States with two sea coasts did not need as many railways as China. Therefore, the Chinese government, with more railways, would make twice the profit.

Zhu summed up by saying that, not counting salt and fish, these six sources would raise, 7,100,000,000 dollars, and that after the national debt was liquidated this would rise to 10,000,000,000. He admitted that this would take place only after thirty or forty years. But, he said, productive organs like mines and railways would be able to provide the government with revenue long before this.[125] This article was described as incomplete, but no further instalment appeared.

Zhu's writing in this piece was very much more pragmatic and specific than Sun's could ever be. This was largely because of the circumstances under which the article was written; Sun would hardly have taken on the task of rebutting Liang's detailed attacks. Sun seems to have felt that it was his task to erect the general structure; it was for others to fill in the gaps. Despite some differences between Zhu's article and Sun's general ideas, Zhu's ideas here seem to have been closer to Sun's than they had been in his articles the year before. In those, Marx was much more in evidence than Sun or Henry George; in the later article the position seems to have been reversed. This must be largely because the problems faced in the two

123. Zhu, "Tudi Guoyou," II, 66–68.
124. Zhu, "Tudi Guoyou," II, 69.   125. Zhu, "Tudi Guoyou," II 69–71.

groups of articles were different. The former articles dealt with revolution as a whole, and therefore emphasized the international socialist movement, while the latter were concerned with China, and had to stress Sun Yat-sen and the Alliance's policies. However, whether or not Zhu had actually attacked Marx, there may also be in this change of emphasis a trace of the swing away from Western socialism and Marxism which seems to have taken place among the Chinese students at the end of 1906 and in early 1907. See below.

The article entitled "Land Nationalization and Finance" was put forward as the official policy of the Revolutionary Alliance. But it is unlike Hu Han-min's article in that there is no proof that it was seen or approved by Sun himself. In fact, it is very unlikely that Sun did see it, as he spent the months during which the two parts of the article were written, April to August 1907, in northern Indo-China, where he was very busy organizing risings in Yunan and Kwangtung. Zhu himself seems to have left Tokyo in the spring and must have written the article in Hongkong or Canton, where he was involved in feverish revolutionary activity.[126]

For all its detail, the policy in Zhu's article does not seem to have contradicted any statement made by Sun at this time or at any time until 1913. This, and the fact that at this time Zhu was in close contact with Hu Han-min, makes it very likely that the views expressed in his article were those of Sun or of his immediate entourage.[127]

This itself raises an interesting point. It seems odd that an article, advocating Sun's most controversial principle, by Zhu, the nephew of Wang Jing-wei and a close supporter of Sun, should have been published in *The People's Journal* at this time. The summer of 1907 was a time at which Zhang Bing-lin, the *Journal's* editor, and most of the other revolutionaries in Tokyo were in the midst of a bitter quarrel with Sun.[128] Its publication indicates that Zhang's need for well-written articles and his interest in social questions and his hatred of Liang Qi-chao were able to over-ride what was undoubtedly a major rift between the two revolutionary factions.

Liang continued the first section of "Another Attack" by com-

126. See Hu, "Hu Han-min Zizhuan," 393; and Zhu, "Zhu Zhi-xin Geming Shiji Shulue," 422.
127. Feng, *Kaiguo shi,* II, 95–96.
128. Chun-tu Hsueh, *Huang Hsing,* 54; and Feng, *Kaiguo shi,* I, 202.

paring the theories of land nationalization and single tax with the French Physiocrats' theory of *l'impôt unique*. An interesting aspect of Sun Yat-sen and the Alliance's choice of the theories of Dove and Henry George on the single tax on land is the similarity between the latter's theories and those of the French Physiocrats, which were themselves at least partly derived from China.

There is no doubt at all about this connection. As De Tocqueville said, "our economists [the Physiocrats] turned their eyes to the Far East, and it is no exaggeration to say that not one of them fails in some part of his writings to voice an immense enthusiasm for China and all things Chinese."[129]

There is also no doubt that part of the Physiocrats' belief that agriculture was the only fundamentally productive element in society came from the traditional Chinese belief in the primacy of agriculture, which Quesnay and the others discovered through the translations of the Jesuits.[130] It was upon this belief that the Physiocrats based their plans for *l'impôt unique,* a system under which only agriculture should be taxed and the agriculturalists would pass on the burden to other sections of society by revising prices.[131]

Henry George, however, developed his theories independently, and was not aware of the ideas of the Physiocrats until his own theories were completely formed.[132] Sun Yat-sen did not emphasize the Physiocrat tradition when he adopted the single tax theory and did not seem to be aware of the Physiocrats' borrowings from China. Liang's attack, and the reply to it, appear to have been the first mention of Physiocrats.

Liang said that the two essentials of any system of taxation were that it should be equitable and extend to all. He thought the revolutionaries' single tax on land was neither. Liang then quoted an abridged version of Voltaire's *L'homme aux quarante écus.* This story was in fact an attack on several contemporary abuses and theories, but its main theme was the contrast between a poor land-

---

129. Alex de Tocqueville, *The Old Regime and the French Revolution,* trans. Stuart Gilbert (New York, 1955, 163.

130. G. F. Hudson, *Europe and China: A Survey of their Relation from the Earliest Times to 1800* (London, (1931), 312–326.

131. H. Higgs, *The Physiocrats,* 43.

132. Henry George, Jr., *Life of Henry George* (New York, 1911), 229.

owner who had to pay heavy taxes, and a rich speculator who had made a fortune but was not liable to any tax because he owned no land.[133] Liang said that the revolutionaries' policy of a single tax on land was hardly different from that of the Physiocrats. He agreed with the revolutionaries that everybody lived off the land directly or indirectly, but those who lived off it indirectly often received more.

If the revolutionaries wanted to take all the rent of 8,000,000,000 *taels,* the peasants would have to pay two hundred times the 40,-000,000 *taels* they were paying at present. This would mean that they would have to pay eighty or ninety per cent of their produce. If the revolutionaries did not set a figure, but charged the peasants rent of at least twenty per cent, while doctors, lawyers, and merchants, who could make hundreds of thousands, would pay next to nothing, this was patently unfair. Liang himself thought that income tax was the most equitable, sales tax the most far-reaching, and business tax the easiest form of taxation to pass on. On the whole, he thought that they should all be practiced together.[134]

Liang then quoted a passage from Hu Han-min's article, which had said that everyone depends on the products of the land, therefore land tax could be passed on to others, who would thus pay tax indirectly. Liang said that this argument was exactly like that of the Physiocrats. Besides, if the peasants raised the prices of agricultural goods, cheaper foreign goods would flood in, and this would mean ruin. If, instead, they had to keep prices down, no one would want to rent land from the government and finance would collapse. It would be suicide either way.

Liang then attacked Hu's statement that smaller forms were more efficient than larger ones. Gustav Schmoller, he said, had often argued against this.[135] He had read that American agriculture was more efficient than European. As for the revolutionaries' theory that their type of taxation would encourage the development of agriculture, Liang thought it quite ridiculous: "There has never been a stranger theory in the world, than that heavy taxation can increase the rate of economic progress." [136]

133. Liang, "Bo Tudi Guoyou," 27–28.
134. Liang, "Bo Tudi Guoyou," 28–30.
135. Liang, "Bo Tudi Guoyou," II, 34.
136. Liang, "Bo Tudi Guoyou," I, 31.

Liang ended this section of his article with a statement that revenue was the main, but not the only, purpose of taxation. All countries except England imposed tariffs to protect home industry, and taxes were often put on luxuries and on poisons like opium and morphine to discourage their use. All of these useful aspects of taxation would be impossible if there were only a single tax on land.[137]

The reply to these arguments came in an article entitled "Denunciation of the Errors of *The Renovation of the People*'s Attack on Land Nationalization." It was written by someone with the pen-name of Tai Qiu, and appeared in *The People's Journal* in October 1907. Tai Qiu in his introduction promised to write three chapters to refute Liang's points one by one, but only the first of these appeared. It was called "The Differences between Our Policy of Land Nationalization and the Theory of Single Tax on Land."[138] He started by putting the arguments for and against taxation in general, coming out with the conclusion that although it was believed necessary for the survival of the state, light taxes were better than heavy taxes, and no taxes better than light taxes. That is why the Alliance's policy of land nationalization was to have no taxes. Then there was the problem of whether it was better to have a single tax on land or multiple taxation. To deal with this, Tai Qiu thought it was necessary to give a short history of the development of the single tax theory.

In this he quoted a series of passages, mainly from un-named sources, for and against the theories of the Physiocrats and Ricardo. At the end of these, Tai Qiu conceded that it would be unfair to tax only the landowners, especially as they would not be able to pass on any of the burden to the consumer because of the competition from imported goods. However, this plan was, he said, not the same as the nationalization of land.

After land nationalization all taxation will not come from land tax; it will come from rent. When the state is the landlord, its rent will make good the total of the nation's taxes and there will be no taxes within the state. . . . Thus foreign imports will not be able to compete.[139]

137. Liang, "Bo Tudi Guoyou," 32.
138. Tai Qiu, "Chi Xinmin Congbao Tudi Guoyou zhi Min," *Min Bao*, XVII, 61.
139. Tai Qiu, 72-72.

According to Tai Qiu this meant that Liang's attempt to attack the Revolutionary Alliance by attacking the Physiocrats was completely unjustified. It also meant that his charge that their policy was inequitable, and his charge that it did not reach everyone, both fell.

Tai Qiu gave an incredibly complicated example of the results of various forms of taxation by taking Liang's hypothetical income figures through all sorts of vicissitudes from multiple tax to single tax, from protection to free trade, and with Liang changing his invested capital from industry (the office of *The Renovation of the People*) to agriculture and back again. Predictably, the final result was that after land nationalization Liang's income figures showed up better than ever before.[140]

Tai Qiu then accused Liang of not understanding that taxation was only one form of revenue and that there were many others. The Japanese economist Kobayashi Ushisaburō was quoted, this time to show the many different possible sources of government revenue, including revenue from commissions, officially owned land, officially owned industries, production monopolies, sales monopolies, fines, confiscations, forced loans, and public debt.[141]

As if choosing a country at random, Tai Qiu showed that only one-tenth of Prussia's revenue in 1898 came from taxation, the rest coming from official property and nationalized industries.[142] He then discussed the proportion of taxation coming from land tax in various countries. In Japan, land tax was over one-third of the total, but in other countries such as Germany and America there was no land tax at all. Tai Qiu reiterated all the benefits that would come from the Alliance policies. He then drew up a list of the differences between their policies and those of the Physiocrats.

I. They believed that all tax should come from land tax.
   We believe that rent should replace all taxes.
II. They used single tax on land, to replace all other taxes without compensation.
   We practice land nationalization, by fixing prices and buying the land; thus there is compensation.
III. They practice single tax on land by putting all the burden on the landlords.

140. Tai Qiu, 76–77.   141. Tai Qiu, 79–80.
142. The figure was quite correct, but Prussia was very exceptional in this respect.

When we practice land nationalization, we not only spare the non-landlords but the landlords as well.[143]

At the end of this article Tai Qiu stated that there was no just method of taxation. It could either be progressive or at a fixed percentage. The latter was fair, superficially, but in fact it was unfair, because under it the rich were taxed lightly and the poor were taxed heavily. Liang had no way to avoid this injustice, but the Alliance had.[144]

The second section of Liang's article, "Another Attack," entitled "To Correct the Mistakes of the Theory of Land Nationalization," assailed the most fundamental beliefs of the land nationalizers. He quoted a short passage from Henry George, in which he had talked about land being made by the Creator and not by man, and of the *right* of society as a whole to enjoy its benefits. Liang said that this argument was based on the concept of *ziran fa* (natural law):

So-called natural law is only a product of history. Thinkers in the eighteenth century widely proclaimed its existence, but in recent years, when research in social history has flourished, the existence of natural law has not been admitted for a long time. So-called laws and justice are only the direct results of social changes. It is not, as the believers in natural law say, that laws and justice are entities that never change.[145]

According to Liang, private property was another such product of history which had existed at least in the higher stages of civilization.

Liang admitted as almost completely true the argument that as the improvement of land was brought about by society and not by the individual, society as a whole should enjoy its benefits. But, he said, this was also true of such things as wages. One could not forbid the private ownership of land and allow it in other things.

Liang said that he believed private property was the fount of all civilization, and that the greatest economic motive was self-interest. In a note Liang accepted Wagner's division of motives into five categories, the first four of which were types of self-interest and only the fifth was altruism. He agreed with Wagner when the later said that the socialist ideal could only be achieved when the fifth motive

143. Tai Qiu, 83.   144. Tai Qiu, 85.
145. Liang, "Bo Tudi Guoyou," II, 2. Liang was right to point out this eighteenth-century static quality in George's theories, a feature that marked him off clearly from Marx and other historically relativist socialists.

had overcome the others, and that socialism could not be put into practice until human nature had changed, which would not be for a long time.[146]

Liang answered another of the revolutionaries' arguments: that because land was a natural monopoly, landlords simply made profits, while other people had to compete to make money. Liang denied this. He said that most land was owned by the tillers, and the concentration of land was not nearly so bad as the concentration of capital. There was plenty of land to be competed for; therefore land could not be called a natural monopoly.[147]

He then divided land into two categories, urban and rural. In every country urban land was only about a thousandth of the total. Therefore, it would be sensible to consider the rural land more important. This the revolutionaries did not do, and their statements were only applicable to urban land; this was one of their mistakes.

Liang himself discussed rural land first. He thought that it could not be a natural monopoly. His reason was that it did not fit any of the types of natural monopoly set up by Ely. According to Liang, Ely had three types. His first was, "They (natural monopolies) occupy peculiarly favored spots or lines of land." Liang said that some areas of land fitted this, but one could not put all agricultural land in this class. Another piece of evidence, to Liang's mind, was that the owner of rich land could only drive out the owner of poor land by damaging his own profit. Ely's second condition was, "When this article or convenience can in general be largely if not indefinitely increased without proportionate increase in plant or capital." This, Liang admitted, was very true of urban, but not of rural land, where in fact the reverse was true. *The People's Journal* itself had talked about the law of diminishing returns in agriculture. According to Liang, increases in the prices of agricultural goods came from increased costs of production, so that the profits of the landlords did not rise. Ely's third type was "When certainty and harmonious

146. Liang, "Bo Tudi Guoyou," II, 4.

147. A survey made in the eighteen provinces of China proper five years later gives an approximate idea of the actual situation. According to this, in 1912 49% of peasants owned their own land, 23% were half owners and half tenants, and 28% were tenants. See *Zhongguo Jindai Jingji shi Ziliao Xuanji,* compiled by Yan Zhongping and others (Peking, 1957), 276, quoted by Xia Dong-yuan in "Lun Qingmo Geming Dang ren Guanyu Tudi Wenti Sixiang," 307.

arrangement, which can only be maintained by unity, are paramount considerations." Liang said that this again was true of urban but not of rural land. Why should the tiny fraction of urban land affect the treatment of all the rural land? Liang thought it was very wrong.[148]

Liang then repeated his earlier arguments that the concentration of land occurred before, not after, the industrial revolution, and that, as the situation was favorable in China, there was no need to fear the concentration of land after industrial development there.

In China, according to Liang, most land was owned by smallholders, and even the landless peasants had the chance to save money and buy land. Why, in that case, should the state rob the peasants of the fruits of their labor, or the labor of their ancestors? Liang noted that working for one's descendants was a large economic incentive. He also thought that land nationalization would have a bad political effect, because it would destroy the class of small landholders who were, he thought, the "foundation stone of the nation."[149]

Liang supplied a possible answer which his opponents might give. They could say that there would be compensation for the land; it would be the same as the Japanese government's paying five per cent bonds for the railways. "If this was not robbery, how could our action be?" Liang's reply to this was that railways, unlike land, are a natural monopoly. With their five per cent bonds, the ex-shareholders were receiving a reasonable profit, particularly as the compensation had been well over the value of the shares. Liang added in a note that if the government paid only the present value it would be robbing the people of their future profit. The revolutionaries had said that they might pay up to double the price. But in this case the national debt would be over 260,000,000,000, so that if the government took all the rent it would not have enough revenue to pay the five per cent interest. Even if rent doubled, the

148. Liang may have been cheating in this list of the types of natural monopoly. Ely in his *Introduction to the Study of Political Economy* (New York, 1889) listed two more "when what they supply is necessary, and when the article or convenience they supply is used at the place, and in connection with the plant or machinery by which it is supplied." The first of these could clearly be applied to rural land and would have weakened Liang's case considerably; see Ely, 251.

149. Liang, "Bo Tudi Guoyou," II, 16.

government would be left with only one-sixth of it. The system could not work unless rent went up three- or fourfold, which was extremely unlikely. Otherwise the government's credit would fail, and the people would be left with worthless scraps of paper in exchange for their land.[150]

Liang had already made the division between rural and urban land. He now made one between unoccupied and occupied land. He thought that unoccupied land should be nationalized, and urban land should be nationalized or municipalized, but that the rest of the land should remain in private hands and be protected as such. The reason why he thought the government should nationalize unoccupied land was that, in the north and west of China, population was very sparse, and he said the nomads there had very little concept of property. Thus the government should settle people (that is, the Han Chinese) there. However, as Liang now believed that "the profits from state-run enterprises are often inferior to private ones . . . particularly in agriculture,"[151] he thought that when the government had settled the land, it should sell it all except for a few model farms and the remaining forests.

On the whole, Liang said, he preferred municipalization to nationalization of urban land, but one or the other should take place, because urban land, unlike rural land, was a natural monopoly. However, later in the article, after more attacks on the financial impossibility of the revolutionaries' schemes, Liang quoted with approval some extreme attacks on public and particularly municipal ownership. He began with some high praise for the entrepreneur, who despite his selfishness helped the country by moving capital to the right place and by taking risks while others were secure. Liang then asked,

Which is better for a business, a private individual or a public group? . . . If everyone worked for the common good without a trace of self-interest, all the organs of production and distribution should go to the center . . . but the level of mankind today is nowhere near this; even the most civilized countries of Europe and America cannot do this, let alone China.[152]

150. Liang, "Bo Tudi Guoyou," II, 15–16.
151. Liang, "Bo Tudi Guoyou," II, 19.
152. Liang, "Bo Tudi Guoyou," II, 52.

Liang then cited a recently written book by a professor from Chicago. In this, the author had listed the six evils of the public ownership of tramways:

1. The great obstacles it put up against technical invention. (According to the author, English inventiveness had deteriorated since 1870 when trams were first municipalized.)

2. American tramways under private ownership had expanded further than English tramways.

3. The result of public ownership was that it was impossible to make a unified system.

4. Since public ownership, bureaucracy had increased.

5. Waste was now worse.

6. Because development had been checked by public ownership, there was more unemployment.[153]

Not content with this, Liang quoted another very similar list of six evils, this time from a New York magazine. After this, he went a little into the theory behind these lists, his main argument being that as officials could not benefit directly from development, they would not take risks and make good pioneers. Thus it was no use founding a public enterprise: "The one or two municipal enterprises which have been successful were bought from privately owned companies and they merely inherited their success." Liang made an even more startling reversal of his old ideas when he continued: "The achievement of Germany's public enterprises which have been acclaimed as excellent also followed this path." Liang turned to the political ill effects of public ownership:

In England, where the political body was good, because of the growth of public enterprises a bureaucratic tyranny is growing, which is gradually corrupting government. In China today, where the people's level of education is far below that of England . . . the official power will be even heavier, and the evil phenomenon of the democratic dictatorship *(minzhu zhuanzhi)*, will be inevitable.

Having denounced public enterprise, Liang said how necessary he thought large industries were, but "only with large capital can one have large enterprises, and vice versa." He continued: "If the State

153. Liang, "Bo Tudi Guoyou," II, 52-53.

does not allow people to devote themselves to large enterprises, they will be finished; if it does allow them, great capitalists are sure to emerge." [154] Great capitalists were, according to Liang, absolutely necessary; the revolutionaries' policy of preventing their emergence would be disastrous to the country.

The passages above mark the high point in Liang's antisocialism. Before this, he had been generally in favor of public ownership, at least of the natural monopolies, on moral and economic grounds, even though he had been cautious in his plans for its application. Most of the time he had followed the German and Japanese arguments for state socialism. But sometimes he had gone so far as to attack the Alliance from a social democratic point of view. In these last pages, on the other hand, he seemed to agree with the most intemperate critics of public ownership, attacking it on economic and political grounds even in such things as tramways, which he had earlier wanted publicly owned. His attack on German state socialism was even more astounding. Some of this change in the appearance of Liang's views can only be explained by his having been carried away by the American material which he had just been reading. However, this article does seem to represent a definite shift in his attitude toward the efficiency or even the morality of public enterprises.

In the third section of the article, "Correcting the Theory of Land Nationalization from the Point of View of the Social Problem," Liang returned some of the way toward his old position. For instance, he stated his support for the Japanese law which vested all mineral rights in the hands of the state, only allowing private individuals to rent them. [155] The section contained very few new ideas but mainly repeated earlier attacks on the policy of land nationalization, the main theme being that the poor people would be worse off than before. His final argument was that it was population pressure, not landlords, which would be the bane of China. Thousands of people had to leave Kwangtung, not because it was like Scotland and had bad landlords, but simply because there were too many people there. He thought that the revolutionaries' land policies would do nothing to solve this, so that even if their land nationaliza-

154. Liang, "Bo Tudi Guoyou," II, 54–56.
155. Liang, "Bo Tudi Guoyou," III, 10.

tion were carried out, the second revolution would be inevitable. He implied, but did not say, that only big industries set up by big capitalists could save the situation.[156]

The tone of this section was not so extreme as the preceding section, but "Another Attack on a Certain Paper's Theory of Land Nationalization" as a whole is very different from Liang's previous articles. It would be fair to say that during the years 1905 to 1907 Liang was gradually moving away from socialism, but if one had to draw a line of qualitative change across this gradual progress it should be between January and April 1907.[157] In "Is Social Revolution Really Necessary in China Today," Liang was expressing a mild evolutionary state socialism; in this last article, he proclaimed his belief in private enterprise for the forseeable future.

The differences between Sun's and Liang's optimism and pessimism and their positions on socialism before 1905 have been described above. However, to a reader from a different culture at a later date, one of the most striking things about the controversy between *The Renovation of the People* and *The People's Journal* is the large number of common assumptions held by the two sides on the subject of social policies. Both Liang and the revolutionaries wanted a strong, prosperous, and technically developed China. Both sides believed in the inevitable material and moral progress of the world in which China was bound to be involved. However, they felt that Western progress and civilization were very mixed blessings. Their misgivings were chiefly based on the existence of a serious class division in the West, which both sides felt was bound to end in a bloody social revolution—a revolution that would probably destroy the society itself. Liang and Sun seem to have disliked class divisions for three reasons: first, that class divisions would eventually destroy society; second, that the privileges of the upper class and the miseries of the lower class offended their sense of justice; third, that they profoundly disapproved of a divided community. Both groups gave the impression that they thought the social revolution in the West was a just reward for the immorality of a divided community. Liang's attack on natural law in his last article did not pre-

---

156. Liang, "Bo Tudi Guoyou," III, 19–20.
157. I can find no evidence to support this in his letters of these months quoted in Ding Wen-jieng, "Liang Nianpu," I, 233–234.

vent his having a very strong sense of absolute justice and injustice. Shared dislike of Western class division meant that both sympathized with all people in the West who tried to end the system, preferring those who attempted to do it peacefully, but not rejecting those who used violent means. It also meant that they were determined that China should do all it could to avoid such a situation. Liang and the revolutionaries agreed that China was not divided in the same way as the West, and that this gave her great advantages. Liang emphasized the point, and the revolutionaries more or less conceded that Chinese society was less stratified than that of the West on the eve of the industrial revolution.

Another great advantage was that China could benefit from the West's experience of industrialization by avoiding its mistakes. To make use of these advantages, conscious planning was necessary; Chinese society must be reorganized in order to adapt to the new methods of industrial production and to build a country strong enough to play her rightful part in the concert of powers. Both sides were agreed that this reorganization should take place as peacefully as possible. Liang wanted very gradual state action, while the revolutionaries pressed for immediate action, chiefly in order to prevent the development of a situation which could only be solved by violence. They called their action social revolution, but it was to be strictly nonviolent.

The specific proposals of the two groups were also remarkably similar. Until his last article, Liang believed in public ownership, state or municipal, for a large segment of the economy. In fact his policy, like that of the revolutionaries, was based on a principle which was commonly held in the West at the time, notably by Ely and the state socialists, but which seems to have been peculiarly suitable to China. The Chinese form of it could be called the principle of *gui*. This word, which is normally translated as "to return," also has the closely related meaning of "to go to its rightful place." Thus, industries which were natural monopolies should *gui* to the state, while those which were naturally competitive should *gui* to private individuals. Everything should *gui* to its proper sphere, public or private. The only difficulty was to discover to which sphere a particular organ of production belonged. This was one reason, for instance, for Liang's long discourse on rural land not being a natural monopoly. Both sides agreed that the transfer from one sphere to another should be gradual. Liang believed that there should be no exception to this rule, while the revolutionaries made the one exception of the nominal transfer of land ownership to the state. Thus the two sides had a large common basis.

There was a great difference between the Revolutionary Alliance's attitude toward racial and political revolution, and that toward social revolution. In their eyes, something was wrong with Chinese society, but there was nothing wrong with the basic character of the Chinese people. The fault lay first with the alien Manchu rulers, and second with the imperial system which had distorted society and crushed the spirit of the Chinese people for two thousand years. To overthrow these twin evils a violent revolution was necessary. Once a decent society was established, people would act rationally and according to their natural benevolence. There would be no need for further violence. The rich would willingly give up some of their chances of future profit, because it was in the common interest, which they would see to be their own. Thus, although the Alliance called their social policies revolutionary, they would not involve any violence, and most of them would only be achieved gradually over a period of years.

As with all revolutionary parties of any seriousness, although belief in the goodness of human nature was the foundation of the Alliance's policies, when they came down to specifics, the party theoreticians showed some inclination to reinforce the "benevolent self-interest" of the rich. Feng Zi-you said bluntly that a military government would be necessary to impose their social policy, while Zhu Zhi-xin and Sun said it would be sensible to make use of unsettled times, when the rich would be more interested in security than in profit. However, they believed their policies could be carried out with the cooperation of, or at least without opposition from, the rich. This meant that they believed the Chinese people would be ready for socialism in the near future.

Liang's attitude toward the readiness of the Chinese people for socialism seems to have changed during the course of the argument. In his early articles he was slightly apologetic when he quoted the Western opponents of socialism, who said that if economic equality were imposed those with ability would not work hard for the community, and so on. However, the way in which he quoted them suggested that he had some sympathy with their views. By the time Liang wrote his last article, he seems to have supported their arguments without hesitation. He quoted Wagner with approval when he said that four-fifths of man's motivation was self-interest, and it would be impossible to practice any type of socialism until there had been a profound improvement in human nature.

Liang's pessimism or caution gave him a fear of the unknown, which meant that he felt that China should, wherever possible, follow existing precedents. The nearest and most applicable precedent for China was that of the modernization of Japan, and Liang seems to have wanted to follow this closely. In fact, as I have said above, the Japanese model is the thread which strings together the seemingly disparate elements of Liang's proposed policy: support for the capitalists at the same time as the nationalization of large sections of industry.

Sun, on the other hand, delighted in the idea of China being a pioneer. He believed in using the experiences of other nations, but in making a blend of his own from all the different countries, a blend which would be distinctively Chinese.

The same dichotomy between the revolutionaries' optimism and Liang's pessimism was reflected in the different attitudes of the two groups toward international relations. Sun was convinced that the foreign powers would see that it was in their interest to have a strong and wealthy China, one with which they could increase trade and every kind of exchange. That is why at that stage the revolutionaries were surprisingly proforeign, welcoming foreign trade and investment in China, and believing that foreign aid could help China's development enormously. Liang, on the other hand, saw the foreign powers as beasts of prey, only held back from devouring China by fear of each other. He thought that they might give China some small amount of help if it were clearly in their own interest, but that the price they would demand would be too high. He often pointed to the example of Egypt and Turkey, where the foreigners had used loans and investments to take over all power. Instead of considering how much help the foreigners could be to China, Liang thought the revolutionaries should concentrate on how to hold back the very real threat of foreign occupation.

Liang's dislike of revolution and his distrust of humanity as a whole seem to have predisposed him toward the solid elements of society: the gentry and the Chinese equivalent of the English yeoman. His plans were for both of these groups to become capitalists and in effect form a capitalist class.

The theoreticians of the Alliance, though mainly from the official class themselves, were for the time being persuaded by Sun and their own revolutionary experiences to sympathize with and support the lower classes and even the members of secret societies—who were often the "gamblers, swindlers," and such whom Liang so hated. However, as they repeatedly stated, they were not mathematically egalitarian; they believed in psychological equality, which in effect meant equality of opportunity. In their new society there would be capitalists and entrepreneurs, but no capitalist class, because everybody would start off on an equal footing.

But Liang would have denied any similarity between his proposals and the European class system and its attendant social problem. The capitalists in European society were the minority. Under his scheme the new capitalists would be the majority of the people, or at least the majority of the respectable people. John Stuart Mill's concept of the tyranny of the majority made no real impact on China, and there was no traditional equivalent for it. Both Liang and his opponents agreed that it was impossible for the majority to be unjust. Furthermore, the concept of a minority without power but with rights had so little foundation in Chinese thought that in many people's eyes the majority became society itself.[158] It was probably in this way that Liang would have reconciled his plan for a large capitalist class with his disapproval of a divided society.

Some of the elements in the controversy between the two parties cannot be usefully explained in terms of optimism and pessimism. The difference in their attitudes toward the European socialist movements is an example. In their earlier articles, both sides tended

158. Yan Fu, in his translation of Mill's *On Liberty (Qun-ji Quanjie Lun)*, stressed the utility of Liberty to strengthen the state and did not emphasize its intrinsic worth. See Schwartz, 130–148. Liang in his "Lun Zhengfu yu Renmin zhi Quanxian" did translate a passage from Mill which included an attack on the tyranny of a government elected by the majority. But he stopped at the point where Mill began to attack the social power of the majority. In this article and elsewhere Liang showed his preference for the integrated free society.

to make socialism in their own images, each on the grounds: we support socialism, therefore socialism is what we support. It is true that by 1905 Liang admitted the concept of complete socialism, with which he sympathized, but which he could not support because he thought it impracticable. But he considered himself a believer in social reformism and German state socialism, the only forms of socialism he thought realistic. Having identified himself with social reformism, Liang tended to describe complete socialism in extreme terms, in order to make it seem utterly impractical.

As we have seen above, the theoreticians of the Revolutionary Alliance had slightly differing conceptions of European socialism. But until Hu Han-min's article in March 1907 many of them considered that they supported true socialism. Feng Zi-you believed in all forms of socialism from Bismarck to Liebknecht, and thought that this was the social policy of the Alliance. Zhu Zhi-xin thought that the Marxist social democrats were the true socialists, and that their theories for the nationalization of capital by a democratic or proletarian government (he was not altogether clear about the distinction between the two) should be applied in China. Sun and Hu, while realizing that land nationalization was only one form of socialism, used the same term to describe their own policies and those of the European socialists. Liang's "Another Attack on a Certain Paper's Theory of Land Nationalization" forced Hu to admit that there was a difference between what Liang called complete socialism and the social policies. However, the leaders of the Alliance still seem to have felt that, although their policy differed from that of the Europeans, they were all part of the same worldwide socialist movement. That is why Hu continued to stress the moderation and the realism of the European socialists.

One reason for the Alliance's reluctance to declare whether they were social revolutionaries or social reformists came from their not wanting to cut themselves off from any type of socialism. Another was a real difficulty in describing their position. They were revolutionaries, and they wanted to make radical changes in the social and economic structure of Chinese society. On the other hand, their kind of social revolution was planned to avoid a real social revolution. It was to be bloodless and almost painless, taking a long time to be carried out.

One of the interesting results of the controversy between Liang and the revolutionaries was that both sides were forced to be fairly specific about their economic policies. Thus, we can reconstruct them with reasonable accuracy from the various articles.

Liang said that his policy was to "encourage the capitalists and protect labor." He mentioned only two ways in which he proposed to encourage the capitalists. One was to impose tariffs to protect Chinese industry; the other was to encourage capital accumulation.

To begin with, all enterprises would be in the hands of the capitalists. But after certain conditions had been fulfilled, the state would nationalize, or the city would municipalize, all natural monopolies. Liang gave no indications of how long he thought the conditions would take to be fulfilled.

Liang's second policy was the protection of labor. To implement this he proposed factory regulations, and compulsory insurance.

Liang's land policy was that urban land was to be municipalized. Rural land was to remain in private hands. But unsettled land, which also happened to be the land of the non-Han peoples of China, was to be colonized with Han people by the government. After this land had become settled, it was to be sold to private ownership. Mineral rights all over the country were to be retained by the government. Mines could be run by the government directly, or by contractors who leased them from the government. Altogether, Liang's economic policy was, as he claimed it to be, very close to the state socialism of Germany and Japan.

The articles of Hu Han-min and Zhu Zhi-xin gave a very clear description of the specific proposals of the Alliance's policy of *ping-jun diquan* (Equal Land Rights) and the principle of *minshengzhuyi*. The first stage of this, which was to come immediately after the political revolution, was the fixing of all land prices. This meant that although the land technically belonged to the state, the original land-owner retained nearly all his rights to it; that is, he could build on it, rent it, let it go fallow, or whatever. However, the government had the right to buy it at any time for the original price. Moreover, if the landowner sold the land to anyone else, the increase on the fixed price would go to the state, but the buyer would have the land. If someone offered a higher price for a piece of land and the owner did not want to sell, he could refuse; but he himself would have to pay to the state the difference between the offer and the fixed price.

The second stage of the plan was for the government to buy the land from the landowners at, or somewhat above, the fixed price. This process would be a very gradual one, taking anywhere from thirty to forty years. The land bought by the state would be let for various periods to the highest bidder, subject to one major condition. This was that the tenant should cultivate the land himself, neither subletting it to others nor leaving it uncultivated. Poor peasants could rent land without having to pay money down. They would be forced to pay only after one or two years. Although there was to be no restriction on the amount of land to be let to the highest bidder, the Alliance spokesmen believed that there was a built-in natural advantage for the small-scale producer: if the government deducted all the differential rent, there would be fair competition, and under fair competition the intensive agriculture of the small peasant was bound to win.

The original landowners were to receive interest-bearing government bonds as compensation. These would be bought back by the state over a period of one hundred years. Funds to back the debt would come from profits gained by the government from the earlier stage of the plan, from the rent of land already in government hands, and from foreign loans. These latter would be easy to obtain, because the government would have the security of the land. During the second stage of the plan, the normal costs of government administration would be borne by the old tax system made more efficient.

As well as buying all the land, the government would retain ownership of such items as certain mines and forests which were already in official hands. It would also nationalize all the other organs of production which came under the heading of natural monopolies: mines, railways, electricity, gas, water, and so on. This would be done partly by the government taking over existing organs, presumably with compensation, but mainly by the government itself developing them on land that it owned. All those sections of industry and commerce which were naturally competitive would remain in private hands. When the process was completed, and the state owned all the natural monopolies, including land, the Chinese government would be quite able to practice single tax, which in effect would simply require the revenue from the state-owned organs of production.

The pattern, which made sense out of the previous jumble of ideas, was that land price fixing, land nationalization, and single tax, were three separate processes, more or less chronologically divided. It is curious that this pattern appeared in print only in Zhu's last article at the very end of the controversy in September 1907. The question arises as to whether Sun had the whole plan in his mind when he first introduced *minshengzhuyi*, in 1905.[159]

One reason to suggest that he did, is that Sun always liked talking in public in general and never in specific terms. Therefore, that he did not describe the full plan in 1905 or 1906 is no reason to suppose that such a plan did not exist. This argument is backed by the fact that in the years 1912-1913, when Sun talked about *minshengzhuyi* he still talked in general terms about similar social policies somewhere between Henry George and collectivism, and he never came down to anything like Zhu's specific plan.

This argument has some foundation. However, the fact that Sun liked talking in vague generalities, and the fact that at this stage he preferred talking to writing, rather suggest that he also liked thinking in vague generalities, and that until more practical people, such as Hu Han-min and Zhu Zhi-xin, put their minds to the problem, Sun had no specific plan of action. That Sun did not mention Zhu's plan after 1911 can be explained first by the likelihood that Sun never read the article, and second, whether he read it or not, it is probable that he would not have been particularly interested in Zhu's specific proposals which had no immediate political relevance. Therefore, he later returned to his old vague ways.

Another reason for supposing that Sun did have something like Zhu's specific plan in his mind, when he first introduced *minshengzhuyi*, is that there were remarkably few discrepancies between the earlier articles and speeches and Zhu's final version. Indeed, the final version would seem to be a chord which linked the earlier vague statements together. However, it could also be that the final version was concocted from the earlier statements, or perhaps from the ideas which lay behind them.

159. Hatano Yoshihiro believes that the policies of Hu and Zhu were different from those of Sun (77). Although conceding that there were differences of emphasis I believe Hatano rather exaggerates them.

The most telling argument is that if there had been a coherent plan in 1905, it was strange that it did not appear earlier, at least in reply to Liang's repeated statements that the Alliance's policy was ambiguous.

The most likely explanation is that most of the ideas, probably more than were written down, existed in Sun's mind when he first introduced Equal Land Rights and *minshengzhuyi*. But during 1906 and early 1907, there were discussions between Sun and his immediate colleagues, and Hu Han-min and Zhu Zhi-xin in particular.[160] In these discussions, some new ideas were introduced, and a coherent pattern began to emerge. The final shaping of the scheme was probably done by Zhu alone. It is just possible that Zhu discussed it with Hu, though not with Sun, in Hongkong during the hectic summer of 1907. The major driving force in this clarification must have been the challenge of Liang, while the main sources of the new ideas seem to have been Ely's works and a general knowledge of Western social democracy.

The following eight ideas can be considered key elements in Zhu's final synthesis:

1. Taxing the increment of land values brought about by social progress.

2. Fixing land prices.

3. Dealing with the social problem before it arose.

4. Having the social revolution at the same time as the political revolution.

5. Single tax of all rent.

6. Land nationalization.

7. Nationalization of all natural monopolies.

8. The coherent arrangement of the others.

The first six of these seem to have been the core of Sun's ideas. He referred to them constantly, both in the period 1905–1907 and the period 1912–1913. Number 7 seems to have been a peripheral part of his scheme.

Nationalization of natural monopolies was first proposed by Feng Zi-you, in his article written in December 1905, and officially by Zhu Zhi-xin in June 1906. However, Sun must have thought about it considerably before then, although it is strange he did not

160. See Hu, "Hu Han-min Zizhuan," 389.

mention it earlier or in his speech in December 1906. It seems quite likely that it was introduced into the party plan by Hu and Zhu under the influence of Ely and the socialists. Sun did mention the idea in 1912 and 1913, although he did not give it so much prominence as the single tax theory, for instance. His relative reluctance to talk about nationalization of any sort may have come from the fear of offending audiences, or from his feeling that it was only a side-stem of his major plan.

The eighth element seems to have been created by Zhu alone. The confusion, dispelled by Zhu's lucid description, returned in all Sun's later speeches. Zhu's synthesis was a crystallizing of Sun's political ideas, but it was probably not made by Sun himself.

It is generally agreed that between 1905–1907 the Reformists, under Liang Qi-chao, lost all remaining support among the students in Tokyo. As Hu Han-min put it: "The flag of the Reformists, was not seen again among the students abroad." [161] Hu was not an impartial observer, but even some Reformists themselves were depressed about the situation.[162] The victory of the Revolutionary Alliance culminated in their wrecking of the foundation meeting of the Political Association, which was a new organization of Liang's. At this meeting on October 17, 1907, a group of alliance students charged the platform, yelling *"Baka"* (Fool) and "Beat him." The Reformists fled, and Liang himself was slightly injured.[163] Zhang Ji, the leader of the rioters, mounted the platform and made a revolutionary speech. According to one reminiscence: "This violent action of the league members was widely acclaimed, and demonstrated the unpopularity of the constitutional monarchists." [164] The relish with which some Chinese historians describe the incident seems to confirm this. It is interesting that

161. "Hu Han-min Zizhuan," 390.
162. See the introduction to Zhang, *Xinhai Geming qian Shilun,* II, 10.
163. Many different dates are given for this meeting. Feng Zi-you says that it was on July 17, 1907. See Feng, *Kaiguo shi,* 202–203; and other writers have followed him. Teng and Ingells' translation of Li Chien-nung's *The Political History of China, 1840–1928* (Princeton, 1956), quotes Zhang Bin-lin's account giving August 25 as the date (217). The version of Zhang's account in *Xinhai Geming,* II, 416, gives October 17, which is confirmed by Guo Ting-yi.
164. Wu Yu-chang, 87.

Zhang Ji, the leader of the student mob, had been in Japan for six years and was considered the most Japanese of all the students in the Alliance, and that he yelled his insults against Liang in Japanese, and that the immediate repercussions of the incident were in Tokyo. This suggests that Zhang may have based his action on a Japanese model, and that the approval he received from students and literati was also partly due to Japanese influence.

This incident seems to have crushed Liang's remaining influence among the Chinese students in Tokyo. This does not mean that Liang failed everywhere. In fact, in 1907 and 1908 the Political Association and Liang's influence were expanding a great deal in China itself among the gentry, who were actively preparing for political struggles in the provincial assemblies which were to be set up under the constitution. However, Liang's annihilation in Tokyo after the incident on October 17 is reflected by the fact that after *The People's Journal,* No. XVII, came out on October 25, the revolutionaries did not bother to reply to the vast amount of criticism still unanswered in Liang's last article.

The other symbol of Liang's defeat in Japan was the death of *The Renovation of the People.* One of the revolutionary students who was in Tokyo at the time, Wu Yu-chang has written: "Under the forcible attack of *The People's Journal,* the new people's journal *(The Renovation of the People)* suffered a complete defeat which led to the cessation of its public action." [165] This description is confirmed by Liang himself. In a letter written to a friend at the time, he admitted that the revolutionaries' polemics were too much for him to handle: "My reasons for wanting to close *The Renovation of the People* have been that with the appearance of the partisan paper I alone have not enough strength to manage our paper and argue with them. It is like a tumor and I have no more spirit." [166]

There is also no doubt that the polemics in *The People's Journal* did impress many of the students and attract them toward the revolutionary cause. However, it is likely that the students, like most of us, were influenced by sections or even phrases in the articles rather than by the whole of the complicated structure of the articles themselves. The fact that virtually no contemporary or later

165. Wu Yu-chang, 86.   166. Ding Wen-jiang, "Liang Nianpu," I, 228.

historian has mentioned Zhu Zhi-xin's brilliant last article would suggest that no one followed the detailed arguments of the two sides except the writers themselves—who had clearly read their opponents' articles with great care. The reasons for this lack of detailed attention seem fairly obvious. Many of the articles are extremely long, and the reader's eye is constantly drawn to the picturesque insult rather than to the somewhat loose arguments themselves.

The arguments on land nationalization were probably not great inducements to entering the revolutionary fold. The reason why it became the dominant issue in the debate was probably as stated above—that Liang felt that land nationalization was the weakest point in the Alliance's defenses. It was not that the two sides felt this to be the critical element in the struggle, though Sun and his immediate entourage felt it to be important. The general disinterest and even hostility to the party's social policies among the revolutionary students is made evident by the fact that during the following three years many devoted revolutionaries tried to jettison the principle of Equal Land Rights altogether. This makes it still less likely that those involved read the articles on social policies at all closely. Both groups of articles on social policy obviously did have a great effect in the long run, however, by introducing many fragments of contemporary European economic and sociological theory as well as a large number of Western arguments both for and against socialism. They also gave currency to some distinctively Chinese syntheses which were to influence Chinese political thought and action. Nevertheless, the immediate effect of all the thousands of characters was less than Zhang Ji's one word *Baka*.

8 | 1907

The explanations for Liang's change of opinion on socialism in early 1907—that he had read American and Japanese writings against it and that he wished to be consistent in his opposition to the Alliance's social policies—have been mentioned above, as has been his defeat in the over-all debate with the revolutionaries. However, other factors must have predisposed him toward arguments that he had previously not accepted. During 1906 and 1907 Liang drew nearer to gentry leaders in China as the movement for a constitution accelerated and organization for local self government—by the gentry—began to be established.[1] This growth of gentry self-confidence vis-à-vis the central government crystallized around the movement for the recovery of railway rights in which provincial gentry organizations tried to gain the right to build extremely profitable railways, rights controlled by the central government and by the foreign companies with which the latter were involved.[2] Thus Liang's increasing contacts with gentry leaders could have inclined him to look more critically at the concept of nationalization which they so bitterly opposed. But there is no evidence to support this supposition.

The only topic with which we know Liang was concerned at the time was the survival of national culture. In March 1907 he wrote a long work on philology and, when asking a friend to write an introduction to it, he lamented that "national studies were so withered."[3] In this Liang was merely joining a widespread movement of cultural conservatism among the upper literati. As its

1. See Levenson, *Liang Chi'i-ch'ao,* 79–80.
2. See E-tu Zen Sun, *Chinese Railways and British Interests, 1898–1911* (New York, 1954).
3. Letter to Jiang Guan-yun in Ding Wen-jiang, *Liang Nianpu,* I, 222.

name—"National Essence" or "National Culture," as opposed to culture pure and simple—suggests, the movement was not traditional but conservative. A useful distinction can be made between the two by stressing the self-consciousness of conservatism, which is aware of alternatives and influenced by them, although its raison d'etre is their rejection. Tradition on the other hand is all-embracing and completely natural to those within it.[4] The forerunner of the Chinese movement was a Japanese one against what its protagonists believed to be the excessive Westernization of the 1880s.[5] The Chinese movement can be said to have begun early in 1905 with the foundation of a magazine, *The Journal of National Essence*, by a group of young scholars, most of them anti-Manchu revolutionaries.[6] Late in 1906 the movement was taken up in a big way by officials. The modernizing Governor General Zhang Zhi-dong began to establish schools to promote national essence.[7] Men like the translator Yan Fu and the educationalists Huang Shao-qi and Kuai Guang-dian, who had previously devoted themselves to expanding knowledge of the West, began to give priority to the promotion of national culture and to the writing of textual and philological studies, though they often used new and foreign approaches for this.[8]

The impetus for this change of attitude seems to have come largely from the abolition of the traditional examination system. Officials like Zhang Zhi-dong, who had been struggling against the institution for years, were suddenly terrified at the thought of the

4. The distinction is Weber's. See Karl Mannheim, *Essays on Sociology and Social Psychology* (London, 1953), 95.

5. See Kenneth B. Pyle, *The New Generation in Meiji Japan: Problems of Cultural Identity, 1885–1895* (Stanford, 1969), 60–69.

6. For the magazine's foundation and its relationship to the Japanese movement, see Martin Bernal, "Liu Shih-p'ei and 'National Essence'" in Charlotte Furth, *The Limits of Change*. See also for Liang's abortive interest in National Essence in 1902.

7. William Ayers, *Chang Chih-tung and Educational Reform in China* (Cambridge, Mass, 1971), 248–251. See also "Liu Shih-p'ei and 'National Essence.'"

8. Late in 1906 Yan attacked youths who had comtempt for ancestral thought and declared himself a conservative. See Yang Tian-shi, "Lun Xinhai Geming qian di Zhongguo Guocuizhuyi Sichao," in *Xin Jianshe* (1965), 2, 67–77, esp. 68. See Schwartz, who sets the date for the break in Yan's thought as 1908, but states that this is an approximation, 212–213. For Huang Shao-qi, see ECCP; for Kuai Guang-dian, see his *Jinsuzhaiji* (Nanking, 1929), and Bernal, "Liu Shi-pei to 1907," Monograph.

extinction of classical studies that would occur with the system's final destruction. There was another lesser but still important factor involved, namely the existence of talented students who were simultaneously political revolutionaries and cultural conservatives. Zhang Zhi-dong and his colleagues, with their intense preoccupation with the young elite, bewailed the sad fact that "many patriots holding the principle of destruction aim at confusion." [9]

It was for this reason that they leapt at the chance to establish a common ground of cultural conservatism with this group of radicals. The outstanding figure in *The Journal of National Essence* group was Liu Shi-pei who, as well as writing the bulk of the group's magazine, had edited *The Alarm Bell,* the chief revolutionary journal in Shanghai until he was forced to flee the city in March 1905. He spent most of 1906 in Wuhu, which became the center of revolutionary activity in the Yangtze valley. Although Liu was ostensibly in hiding, he in fact maintained close contact with high officials with similar cultural tastes, including Kuai Guang-dian who was a close colleague of Zhang Zhi-dong. [10]

The winter of 1906–1907 was catastrophic in central China. There were droughts and huge floods. Tens of millions of peasants lost their homes, and millions died of starvation. In the suffering and confusion there were widespread riots and a number of revolutionary risings, notably one of miners from the coal mines of Anyuan on the Hunan-Kiangsi border. [11] These were crushed with hideous ferocity by Zhang Zhi-dong and the newly appointed Manchu Governor Duan-fang at Nanking. Duan-fang's intelligence in this operation was superb, and it is probable that he was helped in this by Liu Shi-pei, who left Wuhu in November 1906 and only arrived in Japan late in the following February. [12]

While winning over the students in Japan the leaders of the Revolutionary Alliance were distressed by events in China. [13] Their

9. *Zhang Wen-xiang Gong Quanji,* ed. Wang Shu-nan (Peking, 1928), XCVIII, 7b.

10. For details of Liu's movements and activities during this period see "Liu Shi-pei to 1907."

11. Chun-tu Hsueh, *Huang Hsing,* 601; and *Xinhai Geming,* II, 463–522.

12. Duan-fang certainly had other informants. For my reasons for maintaining that Liu may have started working with Duan-fang as early as November 1906, see "Liu Shi-pei to 1907."

13. See, for example, Song Jiao-ren's reactions in *Wo zhi Lishi,* 305.

difficulties were compounded when the Japanese authorities, conceding to pressure from the Chinese government, expelled Sun Yat-sen, with the Japanese hedging their bets by giving him a parting present of 5,000 Yen. Sun and his immediate followers, Hu Han-min and Wang Jing-wei, set off for South East Asia, and Zhu Zhi-xin left for Hongkong soon after to organize revolts in Kwangtung. Their departure symbolized the breakup of the consensus on Westernization that had existed up to 1906 between Liang Qi-chao and the writers for *The People's Journal,* nearly all of whom came from Kwangtung.

During 1907 the preoccupation with national essence and cultural conservatism became widespread, both among the officials and reformers and among the revolutionaries.[14] This tendency gained increasing ground after Liu Shi-pei (considered a revolutionary hero, though probably working for Duan-fang) joined his old friend Zhang Bing-lin in the production of *The People's Journal.* In this new atmosphere, interest in Western socialism among Chinese students abroad declined, and there was a sudden eruption of interest in anarchism.

Naturally, interest in, and knowledge of, anarchism and nihilism had existed in Japan and China long before this. Information on Russian populism became available in Japan within months of its reaching the West. In 1882 and 1883, years of great terrorist activity in Russia, several books on the nihilists were published in Japan. These books, all of which appear to have been based on works available in English and French, included translations of such vivid and sympathetic accounts of the revolutionaries as Stepniak's *Underground Russia.*[15] However, the bulk of the reporting on the nihilists in the Japanese press was as hostile as that of *The Review of*

14. That year a group of writers who had been associated with Liu on *The Alarm Bell* established the Southern Society in Shanghai. For this see Lawrence Schneider, "The Southern Society," in Furth, *Limits of Change.* At the same time Qian Xuan-tong, Lu Xun, his brother Zhou Zuo-ren, and others established a Society for the Promotion of National Studies in Tokyo. See Chow Tse-tsung, *The May Fourth Movement* (Cambridge, Mass., 1960), 53. For Qian, Zhou, and Lu Xun, see BDRC.

15. This was published under the title *Kyomutō jitsu denkiki shushu* (Tokyo, 1883), trans. Miyazaki Muryū. For the others, see the bibliographies of books on Western radicalism: Shimoide Hayakichi in *Meiji Bunka Zenshu,* XXI; and Shioda Shōbei, *Nihon Shakaishugi Bunken Kaisetsu.* This summary of East Asian nihilism and anarchism before 1907 closely follows that given in the "Triumph of Anarchism."

The Times in China. It would be difficult to say how much immediate impact these books had on Japan. The early 1880s, the era of the popular rights movement, were years of violent political struggle, and some contemporaries saw the influence of Russian nihilists in the activities of radical supporters of the Liberal Party.[16] Kōtoku Shusui maintained that Russian nihilism was influential in the foundation of the Eastern Socialist Party. It was more radical than the Liberal Party, but like the Russian terrorists of the time, its radicalism was more political than economic. As the anarchist Kōtoku pointed out, approvingly, it had a clearly antiauthoritarian bent; it was to have no leaders and no headquarters. Kōtoku saw it as the unscientific pioneer of Japanese socialism, in very much the same position as that of Fourier and Weitling in the French and German movements.[17]

The late 1880s and 1890s were years of relative social calm in both Russia and Japan. No books on nihilism appear to have been published in Japan between 1884 and 1902. The Japanese socialist movement, which grew up at the same time as the Russian Social Democratic Party in the late 1890s, was very hostile to anarchism and terrorism. Indeed, the declaration of the Japanese Social Democratic Party in 1901 stated: "It is only the nihilist and the anarchist who brandish a sword and throw bombs. Since our Social Democratic Party resolutely opposes the use of force, we will never imitate the foolishness of the nihilist and anarchist parties."[18]

From 1902 to 1904, however, a number of books were published on anarchism, a word that was beginning to replace nihilism and terrorism as the term for radical assassination. The indiscriminate use of these three words by popular writers in every language had a great effect on Japanese and Chinese radicals who, impressed by nihilist or populist terrorism, turned toward anarchism, which they assumed to be very much the same. The most influential of the new books was *Modern Anarchism* by Kemuyama Sentarō, a teacher at Waseda university and a journalist specializing in Russian affairs. Most of the book was not about anarchism, but was a general

16. See Scalapino, *Democracy and the Party Movement in Prewar Japan*, 77.
17. Kōtoku Shūsui and Ishikawa Kyōkusan, *Nihon Shakaishugishi*, 338, 339.
18. Nobutaka Ike, "Kōtoku, Advocate of Direct Action," *Journal of Asian Studies*, III (1944), 227.

history of the Russian revolutionary movement which was divided into three periods: revolutionary literature, propaganda and agitation; and assassination and terror, a scheme that was later to have great influence on the Chinese revolutionaries.

In 1904 the Russo-Japanese War focused Japanese attention on Russia. Katayama Sen's handshake with Plekhanov at Amsterdam and the exchange of letters between *The Commoners' Newspaper* and the Russian *Iskra* brought the Japanese socialists into direct contact with members of the Russian Social Democratic Party, linking them in opposition to the militarism of their governments. Despite the cordiality of the correspondence, there was an interesting and significant difference between *The Commoners' Newspaper* and *Iskra*, which was then under Menshevik control.[19] Kōtoku and Sakai Toshihiko wrote:

We are neither nihilists or terrorists but social democrats and are always fighting for peace. We object absolutely to using military force in our fighting. We have to fight by peaceful means; by reason and speech. It may be very difficult for you to fight with speech and produce revolution by peaceful means in Russia, where there is no constitution, and consequently you may be tempted to overthrow the government by force. But those who are fighting for humanity must remember that the end does not justify the means.[20]

The condescension in this letter may have come from a feeling held even by antimilitarist Japanese that Japan's victories in Manchuria had proved that the country was more civilized and advanced than Russia. It is hardly surprising that the editors of *Iskra* rejected both the tone and content of this part of the letter:

Force against force, violence against violence! And in saying this we speak neither as nihilists or terrorists. . . . Against terrorism as an improper method of action we have never since the establishment of the Russian Social Democratic Party ceased to fight. But regrettable as it may be, the

19. G.D.H. Cole, III, 2, 935; and Kublin, 239 are mistaken when they say that Lenin may have written the reply. March 1904 is the earliest month in which it could have been written, by which time Plekhanov had brought back Martov and the other Mensheviks, and Lenin had resigned from the editorial board. See I, Deutscher, *The Prophet Armed*, 86; and T. Dan, *The Origins of Bolshevism* (London, 1964), 248. It is possible, however, that it was written by Trotsky.

20. *Heimin Shimbun* (3/20/04), English column.

ruling classes have never submitted to the forces of reason, and we have not the slightest ground for believing that they ever will.[21]

The Japanese comment on the Russian reply appeared to overlook the general challenge to their policy of moderation and gradualism. It treated *Iskra's* position simply as an unfortunate result of the peculiar Russian situation.[22] Like socialists in other countries they continued to imagine that the Russian social democrats were relatively orthodox members of the International. Kōtoku later quoted in *Straight Talk* the resolution passed by the Russian party's first congress in 1898 against violence.[23] Thus the Japanese socialists were able to accept the convenient distinction between social democratic moderation and anarchist and nihilist violence. They, like socialists and others throughout the world, did not see the importance of the Bolsheviks and Trotsky in the revolution of 1905 and overestimated the admittedly significant role of the social revolutionaries.[24]

The year 1903 seems to have been the time when the Japanese term of *museifushugi* (*wuzhengfuzhuyi* in Chinese, "anarchism") was first used in China.[25] Several articles were published describing the feats of anarchists in favorable terms.[26] Also in that year a pamphlet appeared which its translator, Zhang Ji, entitled *Anarchism* in which he described the Western European movement.[27] On the other hand passages on anarchism in the books

21. *Heimin Shimbun* (7/31/04), English column.
22. *Heimin Shimbun* (7/24/04).
23. *Chokugen* (2/19/05).
24. Tanaka Sogorō in *Kōtoku Shūsui ichi Kakumeika no Shisō to Shogai* (Tokyo, 1955), 261, makes this point for Japan.
25. For the earlier translations of anarchism and nihilism see above.
26. See, for instance, "Nujie Guoerman" by Su Man-shu in *Guomin Riri Bao* (10/7–8/03), parts of which are quoted in McAleavy, 7.
27. This pamphlet was generally supposed to have been a translation of Errico Malatesta's *Anarchia* which was first published in 1896. See Zhang Jing-lu, 174. Zhang's evidence for this seems to have been: (1) that advertisements for a pamphlet by Zhang Ji called *Wuzhengfuzhuyi* opened with a quotation from Malatesta. See *Zhongguo Baihua Bao*, 1 (December 1903), Advertisement section, 2. And (2) that Zhang Ji did at some time translate Malatesta's pamphlet. However, a summary of Zhang Ji's pamphlet in *Min Bao*, X, lists contents totally different from Malatesta's original. Furthermore, Zhang Ji says in his memoires that he translated Kōtoku's Japanese version of Malatesta in 1907. See *Zhang Pu-quan Xiansheng Quanji*, 2 vols. (Taipei, 1951–1952), I, 236. This seems likely, as Zhang's only foreign language was

on socialism published that year were written from the hostile viewpoints of social democrats or Christian socialists.

This lack of sympathy was restricted to Western anarchism. In the three years from 1902 to 1904 there was considerable interest in and support for Russian nihilism, for which the Japanese term *kyōmushugi* (*xuwuzhuyi* in Chinese) was now being used. Numerous works touched on the subject, and three books were specifically written about it. The most influential was a translation of Kemuyama's *Modern Anarchism*, which appeared in Chinese in 1904 as *Anarchism*, but which was better known under its later title of *Freedom's Blood*.[28] Nearly all of these works in Chinese deplored the Russian autocracy and expressed sympathy with the terrorist tactics of the nihilists. However, there was no such general support for their goals, if only because the writers were very confused as to whether the nihilists were communists and anarchists or simply political revolutionaries. Liang Qi-chao for instance, who at the time thought they advocated communism, wrote that "the methods of nihilism receive my respect, but I can not support their principles."[29] Most of the other writers seemed to agree with Liang and likewise supported the methods and political aims of the nihilists while opposing or neglecting to mention their social or economic goals.

Liang had no qualms about the use of revolutionary terror in Russia, and in 1903 he believed that these methods could be modified to fit China. The revolutionaries went further. According to them, the situation in China was even worse than in Russia.

In Russia the sovereign and the people are both of the same slow race, but simply because the people cannot bear the poison of autocracy. They are willing to sacrifice millions of lives to obtain freedom. . . . But when I look at my country I cannot control my feelings. For not only has it the same

---

Japanese, and Kōtoku's translation, the first in Japanese, came out only in 1907 or 1908. Thus it appears that Zhang translated a Japanese survey of anarchism in 1903 and Malatesta's pamphlet in 1907. Zhang Bing-lin's introduction written in January 1908 was for the latter. See *Min Bao,* 129.

28. The other works were: Duli zhi Geren (trans.), *Elosi Da fengchao* (1902), which may be a chapter of Kirkup's *History of Socialism.* See Zhang Jing-lu, 171, and *Xuwu Dang,* written or translated by Chen Leng-xue in 1904.

29. "Lun Elosi Xuwu Dang," XMCB, XL–XLI (11/03).

autocracy as Russia but for 200 years we have been trampled on by foreign barbarians.[30]

The anti-Manchu revolutionaries were unlike the Japanese radicals in that their concern with the methods and political aims of the nihilists was not merely academic. In 1903 they began to investigate ways of imitating the Russians. The key figure in this movement of imitation was Yang Du-sheng.[31] In 1902 as a student in Japan he was an editor of the *Translations from Students Abroad.*

From 1903 to 1905 he was deeply involved in revolutionary and terrorist attempts. He also wrote *New Hunan,* a popular pamphlet in which he called for a new spirit in China—which would have to be one of destruction. The examples that appealed to him and others of his generation were the groups that were passionate supporters of the Meiji restoration at the end of the Tokugawa period and the Russian terrorists who appeared to be the epitome of the spirit needed to revive decadent nations.[32]

One of Yang's followers was Wu Yue, a student at the Baoding Higher School.[33] Yang trained Wu in the use of explosives. In the autumn of 1905 they decided to attack five ministers who were about to leave for Europe to investigate possible models for a Chinese constitution. Various difficulties checked the conspirators, but on September 24 Wu, growing desperate, made the attempt on his own and threw a bomb at the ministers just before their departure. The explosion killed Wu and badly frightened the ministers, two of whom withdrew from the mission. Yang managed to avoid

30. Yuan Sun, "Lusiya Xuwu Dang," in *Jiangsu,* IV (7/03), 55.

31. Yang (1872–1911) *zi* Yu-lin, who later changed his name to Shou-ren, came from an official family in Changsha; he was a brother or nephew and companion of Mao's teacher, Yang Chang-ji. He became a *Juren* in 1897 and was involved in the educational activities of Liang Qi-chao and other reformists in Changsha. In 1902 he went to Japan where he studied at the Kobungakuin and Waseda; see the three biographies collected by Cao Ya-bo reprinted in *Xinhai Geming,* IV, 316–324.

32. Yang, *Xin Hunan,* which is reprinted in Zhang Nan and Wang Ren-zhi, I, 2, 612–649.

33. Wu (1878–1905) *zi* Meng-xia came from Tongcheng in Anhwei. His father was an official who left his position to become a merchant. After repeatedly failing official examinations, Wu wandered through the country, finally entering the Baoding Higher School, In 1902 or 1903 he became a Revolutionary but later in 1903, influenced by *Qingyi Bao,* he became a Reformist. By 1904 more revolutionary literature had led him back into the fold. See "Ziyu" in *Tian Tao,* supplement to *Min Bao* (April 1907), 1.

suspicion and escaped from Peking, going to Tokyo where he joined the newly formed Revolutionary Alliance. Wu had clearly seen his attempt as an act of "propaganda by deed." He had written extensively, explaining his political beliefs, hoping that through his action his writings would have a considerable impact, which they did when they were fully published in April 1907.[34] These writings show that the Russian revolutionary tradition had a very great influence on him. We know that he read *New Hunan* and *Freedom's Blood*, and from them and his talk with Yang he had adopted the concept of a period of assassination. However, writing after the outbreak of the Russian revolution, he seemed to believe that this period was coming to an end in Russia. He wrote:

At present nothing in the world attracts so much awe and attention as the fame of the Nihilist Party. In what period is the Russian Nihilist Party today? If I dared to be arbitrary I should say that the last half of the nineteenth century was the nihilist's period of assassination and the first half of the twentieth century is their period of revolution. Without the former how could you obtain today's results? Where are we Han people? Where are we, comrades? We, comrades, are in the period of assassination and future years will bring the Han people's period of assassination.[35]

Like Yang, Wu had been entirely absorbed in the methods of the Russian revolutionaries and their applicability to China. His aims were purely political; at no point did he show the slightest interest in the basic ideas of anarchism or socialism. However, the publication of his writings in April 1907 caused not only a revival of interest in assassination, but also played a considerable part in the awakening of interest in anarchism among Chinese revolutionaries, as did the police official Xu Xi-lin's assassination of the Manchu governor of Anhwei in July.[36]

The first signs of Kōtoku Shūsui's conversion to anarchism

34. A letter attacking plans for a constitution was printed in *Min Bao*, III (4/06). Much longer writings were published in *Tian Tao*.

35. "Wu Yue Yishu," *Tian Tao*, 7–8, and 10. Wu was not consistent in his theory that assassination was simply a preparation for revolution. At another point he suggested that assassination by itself could overthrow the Manchu regime.

36. In fact Xu had attempted to start a revolt, and his shooting of En-ming was only the opening step in this. However, the scheme failed. See Mary Rankin, 179–184.

appeared in February 1905, the month in which he began a five-month prison sentence for the publication of the special anniversary issue of *The Commoners' Newspaper,* the issue which had included the *Communist Manifesto.* In that month he published two articles in *Straight Talk* on Russian revolutionaries, a subject that had become topical since the beginning of the revolution on January 22.[37] The articles concentrated on the Social Revolutionary Party, heir to the nihilist traditions of the 1880s, and Kōtoku was very sympathetic toward both the party and the traditions. These articles contained the first criticisms by a Japanese socialist of a Social Democratic Party: "The moderation of the (Russian) Social Democratic Party being unsatisfactory, a revolutionary socialist party was organized and . . . the majority of the youth were attracted to it." He qualified his attack by saying "I am sure that the Social Democratic Party has had great achievements in strikes and demonstrations."[38] Furthermore, he made it clear that he believed that revolutionary violence was justifiable only in unconstitutional Russia and not in Japan. Nevertheless, it was a step away from parliamentary social democracy.

The clearest way of regarding Kōtoku's change of ideas is as his liberation from the constriction of Marxist social democracy. Lacking the Christian background of many Japanese socialists, Kōtoku had no horror of violence. Indeed, as a Samurai brought up in the strife of the popular rights movement, he seems to have been predisposed toward it and had no particular attachment to the moderation of parlimentary methods. He was born and brought up in Tosa, a *han* with a strong radical agrarian tradition.[39] Furthermore, he was a pupil and biographer of Nakae Chōmin, also from Tosa, the "Japanese Rousseau" who translated *Le Contrat Social.* Thus, throughout his social career Kōtoku chafed against the Marxist emphasis on the urban proletariat and the social democratic belief that socialism could only come after the full development of capitalism. Kōtoku always appears to have preferred the populist

37. "Rokoku Kakumei no Sobo" and "Rokoku Kakumei ga Yo uru Kyōkun," *Chokugen* (2/12/05 and 2/19/05, respectively).
38. "Rokoku Kakumei no Sobo" (2/12/05).
39. See his praise of an assassin in 1889, quoted Notehelfer, 27.

view of a revolution of the majority of the people led by youth *before* the triumph of capitalism.

Given these proclivities it is surprising, not that he became an anarchist, but that he ever called himself a social democrat. The fundamental reason for this was that before 1905 Kōtoku and other Japanese socialists believed that no rational man could deny Marxist socialism. With his economic and historical analysis Marx and Marx alone had raised socialism from a beautiful inspiration to a science. In their eyes pre-Marxist socialists were admirable but impractical. As Kōtoku wrote in 1904, "most of Fourier's schemes failed not because his basic reasoning was bad but because his practical plans were unscientific and unnatural."[40]

In addition to believing that Marxism was the only scientific socialism, Kōtoku also thought that the social democrats were the only true interpreters of Marx. Thus despite his basic prejudices, Kōtoku felt obliged to admit that the Western social democratic parties represented the wave of the future and that anarchism was only a moribund relic of the primitive past. In August 1904 *The Commoners' Newspaper* reported: "As in other countries there has been a decline in the Anarchist Party since the appearance of the [Russian] Social Democratic Party."[41]

Apparently there were three major reasons why by February 1905 Kōtoku had begun to reconsider his position. First, was the closure of *The Commoners' Newspaper* and his sentence to a term of imprisonment. These events increased his skepticism about Japanese constitutional government, and doubts arose in his mind about the possibility of progress by moderate parliamentary means.[42]

Second and most important was the massacre of workers on

40. *Heimin Shimbun*, III (5/8/04). Notehelfer, at 110-112, stresses Kōtoku's interest in the pseudoscientific works of Professor Michael Lane of Boston. This illustrates Kōtoku's great desire to be scientific.

41. *Heimin Shimbun* (8/14/04).

42. See his letter to Albert Johnson (12/30/04) reprinted in Hyppolyte Havel, "Kōtoku's Correspondence with Albert Johnson," *Mother Earth*, VI, 6-7 and 9 (1911), 6, 181. Notehelfer rightly opposes accepting at face value all Kōtoku's statements to Albert Johnson, which were written for foreign consumption, but in this and other cases cited below they are accepted for their plausibility in context, as are statements made for home consumption.

Bloody Sunday, January 9, 1905, and the wave of strikes and demonstrations that opened the revolution in Russia. These events, which were fully reported in *Straight Talk* and the rest of the Japanese press, clearly had a considerable impact on Kōtoku. He believed that the Russian revolution had world-wide significance and would serve as a model, particularly in East Asia:

Russia at the beginning of the twentieth century is like France at the beginning of the nineteenth. As revolutionaries in Western countries looked to a signal from France, now all the lost countries of the East look for a sign from the Russian revolution. . . . Look at China; look at Korea.[43]

Not only did the new manifestations of revolutionary spirit inspire him, but they also cast a retrospective glow on the past activities of Russian revolutionaries. "Going to the people" and terrorism, which had previously seemed the pathetic attempts of unscientific and hopeless idealists, could now be seen as the planting and hoeing necessary for the harvest of revolution.

The third factor in Kōtoku's conversion was his relationship with Albert Johnson, an elderly California anarchist with whom he began a correspondence in the autumn of 1904. Johnson immediately set about converting Kōtoku to his own ideas, sending him anarchist books and pictures of anarchists and social revolutionaries. Like many others, Johnson was mistakenly convinced that the theories of anarchism and the activities of the social revolutionaries were two sides of the same coin. This combination, which Kōtoku accepted, gave to the social revolutionaries the scientific theory of Kropotkin's anarchocommunism and to anarchism an almost irresistible revolutionary glamour.

Kōtoku spent his five months in prison in reading and in intense thought, and his progress toward anarchism continued. In August 1905 he wrote "Indeed, I had gone [to Sugamo prison] as a Marxian socialist and returned a radical anarchist."[44] While in prison Kōtoku decided to work out his new ideas by going to America after his release, and in November he set off for San Francisco.[45] He

43. Kōtoku, quoted by Tanaka Sogorō, in *Kōtoku Shūsui*, 261. Notehelfer does not see the Russian revolution as an element in Kōtoku's conversion.
44. Kōtoku to Johnson (8/10/05), *Mother Earth,* VI, 6, 182.
45. Shioda Shōbei, *Kōtoku Shūsui no Nikki to Shokan* (Tokyo, 1954), 406. For Kōtoku's other motives, see Notehelfer, 116–119.

stayed there for seven months, seeing a great deal of Johnson and studying all the radical groups of the Bay area. The only significant addition to the ideas that he formed in Japan was the concept of "direct action." This compromise between revolution and reform was current in the Industrial Workers of the World, the union founded in June 1905 which had its main strength in the Pacific states. Its leaders rejected the craft unionism of the American Federation of Labor and the electoral tactics of the American Socialist Party. The I.W.W. wanted to overthrow the economic power of the capitalists and the political power of their state by "direct action"—demonstrations and strikes backed by violence and refusal to pay taxes or be drafted. Union leaders maintained that when the working class had become sufficiently class conscious and militant by these means it would be able to start and maintain a general strike that would bring about the collapse of capitalist society. After this the government would be replaced by trade unions, and eventually the world would be federated under "one big union." [46] These ideas, similar but unconnected to those of the French syndicalists, had a great effect on Kōtoku. They provided a policy more immediately applicable to Japan than the assassinations and peasant risings of the Russian social revolutionaries. Thus Kōtoku saw himself as a scientific anarchocommunist identified with social revolutionary tactics in Russia and the "lost countries of Asia," advocating immediate direct action for Japan and the West.

Kōtoku first began to expound his new views while he was still in San Francisco in letters to *Light*, the new socialist journal.[47] But his letters made no impact until his return to Japan on June 22, 1906. Six days later he gave a lecture on "trends in the world revolutionary movement" which caused a sensation. "Kōtoku," it was reported, "just returned from six months abroad studying the new tendencies of socialist parties, came back to Japan carrying a bombshell, his talk about 'direct action' as opposed to parliamentary [methods]." [48] After the meeting Japanese socialists began to absorb the staggering idea that their leading intellectual believed

46. G.D.H. Cole, III, 2, 793–797.
47. See his series "San Furanshisuko yori," in *Hikari*.
48. Tanaka, *Kōtoku Shūsui*, 315. See also Shioda Shōbei, *Kōtoku Shūsui*, 457; and Nishio Yōtarō, *Kōtoku Shūsui* (Tokyo, 1959), 159.

that Marxist social democracy was outmoded and that the wave of the future was direct action and anarchocommunism.

After his speech Kōtoku, whose health was always bad, went to the country because of illness. He did not return to Tokyo until September. Once back, though still ill, he threw himself into the socialist movement. Although he joined with Sakai, Nishikawa, and others in their plans to publish a daily newspaper supported by all socialist factions, he attacked their two main policies, agitation for adult suffrage and for economic help for the workers and unemployed. He gave several speeches in which he argued fiercely and effectively for direct action and anarchocommunism and reinforced his image as a man in touch with the latest European trends by publishing a letter to him from Kropotkin himself.[49]

In January 1907, the political and Christian wings of the socialist movement came together to found a new daily, *The Commoners' Newspaper,* and for the first time the Japanese socialist movement was united under one party with one journal. However, the annual meeting of the Japanese Socialist Party in February revealed the divisions within the movement. The chief motion before the conference was one put forward by the executive amending three points in the party constitution, the most important being the proposed change of Article I from "We advocate socialism within the limits of the law" to "Our aim is the realization of socialism."[50] This radical departure from social democratic legality illustrates the great changes that had taken place within the party. But Kōtoku was not satisfied and in "one of the great orations of our time" he demanded an explicit renunciation of parliamentary methods and that the party should openly support direct action and a general strike. A moderate proposed a countermotion, asking the party to state that "parliamentarianism is the tacit direction of the Japanese socialist movement."[51] He received two votes, the executive 28, and Kōtoku 22. Thus by February 1907, 50 out of the 62 delegates no longer supported parliamentary social democracy, and 22 out of 52 were anarchosyndicalists. After the party's repudiation of authority it was immediately banned by the police, and *The Commoners' Newspaper* did not long survive. In the situation of semilegality

49. *Hikari* (11/25/06), 3.
50. Tanaka, *Kōtoku Shūsui,* 356.   51. Kublin, 195.

that followed, anarchism continued to flourish, until by 1908 Kōtoku and his ideas completely dominated the Japanese socialist movement.

Kōtoku's personality and oratory, together with his convincing claim to be in touch with the latest Western trends, were largely responsible for the rapid change of ideas in the winter of 1906–1907. However, he was effective only because many of his colleagues, particularly the newer younger members, shared his dissatisfaction with social democracy—its emphasis on voting and moderation, its slow staged progress to socialism, and above all its faith in the proletariat and its contempt for youth. Furthermore, his colleagues were strongly moved by the non-Marxist aspects of the Russian revolution which was by no means over in the autumn of 1906. But violence alone was not sufficient to be attractive; it had to be applicable to Japan, and modern and scientific. The concept of direct action satisfied all three requirements. According to Kōtoku direct action was possible in countries where parlimentary progress was blocked but in which conditions were not yet ripe for revolution. Moreover, the concept was backed by Kropotkin's theoretical anarchism which, from a basis in Marxist economics and Darwinian evolution, had developed into something even more modern and scientific. Moderate and old-fashioned Marxist social democracy had no hope against the new movement.

Kōtoku was not completely unaided in his conversion of the Japanese socialists to anarchism. In November 1906 a favorable account of anarchism appeared under the title *Anarchism in Europe and America*. This book, instalments of which had been published earlier in the year in *The Study of Socialism*, was by Kutsumi Kesson, a journalist and an old friend of Kōtoku, who in 1906 was working in Nagasaki. He was a contributor to the socialist journals in Tokyo and a member of the local branch of the Commoners' Press. Before 1906 Kutsumi had the reputation of being "a kind of anarchist," and by that year he had become extremely interested in anarchocommunism.[52] His sympathies with anarchism and populism must have been strengthened by his contact with a small group of Russian social revolutionaries based on Nagasaki. In May 1906 he wrote in *Light,* enthusiastically describing a Captain

52. Nishida Nagashi, Introduction to the reprint of *Hikari*, VII.

Wadezki who had just founded a revolutionary magazine in Russia called *Volia*. He also stated that a Dr. Russel was involved.[53] Kutsumi was not the only Japanese to have contact with the Russian group. The ultranationalist Black Dragon Society also sent its agent to meet and encourage the revolutionaries.[54] The aims of the society, which had been founded in 1900, were to spread Japanese influence to the Amur (Black Dragon) River area and eventually to drive Russia from Eastern Siberia. Since 1902 its members, many of whom were interested in social reform at home, had seen the potential of the Russian revolutionary movement and had considered ways of helping it in order to weaken the czarist regime.[55] It is unlikely, however, that they made any personal contact with the Russian revolutionaries before the war.

During the 1890s there were similar groups working for a reformed East Asia under Japanese leadership, groups that were interested primarily in Korea and China. After 1900 the defeat of the Chinese reformers and revolutionaries and the Russian occupation of Manchuria caused most of the ultranationalists and their influential backers to turn their attention toward the dangers and opportunities coming from Russia.[56] At the same time the Japanese government began to see the advantageous possibilities of cooperation with the Manchu regime. Thus Miyazaki Torazō and his friends' support for Sun Yat-sen continued in the face of coldness and discouragement from the Japanese authorities.

For the group and for Miyazaki in particular the years from 1901 to 1904 were ones of depression.[57] In 1905 affairs brightened and, like radicals everywhere, the Japanese patriots were greatly encouraged by events in Russia. Furthermore, the group's part in the establishment of the Revolutionary Alliance led to their becoming

53. *Hikari* (5/20/06), 2. Russel, whose real name was N. K. Sudzilovski, was born in 1848 and died in 1930. His revolutionary career in Russia, Romania, Bulgaria, California, Hawaii, Japan, the Philippines and China is too fantastic to give in full here. See S. L. Tikhvinsky, *Sun Yat-sen* (in Russian; Moscow, 1964), note on 92-93.
54. Tanaka, *Kōtoku Shūsui*, 366.
55. See D. M. Brown, *Nationalism in Japan: An Introductory Historical Analysis* (Berkeley, 1955), 114.
56. Jansen, *The Japanese and Sun Yat-sen,* 108; and Brown, 136.
57. Jansen, 112.

closely associated with the Alliance though not fully accepted by all the Chinese students.[58] Sun, however, retained complete confidence in his Japanese friends, and in the summer of 1906 he went with a retired officer named Kayano Nagatomo on a journey to South East Asia. On the way south their ship called at Nagasaki, and through the local agent of the Black Dragon Society they were put in contact with Russel who came on board and had a two hour conversation with Sun.[59] Their talk concerned the revolutionary movement in both countries, and it is almost certain that Russel used it to put forward his social revolutionary views as he did in the correspondence between them that followed.[60]

This was not the only instance of the Miyazaki group trying to link the Russian and Chinese revolutions. That same summer, probably inspired by the existence of *The People's Journal* and the newly founded *Volia*, they decided to establish a new journal entitled *The Review of Revolutions*. Kayano stated the factors behind this decision:

At that time, we Japanese who were members of the Revolutionary Alliance believed that China and Russia were the two great autocracies and that their repression was a block to freedom. We also believed that for the advance of civilization it was necessary to overthrow these autocracies. As a change in these regimes was necessary we launched a bimonthly magazine called *The Review of Revolutions* to help the revolutions in China and Russia.[61]

After some delay the first issue of the *The Review of Revolutions* appeared in September 5, 1906. Its contents were listed in English on the front page as follows:

Current topics on the Western Revolutionary movements. (1) Torpidinous measure of Revolution. (2) Open confession of Sasanof. (3) Secret bomb factories. (4) Glimpse of the boiling Russia. (5) Anarchism in Spain. (6) The Tsar's Iron Hell. Modern Revolutionary problem of China. . . . ; Epitome of Revolutionary Heroes—Michael Bakunin; "Crossing the Threshold," a

58. Feng Zi-you, *Kaiguo shi* 1, 309.
59. Luo, *Guofu Nianpu,* I, 163; and Tanaka, *Kōtoku Shūsui,* 367.
60. Two letters from Sun to Russel are reprinted in A. N. Kheifet, "Revolyutsonye svasi Narodov Rossii i Kitaya v Nachale XX Veka," *Voprosi Istorii,* 1956, XII, 91–100.
61. Kayano Nagatomo, *Chūkaminkoku Kakumei Hikyū* (Tokyo, 1941), 85.

novel by Turgenev; The Chinese students in Japan. Appendix: Report of the Society of Equal Land.[62]

Throughout the *Review*'s existence—the tenth and last issue came out on March 25, 1907—almost all the articles in it concerned assassination and the violent aspects of the Russian and Chinese revolutions. There were also articles on Western anarchist activities and about anarchist leaders, including the nonviolent Kropotkin, firmly linking them in the reader's mind to the Russian movement. The writers' belief in this tenuous connection was undoubtedly helped by the increasing interest in anarchism among Japanese after Kōtoku's return. It is not certain how much contact the patriots had with Kōtoku at this time, but Miyazaki Tamizō did have two long conversations with him in September, and it is very likely that the future fascist leader, Kita Ikki, who was working with the Miyazakis at the time, was also seeing Kōtoku.[63]

After the *Review*'s foundation the patriots continued their efforts to put Sun in touch with Russian revolutionaries. In the middle of November 1906, Gregori Gershuni, the founder of the Social Revolutionary Party's "battle group" or assassination squad, and perhaps the Party's most famous leader at the time, escaped from Siberia to Japan.[64] Members of the Miyazaki group contacted him, and on November 15, two days before his departure for Europe, they arranged a meeting with Sun, and the two talked through the night. Gershuni also gave an interview to the *Review* in which he described his adventures, the progress of the Russian revolutionaries and of the Social Revolutionary Party.[65]

Throughout the autumn and winter of 1906 the patriots kept up their close contact with the Chinese students. *The Review of Revolutions* and *The People's Journal* frequently advertised in each other pages, and the calligraphy for the *Review*'s first page was written by the *Journal*'s editor, Zhang Bing-lin.[66] Writers for the *Review* were very much in evidence at the *Journal*'s anniversary meeting in December—an event which received extensive coverage

62. *Kakumei Hyōron* (9/6/06).
63. Shioda Shōbei, *Kōtoku Shūsui*, 408; and Tanaka, *Kita Ikki.*
64. B. I. Nikolayevsky, *Aseff the Russian Judas*, trans. G. Reavey (London, 1934), 202.
65. Wada Saburō, "Gerushyūni," *Kakumei Hyōron* (1/25/07).
66. Kayano, 85.

in the *Review*. From Song Jiao-ren's diary, it is clear that he and his friends were in close and constant contact with the Miyazaki brothers and with Kita Ikki.

There is little doubt that the *Review* was successful in its attempts to influence and inspire the Chinese students. Again, we can rely on Song's diary.

9/6/06. Cloudy . . . received a copy of *The Review of Revolutions*. When I examined it I saw that it contained articles about political and social revolution, novels, and news, though it emphasized the Chinese revolutionary movement, and it said that students in Japan should not be insulted. . . . There were also accounts of Wu Yue and Chen Tian-hua and their self sacrifice for their country. . . . I was so moved that without being aware of it, I cried for a long time.[67]

The chief effect of *The Review of Revolutions* on the Chinese students in Japan was to confirm the link that already existed in their minds between the Russian revolutionary tradition and the situation in China. In addition, two important side effects were the creation of an identification of anarchism with populist terrorism and the mistaken establishment of Bakunin and Kropotkin as heroes of the Russian revolution.

In his article on the introduction of Marxism to China, the modern Chinese historian Rong Meng-yuan states: "From 1907 the articles in *The People's Journal* introducing socialism became very scarce, while articles introducing anarchism increased."[68] A glance at the contents of the *Journal* indicates that he is substantially correct. For the purpose of analysis it is convenient to divide the *Journal*'s life into three stages: first, from November 1905 to June 1906. issues I to V were nominally edited by Zhang Ji but in fact were produced collectively by Hu Han-min, Wang Jing-wei, Zhu Zhi-xin, Wang Dong, and Song Jiao-ren; second, from July 1906 to January 1907, issues VI to XI were edited by Zhang Bing-lin, who worked closely with the original group; third, from March 1907 to October 1908, when the Japanese authorities closed the *Journal*, issues XII

67. Song, 203. In fact, the sections on Wu Yue and Chen Tian-hua did not appear until the seventh issue in January 1907. This means that Song did not write up his diary immediately, which if anything strengthens his report of the impact of *Kakumei Hyōron*.

68. Rong Meng-yuan, 7.

to XXIV.[69] In this last period the original compilers, with the exception of Zhang Ji, had left Japan, and Liu Shi-pei had come to join Zhang Bing-lin, although the two split acrimoniously in the summer of 1908.

During the first period there were ten articles favorable to social democracy, two on the Russian revolution and nihilism, and none on anarchism. During the second there were two articles on socialism, three on anarchism—two of them unfavorable—and two on Russian nihilism. In the third period there were ten articles concerned with anarchism and nihilism, and none on socialism.[70]

A study of the frequency of word use suggests that there was a significant drop in the frequency of terms and names associated with socialism at the end of the first period, and a significant rise in the frequency of terms and names associated with anarchism and nihilism at the beginning of the third.[71] The use of these terms does not, of course, indicate favor or disfavor of them, but it does show

69. Two further issues were produced in 1910 by Wang Jing-wei. For a history of *Min Bao,* see Tang Zeng-bi, "Tongmeng Hui Shidai *Min Bao* Shimo ji," in *Xinhai Geming,* II, 438–459.

70. For the articles on socialism in periods I and II, see chapter 6 above. The pieces on Russian nihilism in the first period were "Eguo Geming Dang zhi Ribao" on *Volia* by Hu Han-min in *Min Bao,* IV; and "Nian Luguo zhi Geming" (translated, 1905, by Song Jiao-ren from an article in *Tokyo Nichi-nichi Shimbun*), 2 pts., *Min Bao,* III and VII. The unfavorable pieces on anarchism in the second period were "Wuzhengfu Dang yu Geming zhi Shuming," by Ye Xia-sheng, *Min Bao,* VII; and "Wuzhengfuzhuyi yu shehuizhuyi" (translated by Liao Zhong-kai from W.D.P. Bliss, *A Handbook of Socialism*), *Min Bao,* IX. The favorable one was from Kutsumi's *O-Bei no Museifushugi,* "Wuzhungfuzhyi zhi er Pai," *Min Bao,* VIII, Liao later translated the whole book. The only article on nihilism apart from Song's second instalment on the Russian revolution was "Xuwu Dang Xiao shi," translated from Kemuyama, by Liao, *Min Bao,* XI, 89–107.

The articles on anarchism and on the issue of "government" in the third period were "Bakuning Zhuan" by Wang Dong, based on Kutsimi, *Min Bao,* XVI; "Guojia Lun," by Zhang Bing-lin, and "Zhengfu Shuo" by Lei Shao-xing, both in *Min Bao,* XVII; "Ji Putaoya Wang bei Ci" by Wang Dong, *Min Bao,* XIX; "Wuzhengfuzhuyi Xu" by Zhang Bing-lin, *Min Bao,* XX. The pieces concerned with Russian nihilism and terrorism were "Sufeiya Zhuan," by Wang Dong, *Min Bao,* XV; "Cike Jiao Junren lun," by Wang Dong, and "Xuwu Dang Xiao shi," translated from Kemuyama by Liao, 2nd instalment, *Min Bao,* XVII; "Diwang ansha zhi shida," by Wang Dong, *Min Bao,* XXI; and "Geming xinli" by Tang Zeng-bi, *Min Bao,* XXIV.

71. The arbitrariness of the selection of words and names from Onogawa Hidemi's *Minpo Sakuin,* 2 vols. (Tokyo, 1970), makes it useless to use complex statistical methods. Even the publication of figures arrived at would give spurious validity to the result.

the degree of concern with the subject. The *Journal's* illustrations show no such change, and there is a constant high frequency of pictures of social revolutionaries and anarchists which is in no way surprising as there had been a growing interest in the Russian revolutionary movement since 1903. By 1907 most of the radical student journals had stopped publication, and *The People's Journal* was *the* journal of the revolutionaries; thus its changes do represent changes among the students in Japan as a whole.

The new elements that appeared between July 1906 and July 1907 were the association of interest in Russian terrorism with interest in anarchist theory and a concern with government and the state as such. There was also an identification of anarchism with true socialism. On August 30, 1907, Liu Shi-pei and Zhang established the Society for the Study of Socialism. At its foundation Liu proclaimed: "Our aim is not only to practice socialism but to have anarchism as our goal." [72] From 1907 to 1911 a considerable number of advanced Chinese intellectuals believed that anarchocommunism was the essence of socialism. In June 1911 Song Jiao-ren, who by this time had detached himself from socialism, wrote: "If you advocate true socialism it will not succeed unless you support anarchism and communism; neither social democracy nor state socialism are worthy of respect." [73]

The new tone was clearly set by the summer or 1907. The foundation of the Society for the Study of Socialism had been preceded by the establishment in June of *The Journal of Natural Justice,* the first Chinese anarchist journal in the Far East. The same month an unrelated group of revolutionaries in Paris founded another anarchist magazine, *The New Era.* [74] The reasons for the simultaneity of the two movements and for the establishment of *The New Era* at this time are obscure, but they are clearly related to the intellectual

72. Liu in "Shehuizhuyi Jiangxi Hui diyici Kaihui Jishi" in *Tianyi Bao,* VI (9/1/07), reprint, 152.

73. Song, "Lun Shehuizhuyi," reprinted in Jiang Kang-hu, *Hongshuiji,* 47. For the anarchist period as a whole, see Scalapino and Yu, *The Chinese Anarchist Movement.*

74. For details of the Chinese anarchist movement in France and its rivalry with the Japanese group see *Chinese Anarchist Movement,* 2–28; Gasster, *Chinese Intellectuals and the Revolution of 1911,* 155–189; and D.W.Y. Kwok, *Scientism in Chinese Thought, 1900–1950* (New Haven, 1965), 3–58.

situations in both China and France. As such they were associated with the world-wide movement toward anarchosyndicalism after 1905. The syndicalist movement in France, the I.W.W. in the United States, the Labor militancy in Britain and Australia, and perhaps even the Soviets (Syndicates) in Russia seem to show a general pattern of radical reaction to parliamentary social democracy. The contradiction was only resolved by Rosa Luxemburg and Lenin. *The New Era,* which survived *Natural Justice* and was not tarnished by the open defection of Liu Shi-pei to the Manchus in 1908, was even more influential than the latter in the consolidation of anarchism among the Chinese students, but it did not initiate the swing toward it.[75]

One of the reasons why some historians have failed to note the change from socialism to anarchism is that Liu Shi-pei and other writers for *Natural Justice*—though not *The New Era* group—continued or even developed Chinese interest in Marxism. Early in 1908 that journal published translations from the Japanese of Engels' 1888 "Introduction to the *Communist Manifesto,*" the first chapter of the *Manifesto* itself, and sections from Engels' *The Origin of the Family.* This interest should not be misunderstood; East Asian socialists wanted any information about the subject, however heterodox. Furthermore, anarchism is by definition eclectic: Kropotkin and the anarchocommunists respected Marx and Engels as the founding fathers of scientific socialism, although they believed that in many respects Marxism had been superseded by more modern and more scientific theories.

This confusion notwithstanding, some historians recognized and deplored the shift toward anarchism.[76] But there have been few attempts to analyze the causes of this change. The most common explanation is that anarchism came in as an adjunct to individual terrorism because of pessimism among the revolutionaries after repeated failures.[77] There is no doubt that there was depression in the revolutionary movement after the failures of the winter of

75. Liu, *Tianyi Bao,* reprint; and Tan Bi-an, "Eguo Mincuizhuyi dui Tongmeng Hui di Yingxiang," *Lishi Yanjiu,* I, 36.
76. Rong Meng-yuan, 11; Tang Leang-li, 54.
77. See for instance Li Zhu, "Lun Shehuizhuyi zai Zhongguo di Zhuanbo," *Lishi Yanjiu,* III, 1–21.

1906–1907. However, there had been sporadic individual terrorist attempts since 1900, whereas their relation to anarchist theory began on a significant scale only in 1907.

A more convincing explanation of the transformation is that it began when Zhang Bing-lin became editor of *The People's Journal,* when he and other central Chinese gained control of the Revolutionary Alliance, replacing Sun and his Cantonese supporters. This theory is supported by the fact that aside from Zhang Ji, who had been interested in the subject since 1903, the leading champions of anarchism in Tokyo were Zhang Bing-lin's friends, Liu Shi-pei, his wife He Zhen, and Wang Dong.[78] Zhang Bing-lin, though not an anarchist himself, was extremely interested in anarchism. There is no doubt that the simplicity of anarchism, its emphasis on morality, its belief in the rural community, and its total rejection of Western society were appealing to men from the more traditional North and Central China, men like Zhang Ji, Zhang Bing-lin, and Liu Shi-pei.

There are a few drawbacks to this scheme. First, interest in social democracy was not confined to Cantonese. Song Jiao-ren, for instance, from tradition-bound Hunan, translated extremely technical articles on the subject. Second, while Liu Shi-pei was preeminently interested in China, he also wrote about Hobbes, Rousseau, and Darwin.[79] Moreover, he published advanced Marxist texts. Third, one should not overemphasize the backwardness of Liu's home in Yangzhou, or Zhang's just outside Hangzhou, or neglect the fact that they had both lived in Shanghai.

There is no doubt, however, that Zhang and Liu were more culturally and psychologically susceptible to anarchism than the group around Sun.[80] Their degree of classical culture and attachment to Chinese tradition was of a different order to that of the Cantonese revolutionaries. Furthermore, both men had been interested in assassination for some time. This seems to have come mainly from the Chinese heroic tradition, but this was reinforced by

78. For Wang Dong, see his "Tongmeng Hui he Min Bao Bianduan Huiyi," *Xinhai Geming Huiyilu,* VI, 23–32.

79. Liu Shi-pei and He zhen, "Lun Zhongzu Geming yu Wuzhengfu Geming zhi deshi," *Tianyi Bao,* VI (9/1/07), reprint, 135–148.

80. One should not neglect the fact that the most cosmopolitan Tongmeng Hui leaders, Liao Zhong-kai and Zhu Zhi-xin, were also interested in anarchism.

Japanese and Russian examples.[81] Late in 1904 Liu Shi-pei had organized an attempt on the life of an extraordinarily corrupt ex-official, Wang Zhi-chun, and months before that he had written an article on "The Advantages of Extremism" under the pen-name of First Extremist.[82] Although Zhang was in prison when the Restoration Society was founded late in 1904, he was very much involved with members of the society, which was founded by his son-in-law Gong Bao-quan specifically as an assassination group.[83] This society also developed to an extremely high level the Russian populist technique of intellectuals establishing relations with, and control of, secret societies.[84]

Zhang Bing-lin became editor of *The People's Journal* immediately after his release from prison in Shanghai and upon his arrival in Japan in July 1906. The beginning of his editorship appears to have marked the end of intense interest in social democracy. However, this is not because Sun's followers ceased writing for the journal: Wang Jing-wei, Hu Han-min, Liao Zhong-kai, and Zhu Zhi-xin were still writing for it in 1907. The students who had been interested in socialism were not forbidden to write, they simply stopped writing about social democracy, either because the editors and readers had lost interest in it, or because they themselves had done so, or for both reasons. Tang Leang-li has stated that since it was Zhu Zhi-xin who introduced socialism, when Zhu left Tokyo to take up revolutionary activities in China, people gave up studying it.[85] In fact, Zhu stopped writing on socialism nine months before he left Japan, and after his return to China in the spring of 1907 he found time to write two articles on Revolutionary Alliance social policies but not on Western socialism. Another indication that Zhu had lost enthusiasm for social democracy is the

81. For the tradition see James Liu, *The Chinese Knight Errant* (London, 1967). See in particular, 118, for a reference to Zhang's teacher, Yu Yue. For its influence in the Lower Yangtze at the beginning of the twentieth century, see Mary Rankin.

82. For the background to this attempt, see "Liu Shih-p'ei," paper presented to the Research Conference on Intellectuals and the Problem of Conservatism in Republican China, held in Dedham, Mass. (August 1972), 11–20.

83. Shen Tie-min, "Ji Guangfu Hui ersan shi," *Xinhai Geming Huiyilu*, IV, 131–142.

84. Mary Rankin, 151–154; and Tao Cheng-zhang, "Zhean Jilue," *Xinhai Geming*, III, 1–22.

85. Tang Leang-li, 54.

statement by his younger brother that Zhu was "clearly influenced by anarchism" in the years before 1911.[86] Liao Zhong-kai provides an even clearer example, for in the early period he translated articles on socialism and Henry George. By the spring of 1907 he was translating Kemuyama Sentarō's *Modern Anarchism*. Thus the disappearance of the Cantonese group cannot explain a change which they themselves took part in.

It was in the spring of 1907, at the time when Zhang Bing-lin and Liu Shi-pei took complete control of the paper, that concern with anarchism rose sharply. Granted that Zhang and Liu were susceptible to anarchism, why did they become interested in it only at this point? Despite his interest in terrorism, Zhang did not write on anarchism before his imprisonment, and Liu had actually written against it.[87] There is no doubt that Zhang's and Liu's intellectual dominance over the revolutionary students and the related wave of cultural conservatism would have brought about shifts in political opinion. However, if anarchism had not been introduced from outside, there is no reason why it need have taken this form. Since it did, the anarchist movement in Tokyo can be seen as an aspect of the same rejection of the West expressed by Zhang's and Liu's cultural conservativism. It was, therefore, the polar opposite of the positivist Westernizing anarchism of the Paris group.

What then were the fundamental causes for the transformation in 1906–1907? Primarily, they were (1) the increase of interest in Russian terrorism stemming from the activities of the social revolutionaries in the Russian revolution and (2) the conversion of the Japanese socialist movement to anarchism—which itself had the same origins. The chief reasons why the Chinese students became particularly aware of the Russian terrorists between July 1906 and July 1907 were the establishment of *The Review of Revolutions* in September 1906 and Sun's meetings with Russel and Gershuni, occurrences which brought Chinese and Russian revolutionaries into direct contact. And in April 1907 Zhang Bing-lin brought out a special supplement to *The People's Journal* which made a great im-

---

86. Zhu Zhi-ru, 422.

87. See his and Liu Xie's "Zhongguo Minyue Jingyi" (1904), reprinted in Liu, *Liu Shen-shu Xiansheng Yishu,* reprinted in 4 vols. (Taipei, 1965) I, 673–713, esp. 688–689.

pact. It featured the writings of Wu Yue with their emphasis on the Russian historical scheme of the three stages of revolutionary activity: literature, agitation, and assassination. The publication also reminded the students of the heroism of this leading Chinese follower of the social revolutionaries. All these factors drew attention to Russia and made the activities of the German social democrats and the Anglo-Saxon land reformers seem very tame and uninteresting.

There is no evidence that Kōtoku met any Chinese before April 1907.[88] However, students listened to his speeches and were aware of his ideas before then.[89] In March 1907 Zhang Ji and Zhang Bing-lin begged Kita Ikki to introduce them to his old friend Kōtoku.[90] By August, enough contact had been established for Kōtoku to suggest the foundation of the Society for the Study of Socialism, modeled on his Socialist Friday Club, and to speak at the Chinese society's inaugural meeting.[91] Kōtoku's campaign removed social democracy's chief attraction in Chinese eyes, that is, its claim to represent the most advanced and scientific thinking in the West.

After the autumn of 1906 the Russian terrorists became attractive not only for their courage and fervor but also because of their alleged possession of the modern, scientific theory of anarchism. No longer did Chinese radicals interested in Western theories have to worry about such aspects of social democracy as class conflict, the need for China to pass through capitalism, the hegemony of the urban proletariat, or the achievement of social justice by parliamentary means. All of these could now be bypassed by anarchism, the true socialism. For the less radical, like Song Jiao-ren, the identification of socialism and anarchism led to a retreat from both. It was in the spring of 1907 that Hu Han-min went to some pains to claim that *minshengzhuyi* was not socialism but demosology, and that not merely socialists but also sociologists were in favor of their land policies.[92] Despite this attempted disassociation, Sun's dif-

88. See Shioda Shobei, *Kōtoku Shūsui*.

89. See for instance the description of one of Kōtoku's meetings by Jing Mei-jiu in *Zuian* (Shanghai, n.d.), sections of which are printed in *Xinhai Geming*, II, 253–256.

90. Tanaka, *Kita Ikki*, 124.   91. Liu, *Tianyi Bao*, VI, 154; and Notehelfer.

92. Hu, "Gao Fei," 126, and 144–146.

ficulties in persuading people to accept his land policies increased from 1907 to 1911.[93] By 1906 socialism and social problems were clearly important questions for both revolutionaries and reformists. However, they were subordinated to their concern over national, constitutional, or even personal issues. Nevertheless, the fact that socialism has played a crucial role in twentieth-century Chinese history gives the Chinese concern with socialism up to 1907 a wider relevance. Even though the early socialist movement was abortive and its influence apparently disappeared in the short run, its long-term effects were greater. This was because the individuals involved played significant political roles in the 1920s when the Soviet revolution made Marx and socialism relevant once again.

The study of socialism in China in the early period helps to clarify several points of general significance. Primarily, it shows the essential irrelevance of pre-Leninist Marxist social democracy to China. It indicates why, after relatively promising beginnings, the study of Marxism should have been aborted until the 1920s. It also helps explain the fact that by 1919 several Chinese thinkers had absorbed Marxist concepts, although Marx himself was hardly mentioned after 1907. This came about either because of writings published before that date or through Marxist elements in the more "modern" theories that followed. There is no doubt that this earlier acquaintance speeded the Chinese response to Marxism after the May 4 Movement. Describing this situation more than forty years later, the anti-Manchu and communist leader Wu Yu-zhang wrote:

In 1903 when I was in Tokyo I read *The Essence of Socialism* by Kōtoku Shūsui and found the new teachings quite novel. But because I had then to study in school on the one hand and take part in practical revolutionary work on the other, I did not make a deep study of these teachings but let them pass. As I came across these teachings again I felt as though I had met an old friend. The noble ideas of equality among all people and the elimination of [the distinction between] rich and poor as described in socialist books, greatly inspired me. They reminded me of Sun Yat-sen's Three Prin-

93. For the dropping of the principle of Equal Land Rights by revolutionary organizations after 1907, see Feng, *Geming Yishi,* III, 214.

ciples of the People and the ancient teaching of *datong*. All these were woven into a picture of the beautiful society to come.[94]

94. Wu Yu-zhang, "Huiyi Wusi qianhou wodi sixiang zhuanbian," *Zhongguo Qingnian,* IX (5-1/1959), 10-15, esp. 10. I am indebted to Mr. David Elliot for this quotation.

Names of Chinese and Japanese Organizations

Association for the Promotion of Labor Unions	Rōdō Kumiai Kiseikai
Black Dragon Society	Kokuryūkai
Chinese Socialist Party	Zhongguo Shehui Dang
Commoners' Society	Heimin Sha
Eastern Socialist Party	Tōyō Shaikaitō
Idealist Band	Risō Dan
Japanese Association for the Study of Social Policies	Nihon Shakai Seisaku Gakkai
Japanese Social Democratic Party	Nihon Shakai Minshutō
Japanese Socialist Party	Nippon Shakaitō
Liberal Party	Jiyutō
Political Association	Zhengwen She
Public People's Party	Gongmin Dang
Restoration Society	Guangfu Hui
Revolutionary Alliance	Tongmeng Hui
Riksha Party	Shakaitō
Socialist Association	Shakaishugi Kyōrai
Socialist Friday Club	Shakaishugi Kinyōbi Kōshūkai
Socialist Party	Shakaitō
Socialist Party	Shehui Dang
Socialist Research Society	Shakaishugi Kenkyūkai
Society for the Promotion of National Studies	Guoxue Zhenqi She
Society for Research into Social Problems	Shakai Mondai Kenkyūkai
Society for Research into the Land Problem	Tochi Mondai no Kenkyūkai
Society for Research into Socialism	Shehuizhuyi Yanjiu Hui

Society for the Restoration of
   Land Rights   Tochi Fukken Dōshikai
Society for the Study of
   Socialism   Shehuizhuyi Jiangxi Hui
Southern Society   Nan She

Names of Chinese and Japanese Journals, Books, and Publishers

The Alarm Bell	*Jingzhong Ribao*
Bookshop for the Diffusion of Knowledge	Guangzhi Zhuji
The China National Gazette	*Guomin Riribao*
The Chinese Daily	*Zhongguo Ribao*
The Chinese Progress	*Shiwu Bao*
Civilization Press	Wenming Chubanshe
Collected Translations	*Yishu Huibian*
The Commoners' Newspaper	*Heimin Shimbun*
Confucius as a Reformer	*Kongzi Gaizhi Kao*
The Daily News	*Yorozu Chōhō*
Datong Translated Book Company	Datong Yishuju
The False Classics of the Xin Dynasty	*Xinxue Weijing Kao*
The Globe Magazine	*Wanguo Gongbao*
The Journal of National Essence	*Guocui Xuebao*
Labor World	*Rōdō Sekai*
Light	*Hikari*
Natural Justice	*Tianyi Bao*
The New Age	*Shin Kigen*
The New Era	*Xin Shiji*
The People's Journal	*Min Bao*
Pure Criticism	*Qingyi Bao*
The Renovation of the People	*Xinmin Xongbao*
The Review of Revolutions	*Kakumei Hyōron*
The Review of the Times	*Wanguo Gongbao*
Revolutionary Army	*Geming Jun*
Spring and Autumn Annals	*Chunqiu*
Straight Talk	*Chokugen*

The Study of Socialism	*Shakaishugi Kenkyū*
Tides of Chekiang	*Zhejiang Chao*
The Translation Magazine	*Yishu Huibian*
Translations from Students Abroad	*Youxue Yibian*
The Universe	*Rikugo Zasshi*

APPENDIX III.

Chinese Forms of Chinese and Japanese Words

Abe Isō	安部磯雄	Datong Xuexiao	大同學校
Anmin	安民	Datong Yishu Ju	大同譯書局
Anmin Xinxue	安民新學	Ding Wen-jiang	丁文江
Ariga Nagao	有賀長雄	Dishui	地稅
Bagong	罷工	Dong Bi-wu	董必武
Bainian yi Jiao	百年一覺	Dong Zhong-shu	董仲舒
Bainian yi Meng	百年一夢	*Dongfang Zazhi*	東方雜誌
Baohuang Hui	保皇會	Dōshisha	同志社
Baozhen	寶琛	Du Lian-zhe	杜聯喆
Bianjian	辨姦	Duan-fang	端方
Byōdō	平等	Duli zhi Geren	獨立之個人
Cai Er-kang	蔡爾康	En-shou	恩壽
Cai Yuan-pei	蔡元培	*Ershi Shiji zhi Zhina*	二十世紀之支那
Chai De-keng	柴德賡	Fabian	法便
Changxing li	長興里	Fang Zhao-ying	房兆楹
Chen Ci-lan	陳紫瀾	Feng Gui-fen	馮桂芬
Chen Du-xiu	陳獨秀	Feng Zi-you	馮自由
Chen Qian-qiu	陳千秋	Fuguo Yangmin Ze	富國養民策
Cheng De-quan	程德全	Fukui Junzō	福井準造
Cheng Jia-sheng	程家檉	Fushen	富神
Cheng Zhung-yi	程鐘伊	Ge Gong-zhen	戈公振
Chokugen	直言	*Geming Jun*	革命軍
Chunqiu	春秋	Geming Junshi Xuexiao	革命軍事學校
Chunqiu Fanlu	春秋繁露	Geren Hui	個人會
Chunzui Shehuizhuyi	純粹社會主義	Gong (public)	公
Cike	刺客	Gong (artisan)	工
Dai Zhen	戴震	Gong Bao-quan	龔寶銓
Dang	黨	Gong Dang	工黨
Datong	大同	Gong Zi-zhen	龔自珍
Datongshu	大同書	Gongchan zhi Lun	共產之論

Gongchan zhi Shuo	共產之說	Hou Tai-wan	侯太館
Gongchanzhuyi	共產主義	Hou Wai-lu	侯外盧
Gongde	公德	Hu Han-min	胡漢民
Gongli	公理	Huang Shao-qi	黃紹箕
Gongmin Dang	公民黨	Huang Xing	黃興
Gongtian	公田	Huaxing Hui	華興會
Gongyang zhuan	公羊傳	Huidang	會黨
Gongyou	公有	Huitou kan	回頭看
Gongzuo zhi Yihui	工作之議會	Ike Kyōkichi	池享吉
Gu Yan-wu	顧炎武	Inukai Ki	犬養毅
Guafen Weiyan	瓜分危言	Ishikawa Kyōkusan	石川旭山
Guangzhi Shuju	廣智書局	Jiang Kang-hu	江亢虎
Gui	歸	Jiang Wei-qiao	蔣維喬
Gui Dan-chi	桂丹墀	Jiang Yong-jing	蔣永敬
Guo Ting-yi	郭廷以	Jiao	教
Guojia Minshengzhuyi	國家民生主義	*Jiaohui Xinbao*	教會新報
Guojia Shehui Zhengze	國家社會政策	Jiaoyu Gonggong	教育公共
Guojia Shehuizhuyi	國家社會主義	Jichanzhuyi	集產主義
Guojia Zhuyi	國家主義	Jiduan Minzhuzhuyi	極端民主義
Guomin Dang (Kuomintang)	國民黨	Jidujiao Shehuizhuyi	基督教社會主義
Guomin Gong Dang	國民公黨	Jieji	階級
Guomin Gongjin Hui	國民共進會	Jiezhi Ziben	節制資本
Hakuai	博愛	*Jingu xuekao*	今古學考
Han	瀋	Jing Mei-jiu	景梅九
Hao you	豪右	Jingji	經濟
Hatano Yoshihiro	波野善大	Jingtian	井田
He Xiang-ning	何香凝	Jingzhong Ribao	警鐘日報
He Xiao-liu	何曉柳	*Jinshi zhi Shehuizhuyi*	近世之社會主義
He Xiu	何休	*Jinsuzhai Yiji*	金粟齋遺集
He Zhen	何震	Jiupin	救貧
Heimin	平民	Jiyū Minken Undō	自由民權運動
Heimin sha	平民社	Jiyutō	自由黨
Heimin Shimbun	平民新聞	Judong	舉動
Heng Bao	衡報	Juluan	據亂
Hequn Junchan zhi Shuo	合群均產之說	Junchan zhi Shuo	均產之說
Hikari	光	Junfu Dang	均富黨
Hong shui Ji	洪水集	Junfuzhuyi	均富主義
Hong Xiu-quan	洪秀全	Junkō	巡耕
Hōsei Daigaku	法政大學	Juntian	均田
Hōsei Gakkō	法政學校	Juren	舉人

Kagaku	科學	Liji	禮記
Kaiming She	開明社	Liu Feng-lu	劉逢祿
Kaishintō	改進黨	Liu Shi-pei	劉師培
Kakumai Hyōron	革命評論	Lixiang	理想
Kao shu	尻書	Liyun	禮運
Katō Hiroyuki	加藤弘之	Longhua Hui	龍華會
Katsura Tarō	桂太郎	Lu Xun	魯迅
Kawakami Kiyoshi	河上清	Luandang	亂黨
Kayano Nagatomo	萱野長知	Luo Da-wei	羅大維
Keizai	經濟	Luo Jia-lun	羅家倫
Kemuyama Sentarō	煙山專太郎	Luotian	羅田
Keti	客体	Lutian	露田
Kexue	科學	Ma Jun-wu	馬君武
Kinoshita Naoe	木下尚江	Man-hua	曼華
Kirisuto Kyō Zasshi	基督敎雜誌	Mao Ze-dong	毛澤東
Kita Ikki	北一輝	Min Bao	民報
Kittei	吉亭	Min De	民德
Kobayashi Ushi Saburō	小林丑三郎	Min-yi	民意
Kokumin no tomo	國民の友	Minjian Yangsheng	民間養生
Kokumin Shimpō	國民新報	Minli Bao	民立報
Kokuryūkai	黑龍會	Minquanzhuyi	民權主義
Kongzi Gaizhi kao	孔子改制考	Minsheng	民生
Kōtoku Shūsui	幸德秋水	Minshengzhuyi	民生主義
Kuai Guang-dian	蒯光典	Minzhuzhuanzhi	民主專制
Kuroiwa Ruikō	黑岩淚香	Minzuzhuyi	民族主義
Kutsumi Kesson	久津見蕨村	Miyazaki Muryū	宮崎夢柳
Kyōkichi	享吉	Miyazaki Ryusuki	宮崎龍介
Lei Fen	雷奮	Miyazaki Tamizō	宮崎民藏
Lei Shao-xing	雷昭性	Miyazaki Torazō	宮崎寅藏
Li	里	Mou	歃
Li Ci-sheng	李滋生	Murai Chishi	村井知至
Li Da-nian	李大年	Muyou	慕友
Li Hong-zhang	李鴻章	Nakai Chōmin	中江兆民
Li Shi-yo	李時岳	Nanhai	南海
Li Yu	李玉	Nidang	尼黨
Li Zhu	黎澍	Nihelisite	尼赫力斯特
Liang Qi-chao	梁啟超	Nihon Shakaiseisaku Gakkai	日本社會政策學會
Liangxin	良心	Niida Noboru	仁井田陞
Liao Zhong-kai	廖仲愷	Nippon Shakai Tō	日本社會黨
Liguo Yiming	利國益民	Nishikawa Kojirō	西川光次郎

Nishio Yōtarō	西尾陽太郎	Sanetō Keishū	さねとうけいしゅう
Nixili	尼希利	Sanminzhuyi	三民主義
Nomura Koichi	野村浩一	Sanshi	三世
Nong Zhen Hui	農賑會	Shakai Minshutō	社會民主黨
Onogawa Hidemi	小野川秀美	Shakai Mondai Kenkyū kai	社會問題研究會
Osaka Asahi	大阪朝日	Shakaishugi	社會主義
Osugi Sakai	大杉榮	Shakaishugi Kenkyū	社會主義研究
Pandang	叛黨	Shakaishugi Kenkyūkai	社會主義研究會
Panyu	番禺	Shakaishugi Kinyobi Kōshukai	社會主義金曜日講習會
Pingdeng	平等	Shakaishugi Kyōkai	社會主義協會
Pingjun Diquan	平均地權	*Shakaishugi Shinzui*	社會主義真髓
Pingmin	平民	Shakaitō	社會黨
Qian Bo-can	翦伯贊	Shakaitō	車界黨
Qian Mu	錢穆	Shang	商
Qian Xuan-tong	錢玄同	Shang Yang	商鞅
Qiang Quan	強權	Shao Ting-yu	邵廷玉
Qingmiao	青苗	She-yuan	社員
Qingyi Bao	清議報	Shehuixuezhe	社會學者
Qiongli	窮黎	Shehui Dang	社會黨
Qun	羣	Shehui Zhengze	社會政策
Qunzhong	羣衆	Shehuizhuyi	社會主義
Ren	仁	*Shehuizhuyi Gaiping*	社會主義概評
Rendao Zazhi	人道雜誌	Shehuizhuyi Jiangxi Hui	社會主義講習會
Rengshu	任屬	Shehuizhuyi Lun	社會主義論
Renlei Gongli	人類公理	Shehuizhuyi Yanjiu Hui	社會主義研究會
Renmin	人民	*Shen Bao*	申報
Renqun zhi Shuo	人羣之說	Shen Tie-min	沈健民
Renxue	仁學	Shengping	升平
Rikugō Zasshi	六合雜誌	Shi Fu (Liu Si-fu)	師復(劉思復)
Risō Dan	理想團	Shihonka	資本家
Rōdō Kumiai Kiseikai	勞動組合期成會	*Shili Gongfa*	實理公法
Rōdō Sekai	勞動世界	Shimada Saburō	島田三郎
Rōdōsha	勞動者	Shimoide Hayakichi	下出隼吉
Rong Meng-yuan	榮孟源	*Shin Kigen*	新紀元
Sai	賽	*Shinsei Dai-i*	真政大意
Saidang	賽黨	Shinshi Batsu	紳士閥
Saigō Takamori	西鄉隆盛	Shioda Shōbei	塩田庄兵衛
Saihui	賽會	Shitsu	恖
Saionji Kimmochi	西園寺公望	*Shiwu Bao*	時務報
Sakai Toshihiko	堺利彥	Shuo Qun xu	說羣序

Song Jiao-ren	宋敎仁	Wada Saburō	和田三郎
Su Bao	蘇報	Wang An-shi	王安石
Su Man-shu	蘇曼珠	Wang De-zhao	王德昭
Su Wang	素王	Wang Jing-wei	汪精衛
Su Xun	蘇洵	Wang Jiong-wu	王烔吾
Subete	凡	Wang Mang	王莽
Sun Chang-wei	孫常煒	Wang Ren-zhi	王忍之
Sun Xiao-hou	孫小侯	Wang Wen-dian	王文典
Sun Yat-sen (wen)	孫逸仙（文）	*Wanguo Gongbao*	萬國公報
Suo	所	Wangtian	王田
Suxier Demokelate	蘇西耳德磨克拉特	Wen	文
Tai-qiu	太邱	Wenming chuban she	文明出版社
Taiping	太平	Wu Tian-min	吳天民
Tan Bi-an	譚彼岸	Wu Xiang-xiang	吳相湘
Tan Si-tong	譚嗣同	Wu Yu-zhang	吳玉章
Tanaka Sogorō	田中惣五郎	Wu Yue	吳樾
Tang Zeng-bi	湯增璧	Wu Ze xi suo Guyouzhe	吾譯昔所固有者
Tao Cheng-zhang	陶成章	Wu Zhi-hui	吳稚暉
Tao Luo-qin	陶樂勤	Wu Zhong-yao	吳仲遙
Tarui Tōkichi	樽井藤吉	Wufen pinfu	無分貧富
Teikokushugi	帝國主義	Wujin	武進
Tian Zi-qin	田梓琴	Wuling	武陵
Tianfu	田賦	Wuzhong zhi Guyouzhe	吾種之固有者
Tiantao	天討	Wuzhengfuzhuyi	無政府主義
Tianxia	天下	Xia Zhong-min	夏重民
Tianyan Lun	天演論	Xian-jie	縣解
Tianyi Bao	天義報	Xiang Da	向達
Tinggong	停工	Xiangshan	香山
Tō	黨	Xiaokang	小康
Tochi Fukken Doshikai	土地復權同志會	Xiaoshan	蕭山
Tochi Kinkō jinrui no Taiken	土地均享人類の大權	Ximin	細民
Tokutomi Sho (Ichirō)	德慶華（一郎）	*Xinghua Boyi*	醒華博議
Tokyō Semmon Gakkō	東京專門學校	Xingzhong Hui	興中會
Tongmeng Hui	同盟會	*Xinmin Congbao*	新民叢報
Tōyō Shakaitō	東洋社會黨	*Xinshi Ji*	新世紀
Tu-fu	屠富	*Xinwen Bao*	新聞報
Tudi	土地	*Xinxue Weijing kao*	新學僞經考
Tudi Guoyou	土地國有	Xixing	犧牲
Tudi Junyou	土地均有	Xu Fo-Su	徐佛蘇
Uchimura Kanzō	內村鑑三	Xu Te-li	徐特立

Xu Xi-lin	徐錫麟	Zhang Wen-bo	張文伯
Xue hui	學會	Zhang Xi-chen	章錫琛
Xuwuzhuyi	虛無主義	Zhang Zhen-wu	張振武
Yamamoto Hideo	山本秀夫	Zhang Zhi-dong	張之洞
Yamanouchi Masaakira	山内正瞭	Zhao Bi-zhen	趙必振
Yan Du-hao	嚴獨鶴	Zhao Jing-qing	趙鏡清
Yan Fu	嚴復	*Zhejiang Chao*	浙江潮
Yan Zhong-ping	嚴中平	Zheng Guan-ying	鄭觀應
Yan-hong	衍鴻	Zhengwen She	政文社
Yanajiside	鴨綠難嘶德	Zhi	貞
Yang Chang-ji	楊昌濟	*Zhixuezhai Congshu*	質學齋叢書
Yang Du-sheng (Shou-ren)	楊篤生（守仁）	Zhong nong pai	重農派
Yang Qu-yun	楊衢雲	*Zhongguo Ribao*	中國日報
Yang Tian-shi	楊天石	Zhongguo Shehui Dang	中國社會黨
Yang Ting-dong	楊廷棟	Zhonghua lixian Minguo	中華立憲民國
Ye Xia-sheng	葉夏聲	*Zhongwai Ribao*	中外日報
Yin yang	陰陽	Zhou Bai-gao	周百高
Yinbingshi	飲冰室	Zhou Zhen-fu	周振甫
Yishu Huibian	譯書彙編	Zhou Zuo-ren	周作人
Yizhen Fajie	一真法界	Zhu Ci-qi	朱次琦
Yorozu Chōhō	萬朝報	Zhu He-zhong	朱和中
Youai	友愛	Zhu Jie-qin	朱傑勤
Youxue Yibian	游學譯編	Zhu Xue-hao	朱學浩
Yuan qiang	原強	Zhu Zhi-ru	朱執如
Yuan Sun	辣孫	Zhu Zhi-xin	朱執信
Yuan-Shi	淵實	Zhuang Cun-yu	莊存與
Zhang Bing-lin (Tai-yan)	章炳麟（太炎）	Zhuti	主體
Zhang Du-xia	張瀆俠	Zi Sheng	資生
Zhang Ji (Pu-quan)	張繼（溥泉）	Ziben	資本
Zhang Jing-lu	張靜廬	Ziran fa	自然法
Zhang Ke-gong	張客公	Ziyou zhi Shuo	自由之說
Zhang Nan	張枬	Zou Lu	鄒魯
Zhang Peng-yuan	張朋園	Zou Rong	鄒容
Zhang Qi-yun	張其昀	Zuo Zhuan	左傳
Zhang Shi-zhao	章士釗		

Western Language Bibliography

Arima Tatsuo. "Uchimura Kanzo: A Study of the Post Meiji Japanese Intelligentsia," Harvard *Papers on Japan*, I, Cambridge, Mass., 1961.

Ayers, William. *Chang Chih-tung and Educational Reform in China*, Cambridge, Mass., 1971.

Balazs, Etienne. *Chinese Civilization and Bureaucracy*, translated M. Wright, New Haven, 1964.

Barker, Sir Ernest (ed.). *Social Contract: Essays by Locke, Hume, and Rousseau*, New York, 1962.

Bellamy, Edward. *Looking Backward*, London and New York, 1888.

Bernal, Martin. "The Triumph of Anarchism over Marxism, 1906-1907," in Mary Wright (ed.), *China in Revolution*, New Haven, 1968, pp. 97-142.

———. "Liu Shih-pei and 'National Essence,'" in Charlotte Furth, *The Limits of Change*, Cambridge, Mass., 1975.

———. "Liu Shih-pei," paper presented to the Research Conference on Intellectuals and the Problem of Conservatism in Republican China, held in Dedham, Mass., August, 1972.

Beston, Arthur E. "Patent Office Models of the Good Society: Some Relationships Between Social Reform and Westward Expansion," in Stanley Katz and Stanley Kutler (eds.), *New Perspectives on the American Past*, Boston, 1969, pp. 444-465.

Biggerstaff, Knight. *The Earliest Modern Government Schools in China*, Ithaca, 1961.

Bliss, W. D. P. *A Handbook of Socialism*, New York, 1895.

Boardman, Eugene Powers. *Christian Influence Upon the Ideology of the T'aiping Rebellion, 1851-1864*, Madison, 1952.

Boorman, Howard. *Biographical Dictionary of Republican China*, 4 vols., New York, 1967-1971.

Brown, D. M. *Nationalism in Japan: An Introductory Historical Analysis*, Berkeley, 1955.

Candler, Warren A.. *Young J. Allen*, Nashville, 1931.

Cantlie, Sir James, and C. Sheridan Jones. *Sun Yat-sen and the Awakening of China,* London, 1912.

Chang Chung-li. *The Chinese Gentry: Studies on Their Role in Nineteenth Century Chinese Society,* Seattle, 1955.

——. *The Income of the Chinese Gentry,* Seattle, 1962.

Chang Hao. *Liang Chi-chao and the Intellectual Transition in China, 1890-1907,* Cambridge, Mass., 1971.

Chen Chi-yun. "Liang Chi-chao's Missionary Education: A Case Study of Missionary Influence on the Reformers," Harvard *Papers on China,* XVI, Cambridge, Mass., 1962.

Ch'eng, Shelley Hsien. "The T'ung-meng Hui, Its Organization, Leadership, and Finances, 1905-1912," Ph.D. Thesis, University of Washington, 1962.

Chow Tse-tsung. *The May Fourth Movement: Intellectual Revolution in Modern China,* Cambridge, Mass., 1960.

Cohn, Norman. *The Pursuit of the Millennium,* London, 1957.

Cole, G. D. H. *A History of Socialist Thought,* 5 vols., London, 1954-1956.

Cole, Margaret. *The Story of Fabian Socialism,* London, 1961.

Cord, Steven B. *Henry George, Dreamer or Realist,* Philadelphia, 1965.

Dan, T. *The Origins of Bolshevism,* London, 1964.

de Bary, Theodore, et. al. *Sources of Chinese Tradition,* text ed., 2 vols., New York, 1964.

de Tocqueville, Alexis. *The Old Regime and the French Revolution,* trans. Stuart Gilbert, New York, 1955.

Deutscher, I. *The Prophet Armed: Trotsky, 1879-1921,* London, 1954.

Dove, P. E. *Elements of Political Science,* Edinburgh, 1854.

——. *Theory of Human Progression: Natural Probability of a Reign of Justice,* Edinburgh, 1850.

Elvin, Mark. *The Pattern of the Chinese Past,* London, 1973.

Ely, R. T. *French and German Socialism,* New York, 1887.

——. *Introduction to the Study of Political Economy,* New York, 1889.

——. *Socialism and Social Reform,* New York, 1894.

E-tu Zen Sun. *Chinese Railways and British Interests, 1898-1911,* New York, 1954.

Feuerwerker, A. et. al. (eds.). *Approaches to Modern Chinese History,* Berkeley, 1967.

Fung Yu-lan. *A History of Chinese Philosophy,* 2 vols., translated Derk Bodde, London, 1953.

Furth, Charlotte. *The Limits of Change: Essays on Conservative Alternatives in Republican China,* Cambridge, Mass., 1975.

Gasster, Michael. *Chinese Intellectuals and the Revolution of 1911: The Birth of Modern Chinese Radicalism,* Seattle, 1969.

George, Henry. *Progress and Poverty*, 5th ed., London, 1883.

George, Henry, Jr. *Life of Henry George*, New York, 1911.

Gide, Charles, and Charles Rist. *A History of Economic Doctrines*, 2nd ed., London, 1958.

Hackett, Roger F., "Chinese Students in Japan, 1900–1910," Harvard *Papers on China*, III, Cambridge, Mass., 1949, pp. 134–169.

Haupt, Georges, and Madeline Reberioux. *La Deuxième Internationale et L'Orient*, Paris, 1967.

Havel, Hyppolyte. "Kōtoku's Correspondence with Albert Johnson," *Mother Earth*, VI, 6–7, and (1911), 181–182.

Higgs, H. *The Physiocrats*, London, 1897.

Ho Ping-ti. *Studies on the Population of China, 1368–1953*, Cambridge, Mass., 1959.

Howard, Richard C. "K'ang Yu-wei (1858–1927): His Intellectual Background and Early Thought," Arthur Wright and Denis Twitchett (eds.), in *Confucian Personalities*, Stanford, 1962, pp. 294–316.

Hsiao Kung-ch'uan. "Kang Yu-wei and Confucianism," *Monumenta Serica*, XVIII, 1959, pp. 96–212.

Hsueh Chun-tu. *Huang Hsing and the Chinese Revolution*, Stanford, 1961.

Hsueh Chun-tu (ed.). *Revolutionary Leaders of Modern China*, London, 1971.

Hudson, G. F. *Europe and China: A Survey of their Relation from the Earliest Times to 1800*, London, 1931.

Hummel, Arthur (ed.). *Eminent Chinese of the Ch'ing Period*, 2 vols., Washington, 1943–1944.

Hyndman, H. M. *The Nationalisation of the Land, 1775–1882*, London, 1882.

Inglis, K. S. *Churches and the Working Classes in Victorian England*, London, 1963.

Jansen, Marius B. *The Japanese and Sun Yat-sen*, Cambridge, Mass., 1954.

Kang Woo. *Les Trois Theories Politiques du Tch'ouen Ts'ieou*, Paris, 1932.

Kang You-wei. *Ta Tung shu, The One World Philosophy of K'ang Yu-wei*, translated by Lawrence G. Thompson, London, 1958.

Katz, Stanley, and Stanley Kutler (eds.). *New Perspectives on the American Past*, Boston, 1969.

Kawakami Kiyoshi. "The Political Ideas of Modern Japan," in *Bulletin of the State University of Iowa, Studies in Sociology, Politics, History* (1903), II, 2, pp. 181–193.

Kheifet, A. N. "Revolyutsonye svasi Narodov Rossii i Kitaya v Nachale XX Veka," *Voprosi Istorii*, 1956, XII, pp. 91–100.

Kidd, Benjamin. *Social Evolution*, London and New York, 1894.

King, F. H. H., and Prescott Clarke. *A Research Guide to China-coast Newspapers, 1822-1911*, Cambridge, Mass., 1965.

Kosaka Masaaki (ed.). *Japanese Thought in the Meiji Era*, translated and adapted by David Abosch, Tokyo, 1958.

Kublin, Hyman. *Asian Revolutionary: The Life of Katayama Sen*, Princeton, 1964.

Kwok, D. W. Y. *Scientism in Chinese Thought, 1900-1950*, New Haven, 1965.

Latourette, K. S. *A History of Christian Missions in China*, London, 1929. *Le Peuple*, Bruxelles.

Legge, J., trans. *Li Ki*, Books I-IX, *Sacred Books of the East*, Volume XXVII, Oxford, 1885.

Lenin, Vladimir Ilyitch. *Selected Works*, 12 vols., London, 1935.

Levenson, Joseph. *Confucian China and its Modern Fate*, I, *The Problem of Intellectual Continuity*, London, 1958.

——. *Confucian China and its Modern Fate*, II, *The Problem of Monarchical Decay*, London, 1964.

——. *Confucian China and its Modern Fate*, III, *The Problem of Historical Significance*, Berkeley and London, 1965.

——. "Illwind in the Well-field: The Erosion of the Confucian Ground for Controversy," in Arthur F. Wright (ed.), *The Confucian Persuasion*, Stanford, 1960, pp. 268-287.

——. *Liang Ch'i-ch'ao and the Mind of Modern China*, rev. ed., London, 1959.

——. "Liao P'ing and the Confucian Departure from History," in Arthur Wright and Denis Twitchett (eds.), *Confucian Personalities*, Stanford, 1962, pp. 317-325, and Joseph Levenson, *Confucian China and its Modern Fate*, III, Berkeley and London, 1965; pp. 3-15.

Li Chien-nung, *The Political History of China, 1840-1928*, translated by Teng Ssu-yu and Jeremy Ingells, Princeton, 1956.

Li Yu-ning. *The Introduction of Socialism into China*, New York, 1971.

Liang Qi-chao. *The Great Chinese Philosopher K'ang Yu-wei*, translated by Dai-ming Lee, San Francisco, 1955.

——. *Intellectual Trends of the Ch'ing Period*, translated by Immanuel C. Y. Hsü, Cambridge, Mass., 1959.

Liew, K. S. *Struggle for Democracy: Sung Chiao-ren and the 1911 Revolution*, Berkeley, 1971.

Liu, James. *The Chinese Knight Errant*, London, 1967.

Lo Jung-pang. *K'ang Yu-wei, A Biography and a Symposium*, Tucson, 1967.

Locke, J. "An Essay Concerning the True Original, Extent and End of Civil Government," in Sir Ernest Barker, *Social Contract: Essays by Locke, Hume, and Rousseau,* New York, 1962.

Lust, John. *The Revolutionary Army: A Chinese Nationalist Tract of 1903,* Introduction and Translation with Notes, Paris, 1968.

McAleavy, Henry. *Su Man-shu, 1884–1918: A Sino-Japanese Genius,* London, 1960.

Macpherson, C. B. *The Political Theory of Possessive Individualism,* Oxford, 1962.

Mallock, W. H. *Memoirs of Life and Literature,* London, 1920.

Mannheim, Karl. *Essays on Sociology and Social Psychology,* London, 1953.

Mao Tse-tung. *Selected Readings from the Works of Mao Tse-tung,* Peking, 1967.

Marx, Karl. "The Eighteenth Brumaire of Louis Bonaparte," *Selected Works,* I, Moscow, 1958, pp. 243–344.

———. *The Poverty of Philosophy,* English ed., New York, 1971, pp. 144–154.

———. *Selected Works,* 2 vols., Moscow, 1958.

Maspero, Henri. *La Chine Antique,* Paris, 1927.

The Masses, Chicago, 1911–1917.

Moore, Barrington, Jr. *Social Origins of Dictatorship and Democracy,* London, 1967.

Mother Earth, New York, 1906–1917.

Muramatsu Yuji. "Some Themes in Chinese Rebel Ideologies," in Arthur F. Wright (ed.), *The Confucian Persuasion,* Stanford, 1960, pp. 241–268.

Needham, Joseph. *Science and Civilisation in China,* I, Cambridge, 1954; II, Cambridge, 1962.

———. *Time and Ancient Man,* London, 1965.

Nikolayevsky, B. I. *Aseff the Russian Judas,* translated by G. Reavey, London, 1934.

Nobutaka Ike. "Kōtoku, Advocate of Direct Action," *Journal of Asian Studies,* III, 1944.

Notehelfer, F. G. *Kōtoku Shūsui: Portrait of a Japanese Radical,* Cambridge, 1971.

Peking Review, Peking, 1958 ———.

Pelling, Henry. *The Origins of the Labour Party, 1880–1900,* Oxford, 1965.

Polachek, James. "Gentry Hegemony: Soochow in the T'ung-chih Restoration," in F. Wakeman, *Conflict and Control,* Berkeley, 1975.

Powles, Cyril H. "Abe Isoo and the Role of Christians in the Founding of the Japanese Socialist Movement, 1895–1905," Harvard *Papers on Japan,* I, Cambridge, Mass., 1961, pp. 89–130.

Pyle, Kenneth B. *The New Generation in Meiji Japan: Problems of Cultural Identity, 1885–1895,* Stanford, 1969.

Rankin, Mary Backus. *Early Chinese Revolutionaries: Radical Intellectuals in Shanghai and Chekiang, 1902–1911,* Cambridge, Mass., 1971.

Richard, Timothy. *Forty-Five Years in China: Reminiscences by Timothy Richard DD,* London, 1916.

Scalapino, Robert A. *Democracy and the Party Movement in Prewar Japan,* Berkeley, 1962.

——. *The Japanese Communist Movement, 1920–1966,* Berkeley, 1967.

——. "Prelude to Marxism: The Chinese Student Movement in Japan, 1900–1910," in A. Feuerwerker et al. (eds.), *Approaches to Modern Chinese History,* Berkeley, 1967, pp. 190–215.

Scalapino, Robert, and George T. Yu. *The Chinese Anarchist Movement,* Berkeley, 1961.

Schäffle, A. E. *The Essence of Socialism,* New York, 1890.

Scheiner, Irwin. *Christians, Converts and Social Protest in Meiji Japan,* Berkeley, 1970.

Schiffrin, Harold Z. "The Enigma of Sun Yat-sen," in Mary Wright (ed.), *China in Revolution: The First Phase, 1900–1913,* New Haven, 1968, pp. 443–474.

——. *Sun Yat-sen and the Origins of the Chinese Revolution,* Berkeley, 1968.

——. "Sun Yat-sen's Early Land Policy," *The Journal of Asian Studies,* XVI, No. 4, 1957, pp. 549–564.

Schiffrin, Harold Z., and R. Scalapino. "Early Socialist Currents in the Chinese Revolutionary Movement," *Journal of Asian Studies, XVIII,* 3 May 1959, pp. 321–342.

Schiffrin, Harold Z., and Pow-key Sohn. "Henry George on Two Continents," in *Comparative Studies in Society and History,* II, 1959–1960, pp. 85–109.

Schram, Stuart, and Helene Carrère d'Encausse. *Marxism and Asia,* London, 1969.

Schwartz, Benjamin. *In Search of Wealth and Power: Yen Fu and the West,* Cambridge, Mass., 1964.

Shih, Vincent Y. C. *The Taiping Ideology: Its Sources, Interpretations, and Influences,* Seattle, 1967.

Single Tax Year Book, New York, 1917.

Smythe, Joan E. "The Tzu-li hui: Some Chinese and Their Rebellion," Harvard *Papers on China,* XII, Cambridge, Mass., 1958, pp. 51–67.

Soothill, W. E. *Timothy Richard of China,* London, 1924.

Tang Leang-li. *The Inner History of the Chinese Revolution,* London, 1930.

Teng Ssu-yu, and J. K. Fairbank. *China's Response to the West: A Documentary Survey, 1839–1923,* Atheneum ed, New York, 1963.

Tikhvinsky, S. L. *Sun Yat-sen* (in Russian), Moscow, 1964.

Tjan Tjae Sam. *Po Hu T'ung, The Comprehensive Discussions in the White Tiger Hall,* 2 vols., Leiden, 1949.

Tucker, William. *J. H. Garrison and the Disciples of Christ,* St. Louis, 1964.

Vooruit, Ghent.

Wakeman, Frederic, Jr. *History and Will: Philosophical Perspectives of Mao Tse-tung's Thought,* Berkeley, 1973.

Wakeman, Frederic, Jr. (ed.), *Conflict and Control: Social Process in Late Imperial China,* Berkeley, 1975.

Wang, Y. C. *Chinese Intellectuals and the West, 1872-1949,* Chapel Hill, 1966.

Wilson, George M. "Kita Ikki, Okawa Shumei and the Yuzonsha: A Study in the Genesis of Showa Nationalism," Harvard, *Papers on Japan,* II, 1963, pp. 139-181.

———. *Radical Nationalist in Japan: Kita Ikki, 1883-1937,* Cambridge, Mass., 1969.

Wright, Arthur F. (ed.). *The Confucian Persuasion,* Stanford, 1960.

Wright, Arthur, and Denis Twitchett (eds.). *Confucian Personalities,* Stanford, 1962.

Wright, Mary. *The Last Stand of Chinese Conservatism: The T'ung-chih Restoration, 1862-1874,* Stanford, 1957.

Wright, Mary (ed.). *China in Revolution: The First Phase, 1900-1913,* New Haven, 1968.

Wright, Stanley F. *Hart and the Chinese Customs,* Belfast, 1950.

Wu Yu-chang. *The Revolution of 1911,* Peking, 1962.

Young, Ernest. "Problems of a Late Ch'ing Revolutionary: Chen Tien-hua," in Chun-tu Hsueh (ed.), *Revolutionary Leaders of Modern China,* London, 1971, pp. 210-247.

Eastern Language Bibliography

Abe Isō. *Shakaishugisha to Naru Made*, Tokyo, 1932.

Cao Ya-bo. "Yang Du-sheng Daohai," reprinted *Xinhai Geming*, IV, pp. 316–324.

Chai De-geng *et al.* (eds.). *Xinhai Geming*, 8 vols., Shanghai, 1957, in the series *Zhongguo Jindaishi Ziliao Congkan*.

Chokugen, Tokyo, 1905, reprinted in the series *Meiji Shakaishugi Shiryō Shū*, 1960.

Ding Wen-jiang. *Liang Ren-gong Xiansheng Nianpu Changbian Chugao*, 2 vols., Taipei, 1962.

Fang Zhao-ying. *Qingmo Minchu Yangxue Xuesheng Timinglu chuji*, Taipei, 1962.

Feng Zi-you. *Geming Yishi*, 5 vols., 1939–1946, Taipei ed., I–II, 1953; III, IV, and V, 1965.

——. "Minghengzhuyi yu Zhongguo Zhengzhi Geming zhi Qiantu," *Min Bao*, IV, 5/1/06, pp. 97–122.

——. *Shehuizhuyi yu Zhongguo*, Hong Kong, 1920.

——. *Zhonghua Minguo Kaiguoqian Gemingshi*, 2 vols., Taipei ed., 1954.

Ge Gong-zhen. *Zhongguo Baoxueshi*, Hong Kong ed., 1964.

Geming di Xianqu, Shanghai, 1928.

Guofu Quanji, 2 vols., Taipei, 1955.

Hatano Yoshihiro. "Shoki ni Okeru Son Bun no 'Keikei Chigen ni tsuite,'" in *Shakai Keizai Shigaku*, XXI, 5.6., pp. 479–502.

He Xiang-ning. "Wodi Huiyi," in *Xinhai Geming Huiyilu*, I, 12–20.

Heimin Shimbun, Tokyo, 1903–1904, reissued in the series *Meiji Shakaishugi Shiryō Shū*, Tokyo, 1961.

Heng Bao, He Zhen, and Liu Shi-pei (eds.), Tokyo, 1908.

Hikari, Tokyo, 1905–1906, reissued *Meiji Shakaishugi Shiryō Shū*, Tokyo, 1961.

Hou Wai-lu. *Zhongguo Lidai Datong Lixiang*, Peking, 1959.

Hu Han-min. "Chi Xinmin Congbao zhi Miuwang," *Min Bao*, V, June 1906, pp. 67–78.

——. "Eguo Geming Dang zhi Ribao," *Min Bao,* IV, May 1906, pp. 93–95.

——. "Gao Feinan Minshengzhuyizhe," *Min Bao,* XII, March 1907, pp. 45–155.

——. "Hu Han-min Zizhuan," *Geming Wenxian,* III, pp. 373–442.

——. "*Min Bao* zhi Liu da Zhuyi," *Min Bao,* III, April 1906, pp. 1–22.

Hubeisheng Zhexue Shehui Kexue Xuehui Lianhehui (ed.). *Xinhai Geming Wushi Zhounian Jinian Lunwen Ji,* 2 vols., Peking, 1962.

Jiang Kang-hu. *Hongshuiji,* San Francisco, 1913 (?).

Jiang Wei-qiao. "Minguo Jiaoyu Zongzhang Cai Yuan-pei," in *Cai Yuanpei Xiansheng Quanji,* Taipei, 1968, pp. 1339–1342.

——. "Zhongguo Jiaoyu Hui Huiyi," *Xinhai Geming,* I, pp. 485–496.

Jiaohui Xinbao, Shanghai, 1868–1874, reprinted in 6 vols. in the series *Qingmo Minchu Baokan Congbian,* Taipei, 1968.

Jing Mei-jiu. *Zuian,* Shanghai, n.d.

Jingzhong Ribao, Liu Shi-pei (ed.), Shanghai, 1904–1905. All except last two months reprinted in 5 vols. in the series *Zhonghua Minguo Shiliao Congbian.*

Kakumei Hyōron, Tokyo, 1906–1907, reprinted *Meiji Shakaishugi Shiryō Shū,* Tokyo, 1963.

Kang You-wei. *Datongshu,* Zhang Xi-chen and Zhou Zhen-fu (eds.), Peing, 1956.

——. "Kang Nan-hai Zibian Nianpu," in *Xuwu Bianfa,* IV, Shanghai, 1957, pp. 107–171.

Katō Hiroyuki, translated by Liang Qi-chao. "Shijiu Shiji Sixiang Bianqian Lun," *Qingyi Bao,* LII, 7/26/1900, pp. 4–5b.

Kayano Nagatomo. *Chūkaminkoku Kakumei Hikyū,* Tokyo, 1941.

Kemuyama Sentarō. *Kinsei Museifushugi,* Tokyo, 1902, reprinted in the series *Meiji Bunken Shiryō Soshō,* 1965.

Kinoshita Naoe. "Yo wa Ika ni Shite Shakashugisha to Nari Shi," *Heimin Shimbun,* 12/12/03, 6.

Kōtoku Shūsui. "Rokoku Kakumei ga Yo uru Kyōkun," *Chokugen,* 2/19/05, I.

——. "Rokoku Kakumei no Sobo," *Chokugen,* 2/12/05, I.

——. "Yo wa Ika ni Shite Shakaishugisha to Nari Shi," *Heimin Shimbun,* 1/17/04.

Kōtoku Shūsui, and Ishikawa Kyōkusan. "Nihon Shakaishugishi," serialized in *Heimin Shimbun,* II–LVII; reprinted in *Meiji Bunka Zenshū,* XXI, Tokyo, 1929, pp. 331–370.

Kuai Guang-dian. *Jinsuzhaiji,* Nanking, 1929.

Li Da-nian. "Xinhai Geming yu Fan Man Wenti," in *Lishi Yanjiu,* 5/1961, and *Xinhai Geming Wushi Zhounian Jinian Lunwen ji,* 2 vols., Peking, 1962, I, pp. 188–203.

Li Shi-yue. "Sun Zhong-shan 'Pingjun Diquan' Zhenggang di Chansheng he Fazhan," *Guangming Ribao*, 10/27/1955.

Li Zhu. "Lun Shehuizhuyi zai Zhongguo di Zhuanbo," *Lishi Yanjiu*, 1954, 3, pp. 1-18.

Liang Qi-chao, "Da Moubao Disihao Duiyu Benbao zhi Bolun," *Xinmin Congbao*, LXXIX (4th year), VII, pp. 1-93.

——. "Guafen Weiyen," *Qingyi Bao* (1899), XV-XVIII.

——. "Jinhualun Gemingzhe Jide zhi Xueshuo," Xinmin Congbao, XVIII, 10/17/02, pp. 17-28.

——. "Lun Kaiming Zhuanzhi Shiyong yu Jinri zhi Zhongguo," 2 pts., *Xinmin Congbao*, LXXV (4th year III), Feb.-Mar. 1906, LXXVII (4th year VI), April 1906, pp. 10-50 and 1-10; part of the series *Kaiming Zhuanzhi lun*.

——. "Lun Qiang-quan," *Qingyi Bao*, XXXI, 10/25/99, pp. 4-7.

——. "Nanhai Kang Xiansheng Zhuan," *Qingyi Bao*, C, 12/21/01, reprint, pp. 6395-6440.

——. "Sanshi Zishu," *Yinbingshi Wenji*, Taipei, 1960, IV, XI, pp. 15-19.

——. "Shehui Geming guo wei Jinri Zhongguo suo biyao hu?" *Xinmin Congbao*, LXXXVI (4th year XIV), December 1906; part of the series *Zada Moubao*, pp. 5-52.

——. "Shehuizhuyi Lun yu," *Xinmin Congbao*, LXXXIX (4th year XVII), pp. 35-37.

——. "Shenlun Zhongzu Geming yu Zhengzhi Geming zhi Deshi," *Xinmin Congbao*, LXXVI (4th year IV), April 1906, pp. 1-73.

——. "Waizi Shuru Wenti," *Xinmin Congbao*, LII, LIII, LIV, LVI, 9/10/04, 9/24/04, 10/9/04, 11/7/04.

——. *Xin Dalu Youji*, supplement to *Xinmin Congbao*, 2/04.

——. "Xixue Shumubiao," *Zhixuezhai Congshu*, 1896, III.

——. *Yinbingshi Wenji*, 15 vols., Taipei, 1960.

——. "Zaibo Moubao zhi Tudi Guoyou Lun," 3 pts., XC, XCI, and XCII, *Xinmin Congbao*, 4th year, XVIII, XIX, and XX, pp. 1-34, 1-57, and 1-22.

——. *Zhixuezhai Congshu*, 1896.

Liao Zhong-kai. "Shehuizhuyi Shi Dagang," *Min Bao*, VII, 9/5/06, pp. 101-130.

——. "Xuwu Dang Xiao Shi," 2 pts., *Min Bao*, XI, 3/9/07, pp. 89-109; and *Min Bao*, XVII, 11/18/07, pp. 121-148.

Liu Shi-pei. *Liu Shen-shu Xiansheng Yishu*, reprinted, 4 vols., Taipei, 1965.

——. "Shehuizhuyi Jiangxi Hui diyici Kaihui Jishi," *Tianyi Bao*, VI, 9/1/07, reprint, p. 152.

Liu Shi-pei and He zhen. "Lun Zhongzu Geming yu Wuzhengfuzhugi, Geming zhi deshi," *Tianyi Bao*, VI, 9/1/07.

Luo Jia-lun. *Guofu Nianpu*, Taipei, 1965.

Ma Jun-wu. "Mile Yohan zhi Xueshuo," *Xinmin Congbao*, XXX, 4/26/03, pp. 9–14.

——. "Shengximen zhi Shenghuo ji qi Xueshuo," *Xinmin Congbao*, XXXI, 3, 5/10/03.

Macklin, W. E. (Malin). "Di, Gong, Ben, Sanshuo," *Wanguo Gongbao*, CXXIV, 5/99, pp. 5–9.

——. "Lun Dizu Guigong zhi Yi," *Wanguo Gongbao*, CXXV, 6/99, 10b–12b.

——. "Yi Dizu Zhengshui Lun," *Wanguo Gongbao*, LXXI, 12/94, 4b–5b.

Min Bao, Tokyo, 1905–1908 (1910), reprinted in 4 vols., Peking, 1957.

Minli Bao, Shanghai, 1910–1913.

Miyazaki Ryusuke. "Oji Tamizō no koto domo," in *Jimbutsu Kenkyū Shiryō*, 2 vols., Tokyo, 1966, I, pp. 110–113.

Miyazaki Tamizō. "Ou Mei Shehui Geming Yundong zhi Zonglei ji Pinglun," *Min Bao*, IV, 5/1/06, pp. 123–133.

——. *"Tochi Kinkō" Jinrui no Taiken*. Reprinted in *Meiji Bunka Zenshū*, XXI, pp. 199–229.

Miyazaki Torazō. *Sanjusannen no Yume*, Tokyo, 1941.

Nankai Daxue Lishixi. *Bakuning*, Peking, 1972.

Nishida Nagashi. "Hikari Kaisetsu," *Hikari*, reprinted, Tokyo, 1961.

Nishikawa Kōjiro. *Shehui Dang*, translated by Zhou Bai-gao, Shanghai, 1903.

Nishio Yōtarō. *Kōtoku Shūsui*, Tokyo, 1959.

Onogawa Hidemi. *Minpo Sakuin*, 2 vols., Tokyo, 1970.

Osugi Sakai. "Bankoku Shakaitō Taikai Ryakushi," *Shakaishugi Kenkyū*, I, 3/15/06, pp. 58–73.

Qian Bo-can (ed.). *Xuwu Bianfa*, 4 vols., Shanghai, 3rd ed., 1961, in the series *Zhongguo Jindaishi Ziliao Congkan*.

Qian Mu. *Zhongguo Jin Sanbainian Xueshu shi*, 3rd ed., Shanghai, 1948.

Qingyi Bao, Liang Qi-chao (ed.). Yokohama, 1898–1901, reprinted in 12 vols., Taipei, 1967.

Rong Meng-yuan. "Xinhai Geming qian Zhongguo Shukanshang dui Makesizhuyi di Jieshao," in *Xin Jianshe*, 1953, III, pp. 5–12.

Sakai Toshihiko. *Nihon Shakaishugi Undō Shi*, reprinted in *Nihon Kindaishi Sōsho*, Tokyo, 1954.

——. "Tochi Fukkensetsu," in *Shakaishugi Kenkyū*, II, 4/15/06, p. 53.

Saneto Keishō. *Chūkokujin Nihon Ryūgakushi*, Tokyo, 1960.

Shakaishugi Kenkyū, Tokyo, 1906, reissued in *Meiji Shakaishugi Shiryō Shū,* Tokyo, 1961.

Shen Tie-min. "Ji Guangfu Hui ersan shi," *Xinhai Geming Huiyilu,* IV, pp. 131–142.

Shimoide Hayakichi. "Shakai Bunken Nempyō," in *Meiji Bunka Zenshū,* XXI, pp. 603–621.

Shioda Shōbei (ed.). *Kōtoku Shūsui no Nikki to Shokan,* Tokyo, 1954.

Shioda Shōbei. *Nihon Shakaishugi Bunken Kaisetsu,* Tokyo, 1958.

Shiwu Bao, Liang Qi-chao (ed.). Shanghai, 1896–1898, reprinted, Taipei, 1966.

Song Jiao-ren. *Cheng Jia-sheng Geming Shilue,* Shanghai, 1912.

——. "Lun Shehuizhuyi," reprinted in Jiang Kang-hu, *Hongshuiji,* pp. 45b–49.

——. (trans., 1905). "Nian Luguo zhi Geming," 2 pts., *Min Bao,* III, April 1906, Section III, pp. 1–9, and *Min Bao,* VII, September 1906, pp. 63–74.

——. "Wanguo Shehui Dang Dahui Lueshi," *Min Bao,* V, 6/26/06, pp. 79–106.

——. *Wo zhi Lishi,* reprinted, Taipei, 1962.

Su Bao, Shanghai, 1898–1903, 2–5/1903, reprinted in *Zhongguo Shixue Congshu,* Taipei, 1964; 5–7/03, reprinted in *Zhonghua Minguo Shiliao Congbian,* Taipei, 1968.

Sun Chang-wei (ed.). *Cai Yuan-pei Xiansheng Quanji,* Taipei, 1968.

Sun Yat-sen. "Fakan ci," *Min Bao,* I, 11/26/05, pp. 1–3.

——. "Jingzhe Yao You Qi Tian," *Guofu Quanshu,* Taipei, 1960, pp. 1004–1006.

——. Letter in *Jingzhong Ribao,* 4/26/04, p. 2.

——. "*Min Bao* Zhounian Jinian Yanshuo ci," *Min Bao,* X, 12/20/06, pp. 83–96.

——. "Shang Li Fuxiang Shu," *Wanguo Gongbao,* LXIX, pp. 3–6, and LXX, 11/94, pp. 9–12.

Tai Qiu. "Chi Xinmin Congbao Tudi Guoyou zhi Min," *Min Bao,* XVII, October 1907, pp. 61–85.

Takenouchi Minoru (ed.). *Mō Takutō Shū,* Tokyo, 1970.

Tan Bi-an. "Eguo Mincuizhuyi dui Tongmeng Hui di Yingxiang," *Lishi Yanjiu* (1959), I, pp. 35–44.

Tan Si-tong, *Renxue,* Shanghai, 1958.

Tanaka Sogorō. *Kōtoku Shūsui ichi Kakumeika no Shisō to Shōgai,* Tokyo, 1955.

——. *Nihon Fasshizumu no Genryū, Kita Ikki no Shisō to Shōgai,* Tokyo, 1949.

Tang Zeng-bi. "Tongmeng Hui Shidai *Min Bao* Shimo ji," *Xinhai Geming,* II, pp. 438–459.

Tao Cheng-zhang. "Longhua Hui Zhang Cheng," reprinted in *Xinhai Geming*, I, pp. 534–544.

——. *Zhean Jilue*, reprinted in *Xinhai Geming*, III, pp. 1–22.

Tianyi Bao, Tokyo, 1907–1908, reprinted (incomplete) in the series *Chukoku Shoki Shakaishugi Bunken Shū*, Tokyo, 1966.

Wallace, J. B. (Hualashi). "Xinghua Boyi," *Wanguo Gongbao*, 1/99, pp. 1–3b.

Wang De-zhao. "Tongmeng Hui Shiqi Sun Zhong-shan Xiansheng Geming Sixiang di Fenxi Yanjiu," in *Zhongguo Xiandaishi Congkan*, I Taipei, 1960.

Wang Dong. "Tongmeng Hui he Min Bao Bianduan Huiyi," *Xinhai Geming Huiyilu*, VI, pp. 23–32.

Wang Shu-nan (ed.). *Zhang Wen-xiang Gong Quanji*, Peking, 1928.

Wanguo Gongbao, Shanghai, 1875–1882, 1889–1906, reprinted, 40 vols., in the series *Qingmo Minchu Baokan Congbian*, Taipei, 1968.

Wu Xiang-xiang. *Song Jiao-ren*, Taipei, 1964.

Wu Yu-zhang. "Huiyi 'Wusi' qianhou wodi sixiang zhuanbian," *Zhongguo Qingnian*, IX, 5-1-59, pp. 10–15.

Wu Yue. "Wu Yue Yishu," *Tian Tao*, supplement, pp. 1–31.

Wu Zhong-yao. "Shehuizhuyi Lun," *Xinmin Congbao*, LXXXIX (4th year XVII), Feb.–Mar. 1907, pp. 35–56.

Xia Dong-yuan. "Lun Qingmo Geming Dang ren Guanyu Tudi Wenti Sixiang," in *Xinhai Geming Wushi Zhounian Lunwenji*, 2 vols. (Peking, 1962), I, pp. 299–322.

Xiang Da et al. (ed.). *Taiping Tianguo*, 4 vols. Shanghai, 1954, in the series *Zhongguo Jindaishi Ziliao Congkan*.

Xin Shiji, Paris, 1907–1910, reprinted *La Tempoj Novaj*, Shanghai, 1947.

Xinhai Geming, 8 vols., Shanghai, 1957.

Xinhai Geming Huiyilu, 6 vols., Peking, 1961.

Xinmin Congbao, Liang Qi-chao (ed.), Yokohama, 1902–1907, reprinted in 17 vols., Taipei, 1966.

Yamamoto Hideo. "Son Bun Shugi Tochi Kakumei Riron no Hatten Kozō," in *Kindai Chūkoku no Shakaitō Keizai*, Niida Noboru (ed.), Tokyo, 1951, pp. 160–163.

Yan Du-hou. "Xinhai Geming Shiqi Shanghai Xinwenjie Dongtai," in *Xinhai Geming Huiyilu*, IV, pp. 78–85.

Yan Zhong-ping et. al. *Zhongguo Jindai Jingii shi Ziliao Xuanji*, Peking, 1957.

Yang Du-sheng. *Xin Hunan*, reprinted in Zhang Nan and Wang Ren-zhi, I, pt. 2, pp. 612–649.

Yang Tian-shi. "Lun Xinhai Geming qian di Zhongguo Guocuizhuyi Sichao," *Xin Jianshe*, 1965, 2, pp. 67–77.

Yang Zhi-jun. "Zhang Tai-yan di Lishiguan he tadi Fajia Sixiang," *Wenwu,* III, 1975, 14–18.

Ye Xia-sheng. "Wuzhengfu Dang yu Geming Dang zhi Shuoming," *Min Bao,* VII, Sept. 1906, pp. 111–123.

Yishu Huibian, Tokyo, 1900, issues I, II, VII, and VIII, reprinted in the series *Zhongguo Shixue Congshu,* Taipei, 1966.

Zhang Bing-lin. *Kaoshu,* Shanghai, 1904, reprinted in the series *Zhonghua Minguo Shiliao Congbian,* Taipei, 1968.

Zhang Ji. *Zhang Pu-quan Xiansheng Quanji,* 2 vols., Taipei, 1951–1952.

Zhang Jing-lu. *Zhongguo Jindai Chuban Shiliao,* 2 vols., Peking, 1957.

Zhang Nan, and Wang Ren-zhi (eds.). *Xinhai Geming qian Shinianjian Shilun Xuanji,* 2 vols., 2 sections each, Peking, 1963.

Zhang Peng-yuan. *Liang Qi-chao yu Qingji Geming,* Taipei, 1964.

Zhang Qi-yun (ed.). *Guofu Quan-shu,* Taipei, 1960.

Zhang Shi-zhao. "Shu 'Huang-di Hun,'" in *Xinhai Geming Huiyilu,* 6 vols. (Peking, 1961), I, pp. 217–304.

Zhang Wen-bo. *Wu Zhi-hui Xiansheng Zhuanji,* Taipei, 1965.

Zhejiang Chao, 5 vols., Tokyo, 1903, reissued in the series *Zhonghua Minguo Shiliao Congbian,* Taipei, 1968.

Zhongguo Baihua Bao, Shanghai, 1903–1904.

Zhu He-zhong. "Ouzhou Tongmeng Hui Jishi," in *Geming Wenxian,* joint vols., I–III, Taipei, 1958, pp. 251–270.

Zhu Jie-qin (ed.). *Gong Ding-an (Zi-zhen) Yanjiu,* Hong Kong, 1971.

Zhu Xue-hao. "Ma Jun-wu Zhuan," *Guoshiguan Guankan,* I, 3, 8/1948, pp. 120–122.

Zhu Zhi-ru. "Zhu Zhi-xin Geming Shiji Shulue," *Xinhai Geming Huiyilu,* II. pp. 422–429.

Zhu Zhi-xin. "Cong Shehuizhuyi Lun Tiedao Guoyou ji Zhongguo Tiedao Guanban Siban," *Min Bao,* IV, 5/1/06, pp. 45–56.

——. "Deyizhi Shehui Geming jia Xiaozhuan," 2 pts., *Min Bao,* II, 1/22/06, sect. 3, pp. 1–13; *Min Bao,* III, 4/5/06, sect. 6, pp. 1–19.

——. "Lun Shehui Geming dang yu Zhengzhi Geming Bingxing," *Min Bao,* V, 6/26/06, pp. 43–66.

——. "Tudi Guoyou yu Zaizheng," 2 pts., *Min Bao,* XV and XVI, July and September, 1907, pp. 67–99 and 33–71.

——. "Yingguo Xin Zongxuanju Laodong Dang zhi Jinbu," *Min Bao,* III, 4/5/06, *Shiping* sect., pp. 6–11.

Zou Lu. *Zhongguo Guomin Dang Shikao,* Taipei, 1965.

Index

256   Index

Chinese Socialism to 1907

Designed by R. E. Rosenbaum.
Composed by Jessamy Graphics, Inc.
in 10 point VariTyper AM 748 Times Roman, 2 point leaded,
with display lines in Optima.
Printed offset by LithoCrafters, Inc.
on Warren's No. 66 Antique Offset, 50 pound basis.
Bound by LithoCrafters
in Columbia book cloth
and stamped in All Purpose foil.